# ASSESSMENT FOR INSTRUCTION IN EARLY LITERACY

*edited by:*

## Lesley Mandel Morrow
*Rutgers, The State University of New Jersey*

## Jeffrey K. Smith
*Rutgers, The State University of New Jersey*

Prentice Hall, *Englewood Cliffs, New Jersey 07632*

*Library of Congress Cataloging-in-Publication Data*

Assessment for instruction in early literacy / edited by Lesley Mandel
  Morrow, Jeffrey K. Smith.

    p.  cm.  —(Rutgers symposium on education)
    Includes bibliographical references.
    ISBN 0-13-050428-9
    1.  Language arts (Primary)—United States—Congresses.
2. Language acquisition—Evaluation—Congresses.  3. Literacy—
United States—Congresses.  I. Morrow, Lesley Mandel.  II. Smith,
Jeffrey K.  III. Series.
LB1529.U5A88  1990
372.6—dc20                           89-36310
                                             CIP

Editorial/production supervision and
  interior design: John Fleming
Manufacturing buyer: Peter Havens

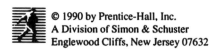
Printed in the United States of America

10  9  8  7  6  5  4  3  2  1

ISBN 0-13-050428-9

Prentice-Hall International (UK) Limited, *London*
Prentice-Hall of Australia Pty. Limited, *Sydney*
Prentice-Hall Canada Inc., *Toronto*
Prentice-Hall Hispanoamericana, S.A., *Mexico*
Prentice-Hall of India Private Limited, *New Delhi*
Prentice-Hall of Japan, Inc., *Tokyo*
Simon & Schuster Asia Pte. Ltd., *Singapore*
Editora Prentice-Hall do Brasil, Ltda., *Rio de Janeiro*

# RUTGERS SYMPOSIUM ON EDUCATION

Louise Cherry Wilkinson, Series Editor

*Research Perspectives on the Graduate Preparation of Teachers*
Anita E. Woolfolk, Editor

*Assessment for Instruction in Early Literacy*
Lesley Mandel Morrow and Jeffrey K. Smith, Editors

# CONTENTS

# SERIES FOREWORD

The *Rutgers Symposium on Education* focuses on vital issues in current education in the United States. The series takes an interdisciplinary perspective and provides a synthesis and interpretation of high-quality educational research on topics of interest to practitioners and policymakers. The focus of each volume is upon a problem, such as the education of teachers, the structure of schools, and the relationship between assessment and instruction in literacy education. Each volume in the series provides an interdisciplinary forum through which scholars can disseminate their original research and extend their work to potential applications for practice, including guides for teaching, learning, assessment, intervention, and policy formulation. We believe that the series will significantly increase the potential for perceptive analysis and the potential for positive impact on the domains of theory and practice.

The purpose of this text is to provide a sythesis and interpretation of current research, theory, and practical information about ways to assess literacy development in early childhood. Underlying each chapter is a summary of what we know about young children's knowledge of literacy. Each chapter includes a discussion of ways to assess this knowledge and how literacy can be best taught and learned. The editors of the book believe, as I do, that assessment enhances a teacher's ability to see and understand children's learning. The editors have set three goals:

1. To define and explore the concept of emergent literacy as it relates to assessment.
2. To offer alternatives to formal evaluative procedures.
3. To expand ideas related to emergent literacy and assessment.

It is with great pleasure that I introduce the second volume of the series, the *Rutgers Symposium on Education*. Our expectation is that this text will catalyze debate about the issues presented and to help clarify what the next steps for both research and training must be.

*Louise Cherry Wilkinson*
*Professor of Educational Psychology*
*Dean of the Graduate School of Education*
*Rutgers, The State University of New Jersey*

# FOREWORD

This book provides the reader with at least five perspectives that focus on emergent literacy, a fundamental construct that has emerged during the past two decades as a major shift in thinking about early reading. The five perspectives are historical, developmental, psychometric, sociolinguistic, and pedagogic.

Historically, reading has mirrored the various views that society has held about the learner, the teacher, what should be taught, and how the learner should be assessed. This volume is mainly concerned with assessment of emergent literacy in youngsters from 2 to 7 years old. This was not always an area of concern. In fact, G. Stanley Hall (1904) and a student of his, Arnold Gessell (1928), believed that a youngster's behavior had a predetermined order of development that could not be altered. These views influenced educational practices through the 1950s. A more dynamic cognitive role for the learner and teacher was introduced in the early 1960s by Ausubel (1959), Bruner (1960), and Bloom (1964). In the 1970s, the accountability movement driven by behavioristic views sought to break down reading into subskills. At the same time, through the work of Clay (1966) and others, we saw an increasing shift toward a naturalistic contextual setting, acknowledging the important role of literacy in the home and school. In addition, we are reminded throughout the various chapters that standardized testing has essentially remained unchanged and unaffected by these new emergent literacy developments that link testing directly to instructional purposes in the classroom.

A developmental perspective emerges from the authors, who themselves have conducted the key studies in their respective areas, that emergent literacy is not just "decoding" or "phonics." Young learners already are aware of certain concepts about literacy, knowledge of letters and words, language competence, and writing. We also find a developmental framework for five of the most frequent forms of writing, beginning with scribbling; going through, either sequentially or concurrently, drawing, nonphonic letter stages, and inventive spelling; and culminating in conventional orthography. Much of the emergent literacy draws upon Wittrock's (1974) generative learning, Vygotsky's (1978) definition of higher mental functioning internalized through social relationships, Holdaway's (1979) developmental theory of literacy, Leont'ev's (1981) concept of activity, and Teale's (1982) emphasis on the socially interactive and emulative behavior of reading development. Essentially, these theoreticians provide us with a framework of the dynamic interactive processes that go on in the reader's head as the reader adjusts and relates to various contexts.

Psychometrically, emergent literacy embraces ethnographic and naturalistic methodologies, emphasizing the concurrent interrelatedness of listening, speaking, reading, and writing that develops very early. At present, this holistic view is most validly assessed by informal testing, whereas formal testing predominantly used today assesses subskills outside the contexts in which they need to be interpreted. The researchers and writers are willing to risk some bias and unreliability to achieve more effective instruction. The more fundamental issue, however, comes down to how we define reading and what should be emphasized, a narrowly prescribed set of subskills or the evaluation of the reader in meaningful contexts.

Sociolinguistic perspectives that emphasize spontaneous speech in natural contexts emerged in the early 1980s. A model of the effective speaker by Wilkinson (1982) continues to appear to be a promising approach to assess individual and group communication in a classroom setting.

Pedagogical perspectives are also apparent in an effort to assess how teachers spend their time on literacy, classroom management, discipline, play, feedback, social interaction, and other instruction. Large variations characterize allocations of time and effort within and between various school settings in regard to these classroom variables.

Taken together, these five perspectives present us with some of the latest and best thinking and research in the rapidly developing emergent literacy construct. It would be most interesting to combine all these informal ethnographic methodologies with more formal standardized tests in a comprehensive design which could be applied in various home and school settings.*

*Martin Kling*
*Professor and Chair*
*Department of Learning and Teaching*
*Graduate School of Education*
*Rutgers, The State University of New Jersey*

*References in the Preface are cited in the bibliographies throughout the text.

# ACKNOWLEDGMENTS

Many people worked on this project to make it possible. Dean Louise Cherry Wilkinson established the Rutgers Invitational Symposium on Education and supported this second effort from the beginning to end. Thank you to the authors for their excellent chapters and the guidance they gave for revisions of each other's work. Jo-an' Van Doren helped to coordinate the conference part of this RISE project, attending to every detail. She was assisted by Barbara Knoblock and Sheryl Bell. Jane Sherwood attended to the conference correspondence. She, along with Kristine Spaventa did all the typing of the manuscript. Carol Wada, editor at Prentice Hall, supported the project and helped to move it along efficiently and effectively as did John Fleming, the production editor. To all these friends and colleagues, we are extremely grateful. Thank you.

# 1

# INTRODUCTION

*Lesley Mandel Morrow and Jeffrey K. Smith*
*Rutgers, The State University of New Jersey*

The context for this volume is change. In the area of early literacy, concepts such as reading readiness, which have been bedrock to the field of reading, are undergoing serious reexamination. Many scholars believe that these ideas do not provide the foundation we thought they did. A competing set of concepts have been introduced under the banner of "emergent literacy," and what was stable is now in flux. The battles are not over, but the impetus for change is strong and the promise of the new perspective is alluring. If this collection of writings has a unifying theme (if not a singular perspective), it is direction. The authors are all making an effort to say, "This is where we are and that is where we should be going." They will not all take you to the same place, but like any worthy guide, they argue with sincerity for the attractiveness of their destinations.

During the past 20 years, researchers have produced a wealth of information relevant to how young children learn language and literacy. The new research has strong implications for changing deep-rooted practices. Instruction that separated "prereading" and "prewriting" from formal reading and writing are being challenged by a theory that does not impose such delineation. In this model, the early years are no longer viewed as the approach to readiness for reading and writing. Learning literacy is seen as a continuous process, beginning in infancy with exposure to oral language, written language, books, and stories beginning in the home and extending to other environments. Although preschoolers and kindergartners may not be literate in the skilled or conventional way that adults are, they have knowledge about literacy which has implications not only for instruction but also for assessment and measurement practices.

With insights from this research, scholars are formulating new perspectives of early childhood literacy development:

1. Literacy development begins long before children start formal instruction in school.
2. School personnel should recognize the knowledge about literacy that children bring to school with them and build early reading and writing experiences on this existing knowledge.
3. Literacy involves the concurrent and interrelated development of oral language, reading, and writing.
4. Learning is promoted when literacy is based on functional experiences in which there is a need to read and write.
5. Learning is promoted in social settings as children interact with adults and peers during literacy activities.
6. Although children's learning about literacy can be described in terms of generalized stages, children can pass through these stages in a variety of ways and at different ages.
7. Adults serve as models for literacy behavior, by demonstrating the use of books and print themselves (IRA, 1985)

## DIFFERENCES BETWEEN EMERGENT LITERACY AND READING READINESS

Emergent literacy, a term first used by Marie Clay (1984), places a much stronger emphasis on the knowledge that the child acquires about language, reading, and writing before coming to school. Literacy development begins early in life and is ongoing. There is a dynamic relationship among the communications skills: each influences the other in the course of development. Development occurs in everyday contexts of the home and community. Even young children possess certain literacy skills, though these skills are not fully developed or conventional, as we recognize mature reading and writing (Teale, 1986). For example, emergent literacy acknowledges children's scribble marks on a page as rudimentary writing, even if formal letters are not discernible. Similarly, a child is involved in legitimate literacy behavior when he or she narrates a familiar storybook while looking at the pictures and occasionally at the print. Although the reading is not conventional, there is the impression of reading through the tone of the child's voice, and the attention given to every page and illustration in a left to right progression across the pages (Sulzby, 1985).

Emergent literacy can be contrasted to a reading readiness model where these behaviors are not viewed as reading itself, but as precursors to reading. They are considered necessary to master before formal reading can begin. Reading skills are taught in a systematic and hierarchical fashion in the assumption that all children need to master the components of reading to become literate. These components, or subskills, can become quite isolated from the notion of deriving meaning from text. Therefore they often have little intrinsic value for the child (Teale & Sulzby, 1986).

Teale (1986) views the development of early literacy as the result of children's involvement in reading activities mediated by more literate others. It is the social interaction accompanying these activities that makes them so significant to the child's development. Not only do interactive literacy events teach children the societal function and convention of reading; they also link reading with enjoyment and satisfaction and thus increase children's desire to engage in literacy activities. Teale's emphasis on the social aspects of reading development reflects Vygotsky's (1979) more general theory of intellectual development. Vygotsky asserted that "all higher mental functions are internalized social relationships." Vygotsky's influence can be seen in Holdaway's (1979) theory of literacy development:

> The way in which supportive adults are induced by affection and common sense to intervene in the development of their children proves upon close examination to embody the most sound principles of teaching. Rather than provide verbal instructions about how a skill should be carried out, the parent sets up an emulative model of the skill in operation and induces activity in the child which approximates toward use of the skill. The first attempts of the child are to do something that is like the skill he wishes to emulate. This activity is then "shaped" or refined by immediate rewards (p. 22).

Holdaway (1979) explains four processes that enable young children to acquire literacy abilities. The first is observation of literacy behaviors, being read to, for example, or seeing adults read and write themselves. The second is collaboration with an individual who interacts with the child, providing encouragement, motivation, and help. The third process is practice. The learner tries out alone what has been learned, role playing, for instance, or invented spelling while writing and experiments without direction or adult observation. Practice gives children opportunities to evaluate their performances, make corrections, and increase skills. In the fourth process, performance, the child shares what has been learned and seeks approval from adults who are supportive and interested (Clark, 1984; Holdaway, 1979; Smith, 1978).

## EMERGENT LITERACY AND ASSESSMENT ISSUES

With the new theories and resulting practice in early literacy instruction there has been concern about commonly accepted practices for assessing the literacy development of young children. The concern is valid since decisions about placement of children, selection of instructional strategies for youngsters, and evaluation of programs are often made based on the scores received in a testing situation.

Assessment and measurement should match educational goals and practice. Many early literacy researchers argue that traditional standardized tests do not reflect the practice that has evolved from the new theories based on research. In addition, standardized tests are only one form of measurement; we have come to realize that these alone are not adequate assessments of total literacy development. Thus, the topic of assessing early literacy development is extremely important to address at this time. For example, many states now have on the books, or pending, legislation providing public school programs for "at-risk" 4-year-olds. Also there is increasing pressure toward pushing reading instruction into the kindergarten. Indications are such that these trends will intensify. Concomitant with this thrust toward providing more formal reading readiness instruction for children that are younger and younger is the tendency to assess those children's abilities. In the International Reading Association's Policy Statement on Literacy Development and Pre-First Grade, a recommendation is made:

> Use evaluative procedures that are developmentally and culturally appropriate for the children being assessed. The selection of evaluative measures should be based on the objectives of the instructional program and should consider each child's total development and its effect on reading performance.

The statement also issues a concern related to the assessment issue:

> The pressure to achieve high scores on standardized tests that frequently are not appropriate for the kindergarten child has resulted in changes in the content of programs. Program content often does not attend to the child's social, emotional, and intellectual development. Consequently, inappropriate activities that deny curiosity, critical thinking, and creative expression occur all too frequently. Such activities foster negative attitudes toward communication skill activities.

The purpose of this book is to present current research, theory, and practical information about assessing literacy development in early childhood. Underlying all the chapters will be the knowledge base gained from research on young children's literacy learning. Each chapter will discuss assessment or measurement strategies linking them closely with instruction since we have learned, it is almost impossible to separate the two. The book has the following major goals.

1.   First, to define and explore the concept of emergent literacy as it relates to assessment. The authors will not agree on the nature of this relationship even as they all acknowledge the potential of emergent literacy. The reader will find here arguments ranging from the notion that an emergent literacy perspective and formal testing are fundamentally incompatible to arguments for a standardized measure based on emergent literacy.

2.   Second, alternatives to formal evaluative procedures will be offered. Practical advice based on research studies will be presented along with problems and pitfalls of informal procedures.

3.   Third, the ideas of emergent literacy and assessment are expanded in several directions. Several authors move toward instructional consequences or toward examining an extended definition of literacy to speaking and writing activities. Others start from early literacy and look ahead toward the assessment of older children.

Thus, this volume might be considered to consist of three concentric circles of ideas. The core is the critique of formal measurement from an emergent literacy perspective. The next circle is an examination of the consequences of that critique, both in terms of modifying current practices and turning toward informal approaches. The third circle addresses the issues of the next level of consequence of this perspective. What does emergent literacy mean for other aspects of schooling and assessment?

Roughly paralleling the conceptual structure, the book has been divided into three major sections. The first is entitled *Issues and Perspectives in Early Literacy Assessment*. This portion of the book begins with a chapter by Anne Stallman and P. David Pearson in which they review and evaluate the tradition of assessing early literacy with formal tests, such as standardized readiness tests, individual placement and diagnostic tests, and criterion-referenced tests of component reading or readiness skills. Next William Teale discusses alternative approaches to assessment and the necessity for linking assessment and instruction in early childhood classrooms. Specific procedures for assessing young children's reading and writing are described. Jeffrey Smith discusses measurement issues in early literacy and addresses the controversy over whether standardized, formal techniques should be used, or whether informal, nonstandardized approaches are superior. The purpose of this chapter is to explore the measurement considerations inherent in both positions. This part concludes with a reflections segment by Robert Parker concerning issues and perspective in early literacy assessment, taking into consideration the discussions of the authors presented in this section of the book.

The second part of the volume is entitled *Ways of Assessing Early Literacy in the Classroom*. Each author focuses upon areas of development in emergent literacy and links instruction and assessment. Elizabeth Sulzby focuses on assessment of writing in early literacy contexts. She emphasizes the importance of assessing writing within the context of the language that surrounds it, distinguishing oral and written language as phenomena. Next Lesley Morrow deals with assessing children's comprehension of story through the construction of meaning during story reading and the reconstruction after the story has been read. Again instruction of comprehension and assessment are closely linked. Connie Juel addresses the controversial area of decoding. This is not a topic that is often addressed in emergent literacy contexts. However she is able to share the importance of decoding in early literacy development, and she discusses appropriate instruction and assessment issues. Last in this segment is a chapter by Jana Mason and Janice Stewart. These authors outline four major aspects that have emerged from the literature concerning early literacy development. They are defined with implications for instruction and assessment. The chapter incorporates some of the aspects within the first three in that section. To reflect on this portion of the book Irene Athey draws upon the contents of the individual chapters and adds her own insights concerning the discussion of new ideas for assessing early literacy in the classroom.

The final part in the book is entitled *Classroom Contexts*. Here Louise Cherry

Wilkinson discusses the communicative competence of young children within the different contexts in which they use language within the classroom. Dorothy Strickland and Donna Ogle complete this part by describing classroom practices reflecting an emergent literacy perspective. They take us into classrooms where teachers had the opportunity to report on their daily practices and discusses how they can evaluate their own programs by studying their own behavior during the school day. Janet Emig provides the concluding chapter in the book by discussing issues raised in the text. Then she places emergent literacy in the broader context of the national political and philosophical debates concerning literacy.

As mentioned in the beginning of this introduction, this is an issue in flux. Although most of the writers in this volume engage in empirical research, the chapters involve philosophical, historical, sociological, and political arguments as well as psychological, educational, and simply practical ones. In ten years, more evidence will be available, positions will change, and challenges to these ideas as yet unknown will no doubt emerge. That is not sufficient reason to delay this effort. It is important to document the change that has occurred thus far, and point to the most promising path for the future. Our goal in this volume is to stop briefly in our effort to say, "This is where we have been and this is where we should go." If we are not in perfect agreement, we are no different from other explorers, either scientific or geographical. The truth does not seek the consensus of scholars. We hope these chapters are as stimulating for the reader as our interactions have been for us.

## REFERENCES

CLARK, M. M. (1984). Literacy at home and at school: Insights from a study of young fluent readers. In J. Goelman, A. A. Oberg, & F. Smith (Eds.) *Awakening to literacy,* 122-130. London: Heinemann.

CLAY, M. M. (1978). *Reading: The patterning of complex behavior.* Auckland, New Zealand: Heinemann.

HOLDAWAY, D. (1979). *The foundations of literacy.* Sydney, Australia: Ashton Scholastic.

INTERNATIONAL READING ASSOCIATION (1985). Literacy Development and Pre-First Grade. Newark, DE: International Reading Association.

SMITH, F. (1978). *Understanding reading* (2nd ed.) New York: Holt Rinehart and Winston.

SULZBY, E. (1985). Children's emergent reading of favorite storybooks: A Developmental study. *Reading Research Quarterly, 20,* 458-481.

TEALE, W. H. (1986). Home background and young children's literacy development. In W. H. Teale & E. Sulzby (Eds.) *Emergent literacy: Writing and reading.* Norwood, NJ: Ablex.

TEALE, W. H. & Sulzby, E. (Eds.). (1986). *Emergent literacy: Writing and reading.* Norwood, NJ: Ablex.

VYGOTSKY, L. S. (1978). *Mind in society: The development of psychological processes.* Cambridge, MA: Harvard University Press.

# 2

# FORMAL MEASURES
# OF EARLY LITERACY

*Anne C. Stallman and P. David Pearson*

*Center for the Study of Reading*
*University of Illinois*

### Abstract

Anne Stallman and David Pearson conducted an extensive, quantitative and qualitative review of the tests of early reading development which are available in America today. They show that these measures tend to be group administered, rely heavily on the multiple-choice format, and stem from a componential, or skills, approach to reading instruction. They conclude that these measures are too similar to one another to offer much in the way of alternatives to educators and that they are not reflective of current thinking in the field of early literacy development.

The purpose of this chapter is to describe and evaluate formal measures of early literacy in relation to changing perspectives on how young children learn to read and write. Our ultimate goal is to be able to make recommendations about how, if at all, they should be used by educators.

Our plan for the essay is to trace historically the relationship of such measures to the child development theories which prevailed during their inception. The historical perspective will serve as a foundation for the major focus of the essay—a detailed analysis of those measures currently available for educators to use in making decisions about young children's "readiness" for literacy instruction. That analysis will provide the evidence to support whatever conclusions we reach about their potential usefulness.

## THE HISTORY

While concern for the instruction of young children can be traced back to the early Greeks—Aristotle and Plato advocated teaching fables to young children in order to promote goodness and development of the soul (Mason, 1984)—the concept of "reading readiness" is a relative newcomer to the field of education. The ancient Greeks were not concerned about prereading skills because learning to read was not considered to be a task difficult enough to merit a readiness stage; after all, it only involved learning the letters of the alphabet (Venezky, 1975). In fact, Socrates described learning to read in this way:

> Just as in learning to read, I said, we were satisfied when we knew the letters of the alphabet, which were very few, in all their recurring sizes and combinations; not slighting them as unimportant whether they occupy a space large or small, but everywhere eager to make them out; and not thinking ourselves perfect in the art of reading until we recognized them wherever they are found. (Plato, *The Republic*, III, 402a)

This view of reading prevailed until the 1900s when Huey put forth the idea that there was more to learning to read than alphabet identification (Huey, 1908). Although Huey's ideas represented a shift in thinking about the skills involved in the reading process, little attention was given to *when* reading instruction should begin. Many educators, including Huey and John Dewey, thought that age 8 was optimal for beginning reading instruction, because then, the child might have a rich enough store of concepts to be able to understand the ideas in texts.

Beginning in the 1920s, as a result of the scientific measurement and testing movement, educators became concerned about the number of children who were unsuccessful in first grade, usually due to a lack of reading skills. There were many studies conducted during the 1920s and 1930s to determine the reasons for children's failure in first grade (e.g., Dickson, 1920; Holmes, 1927; Smith, 1928; Monroe, 1932). This type of research is typified by a study by Morphett and Washburne (1931). In the summary of their study they recommended that teachers could reduce the possibility of children failing to learn to read by postponing reading instruction until the children reach a mental age of 6 ½ years, as measured on the Detroit First-Grade Intelligence Test. Overall, studies of this type found that the reason children were having difficulty learning to read was that they were not ready to learn to read when instruction began (Durkin, 1989). It was during this time that the term "reading readiness" began to appear in the literature (Venezky, 1975). The idea of reading readiness was reflective of the research of the time as well as the philosophy of the educators and psychologists of the period. One of the leading psychologists at the turn of the century was G. Stanley Hall. As the field of child development progressed, Hall exerted a profound influence on what came to be known as reading readiness. In his theory of recapitulation, he hypothesized that as individuals develop, they pass through the same stages through which the human race has passed in its development. All people pass through these stages in a predetermined order that cannot be changed.

According to this view, performance is determined by heredity (Hall, 1904). This view was taken one step farther by a student of Hall, Arnold Gesell. Not only did Gesell believe that the course of human development was predetermined, but he also proposed that advancement from one stage to the next was a result of what he called "neural ripening" or "automatic and unfolding behavior." He believed that movement from one stage to the next would occur only when an individual had reached a specific level of development, and this could not be accelerated (nor could the order in which these stages were encountered be altered). Movement from one stage to the next occurred naturally as a result of the passage of time (Gesell, 1925, 1928, 1940). This kind of thinking was clearly consistent with views like those of Morphett and Washburne. Many reading educators felt that children would learn to read only when they had reached the appropriate stage in their development and that reading instruction should be postponed until then. It is interesting to note that Hall and Gesell did not specify the stage at which reading readiness occurred; however, armed with the convincing data from Morphett and Washburne's work and buoyed by the popularity of the scientific measurement movement, educators pinpointed that stage at a mental age of 6.5.

The idea that a mental age of 6.5 was a necessary prerequisite for learning to read gained widespread acceptance during the 1930s and continued to dominate beginning reading instruction programs for the next 30 years. Objections to the mental age concept of reading readiness began as early as 1936 when Arthur Gates pointed out that the type of reading program is an important determinant of its success, and the child's mental age is a relatively insignificant factor, correlating about .25 with reading achievement scores at the end of first grade (Gates, 1937; Gates & Bond, 1936; Gates, Bond, & Russell, 1939). Betts (1946) likewise viewed instruction as a viable alternative to waiting. However, objections of this type went virtually unnoticed by educators, who continued to support the use of mental age scores as the indicator of reading readiness.

In a very important sense, readiness tests were developed as an alternative to the mental age philosophy of just waiting. The early reading readiness tests were seen to have several desirable features. These tests were "designed to measure the traits and achievements of school beginners that contribute to their readiness for first grade instruction" (*Metropolitan Readiness Tests*, 1933). Not only were they designed to measure overall readiness for beginning reading, but they were also to be used "to predict the rate of development of reading ability, and to diagnose the pupil's status and thus reveal his needs in each of several of the most important abilities required in learning to read" (*Gates Reading Readiness Tests*, 1939). Presumably, Gates and others (e.g., Betts, 1946) thought that teachers could do something instructionally to promote readiness; they did not have to adhere to a "just wait" philosophy. The one feature that readiness tests shared with the mental age approach is that they, like intelligence tests, represented a nonsubjective way to measure a child's readiness for reading, an important criterion in the scientific measurement movement so dominant during this era.

The early readiness tests were paper and pencil, group-administered instruments that focused on vocabulary knowledge; visual discrimination of pictures, objects, letters, or words; auditory discrimination (usually in the form of identifying rhyming words); and copying, which was thought to be indicative of mental maturity as well as physical development (*Metropolitan Readiness Tests*, 1933). As we have suggested, the intent of these tests was to diagnose individual children's strengths and weaknesses so that they could receive instruction in areas in which they were weak. However, in practice this was not the case. Schools tended to use total scores as indicators of overall readiness for reading instruction; as a result, many children were simply labeled as ready or not ready without any indication of what could be done to help those who were not ready for reading instruction. That was left up to whatever readiness program the school or teacher happened to be using (Durkin, 1989). Tests of this type continued to be developed through the 1940s and 1950s with relatively few changes in format, underlying philosophy, or use.

The 1960s brought changes in the philosophy of early reading instruction as well as some changes in the readiness tests. The American public was greatly shaken by the Soviet Union's launch of *Sputnik I* in 1957, and it brought to the foreground public concern over the quality of public school education in the United States. Not only did people feel that the schools should be teaching more, but teaching of basic skills should begin earlier (Durkin, 1989). Coincidentally, the thinking of psychologists and educators of the time supported the public's notion that children could and should be taught to read at an earlier age. Among the most prominent and influential thinkers of the time were Benjamin Bloom, Jerome Bruner, and David Ausubel. Bloom (1964) made two important discoveries: (1) preschool children have the ability to learn many kinds of skills, and (2) intelligence develops most rapidly during the first five years of life. Bruner put forth the popular hypothesis that "any subject can be taught effectively in some intellectually honest form to any child at any stage of development" (Bruner, 1960, p. 33). This was supported by Ausubel's definition of readiness as "the adequacy of existing capacity in relation to the demands of a given learning task" (Ausubel, 1959, p. 246). This type of thinking implied that the reason children were having difficulty learning to read lay in the quality of the instructional programs, not in the presence or absence of any predetermined level of readiness or mental age. This view echoes Gates's comments about readiness in the 1930s (Gates, 1937). William S. Gray (1969) pointed out that the generally accepted correlation of .65 between mental age and progress in learning to read indicates that there are factors other than mental age which influence learning to read. All this research stressed the importance of the child's early environment and the necessity of working with the child to get him or her ready to read rather than simply waiting for the child to reach an appropriate level of readiness as a result of the passage of time. This kind of thinking, in concert with the social revolution that occurred in the 1960s, led to the inception of Head Start programs. These extremely popular preschool programs were designed as intervention programs to help "culturally disadvantaged" children prepare for school and thereby ensure equal opportunities for success in school for all children

(Durkin, 1989; Teale & Sulzby, 1986). This effort to teach more to children and to do it earlier was manifested in the schools in two ways. First, the idea that it is necessary to teach prerequisite skills for reading became an integral part of the philosophy of basal reading programs; it took the form of a subskills approach to reading instruction, even in the kindergarten program. A second outgrowth of this period was that to accommodate the teaching of reading in kindergarten, the curriculum was simply pushed back—the skills and materials that had been used at the start of first grade were now part of kindergarten programs. The use of reading readiness programs, usually from basal reading series, became a staple of kindergarten curricula (Teale & Sulzby, 1986).

However, readiness tests of the 1960s tended to reflect only a few of the changes in the ways people thought about readiness at that time. Overall, tests continued to be made up of subtests of vocabulary, visual and auditory discrimination, and copying (*Metropolitan Readiness Tests*, 1964, 1966, 1969). There were some exceptions, such as the *Murphy-Durrell Diagnostic Reading Readiness Test* (1964) in which the subtests consisted of phoneme identification (identifying sounds in spoken words), recognition of letter names, and a learning rate test in which the child was tested on the number of words that he could remember after an hour of formal instruction. In general, despite an awakening of programs for early literacy, the readiness tests of the 1960s continued the tradition of the previous 30 years.

In the reading field, and in other curricular areas, the 1970s ushered in the era of mastery learning and skills management approaches to curriculum. Ultimately, these movements were to provide a more favorable climate for readiness tests because they, like the readiness tests that had evolved, were based upon a componential assumption about the nature of the reading process. The readiness tests of the 1970s included most of the subtests that were found in previous readiness tests—vocabulary knowledge, and visual and auditory discrimination, but they were organized in a slightly different way and included some new subtests. Visual and auditory discrimination tasks were subdivided into components. Visual discrimination of printed symbols was tested separately from letter recognition, and rhyming was tested separately from auditory memory (ability to recall a series of spoken words). Subtests of knowledge of letter-sound correspondences appeared consistently on the tests of the 1970s in contrast to the 1960s, where they appeared only sporadically. The new additions to these readiness tests were subtests on school language (the language of instruction as well as knowledge of standard English) and quantitative language and operations (math). Subtests that required copying were either dropped or rendered optional, mainly because writing was considered to be a skill that followed, not preceded, learning to read. The standardized readiness tests continued to be designed to permit diagnosis of strengths and weaknesses. In practice, however only total scores were used, and then only as a basis for placing children in groups for basal instruction. Once children began in the basal program, they usually completed it in its entirety regardless of their relative strengths or weaknesses. The driving force for basal instruction tended to be end-of-level tests included in the basal kindergarten programs, which, while uncannily similar to standardized readiness tests, were curriculum specific and, therefore, potentially greater in diagnostic value.

While the readiness tests and classroom instruction of the 1970s were most closely aligned with the philosophy of a subskills approach to reading, the research was not. Beginning in the late 1960s and continuing through the 1970s and into the 1980s was a new approach to looking at beginning reading. Both the maturational and subskills approaches to beginning reading were rejected. In 1966 Marie Clay coined the term that would come to characterize this new approach to beginning reading, *emergent literacy*. The emergent literacy perspective takes into account all of the child's interactions with books, print, reading, and writing as important steps in becoming an independent reader/writer (Teale & Sulzby, 1986). This view also suggests that in a print-rich environment, such as the one in which American children grow up, learning to read and write can be as natural as learning to speak in language-rich environments (Y. Goodman, 1967, 1984; K. Goodman, 1967, 1968; Goodman & Goodman, 1979). The term emergent literacy is appropriate for this movement because children are viewed as being "in the process of becoming literate" through active engagement with their world in reading and writing situations (Teale & Sulzby, 1986). Conversely, the term readiness is inappropriate because it implies that there is a stage in which the child is not yet a reader. Clearly, such an implication is unacceptable to the emergent literacy perspective.

Given the lack of consistency between dominant philosophies of beginning reading and formal measures of early literacy documented thus far, we should probably not expect to find a match between emergent literacy views and current measures of early reading. To determine whether we will, we now turn to the major task of this study—to analyze the crop of tests currently available for evaluating early literacy.

## METHOD

To analyze formal measures of early reading (or readiness), we first had to determine what was currently available on the market. We started with this operational definition of readiness tests: of those tests listed in the reading readiness section of *The Ninth Mental Measurements Yearbook* (Mitchell, 1985). We augmented that definition by calling all the publishers that we either knew published, or suspected might publish, readiness tests. We ordered copies of all the readiness tests that were uncovered in this search. In this way we received most of the readiness tests readily available to school personnel in the United States today.

Thus, our definition of *formal measure* included commercially available tests and inventories. Even at this early level, we found that most of the *tests* available employ some sort of multiple-choice, machine-scorable format, although a few require students to construct responses and test administrators to make judgments about the correctness, appropriateness, or sophistication of those responses. *Inventories* almost universally take the form of checklists that teachers or evaluators are supposed to use as they observe children's psychomotor, cognitive, social, and emotional development in either natural or controlled settings.

Once we had the tests and inventories, we had to find a way to look at them that would allow us to compare features across tests while depicting the essence of each test fairly. We began with what was essentially a discovery approach, asking ourselves what categories of information we needed to characterize each test accurately and to distinguish it from other tests. We listed characteristics we found, and then we sorted the characteristics into areas that seemed to capture the essence of the tests. These characteristics fell into four broad categories: general test characteristics, skills tested, presentation factors, and response characteristics. Then, each of the four categories were subdivided to capture the aspects of each test that were unique to particular tests, as well as those aspects that were common across tests. The subcategories of these four broad categories are listed in Table 1.

**TABLE 1    Complete List of Test Categories, Subcategories, and Areas**

| | |
|---|---|
| I.  General Test Characteristics | 13. Vowel Digraphs |
| A. Copyright | 14. Dipthongs |
| B. Age | 15. Phonetic Rules |
| C. Administration | 16. Syllables |
|    1. Group | 17. Spelling |
|    2. Individual | 18. Rhyming |
| D. Time | 19. Auditory Discrimination |
| E. Format | 20. Memory |
|    1. Checklist | 21. Printing |
|    2. Multiple Choice | C. Literacy and Language Concepts |
| F. Number of Items |    1. School Language |
| G. Stimulus Size |    2. Syntax (Including Negatives) |
| II. Skills Tested |    3. Compound Words |
| A. World Knowledge |    4. High-Frequency Words |
|    1. Vocabulary/Picture Identification |    5. Word Recognition (Auditory) |
|    2. Sequencing |    6. Decoding Printed Words |
| B. Sound and Symbol Concepts |      in Spoken Context |
|    1. Visual Matching and Embedded |    7. Environmental Print |
|      Patterns |    8. Orientation |
|    2. Uppercase Letters |    9. Directionality |
|    3. Lowercase Letters |   10. Concept of a Letter |
|    4. Matching Upper- and Lowercase |   11. Concept of a Word |
|      Letters |   12. Message |
|    5. Upper- and Lowercase Letters, |   13. Alphabetical Order |
|      Mixed | D. Comprehension |
|    6. Letter-Sound Correspondences |    1. Auditory Comprehension |
|    7. Initial Consonant Sounds |    2. Reading |
|    8. Final Consonant Sounds | E. Others |
|    9. Consonant Digraphs |    1. Colors |
|   10. Consonant Blends |    2. Shapes |
|   11. Short Vowel Sounds |    3. Mathematics |
|   12. Long Vowel Sounds |    4. Quantitative Language |

**TABLE 1    (Cont.)**

| | |
|---|---|
| III. Presentation | 3. Production |
| A. Mode | B. Unit of Response |
| 1. Auditory | 1. Picture |
| 2. Visual | 2. Letter |
| 3. Production | 3. Word |
| B. Unit of Presentation | 4. Nonsense Word |
| 1. Graphemic | 5. Phrase |
| 2. Phonemic | 6. Sentence |
| 3. Syllabic | 7. Connected Discourse |
| 4. Word | 8. Book |
| 5. Phrase | 9. Numerical |
| 6. Sentence | 10. Objects |
| 7. Connected Discourse | C. Student Response Activity |
| 8. Patterns | 1. Underline |
| 9. Numerical | 2. Mark |
| 10. Picture | 3. Point |
| 11. Book | 4. Fill in the Circle |
| IV. Response | 5. Write |
| A. Level of processing | 6. Draw |
| 1. Recognition | 7. Manipulate |
| 2. Identification | 8. Oral |

### General Test Characteristics

The category of general test characteristics focused on the aspects of the tests that were basically descriptive of tests in general—copyright, age, administration, time, format, number of items, and stimulus size. While all the tests used in this analysis are currently in print, the copyright dates ranged from 1976 through 1988. Whenever more than two copyrights were still being marketed, only those versions with the most current copyright date were included in our analysis.

*Age* refers to the age of the child for which the publisher recommends administration of the test to be appropriate. *Administration* refers to the setting in which the test is designed to be used, individual or group. All the group tests could be given to children individually, but the individual tests are not appropriate for use with more than one child at a time. *Time* indicates the amount of time that the publisher or author of the test recommends for administration of that test. In terms of *format*, a test could either have a multiple-choice format or a checklist format. In a checklist format, the examiner was usually directed to check off the appropriateness or occurrence of student responses to test items on a predetermined list.

The last two subcategories were the number of items used to test each skill and the size of the stimuli. The *number of items* used to test a child's knowledge of individual skills ranged from 1 to 54. The *size of the stimuli* that the child responds to was also categorized. The stimuli ranged from 1/8 inch to 10 inches, with almost 80 percent of the stimuli measuring one inch high or less.

### Skills Tested

In this category each subtest was classified according to the skill that was being assessed. These skills fell into five major areas: world knowledge, symbol and sound concepts, literacy and language concepts, comprehension, and others.

In our scheme, *world knowledge* includes the specific skills of vocabulary, picture identification, and sequencing. Regardless of the specific skill label, it is most often assessed by asking the child to identify pictures that represent general vocabulary or conceptual knowledge about everyday things or occurrences. For example, an item of this type might ask the child to "mark the picture of the truck that came to put out the fire" (see Figure 1a) or "mark the picture of the fan" (see Figure 1b).

The second major area that is assessed on readiness tests is the child's knowledge of *symbol and sound concepts*. It includes most of what we would normally label

---

**FIGURE 1**    World Knowledge Items

Example 1a
Item testing world knowledge

**What the child sees:**

**What the child hears:** *Look at the pictures of the three trucks.   Listen carefully. Yesterday there was a fire at Jones' Garage. Mrs. Jones called the fire department. Which truck came to put out the fire?*

Example 1b
Item testing vocabulary knowledge

**What the child sees:**

 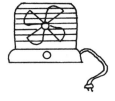

**What the child hears:** *There are pictures of an iron, a toaster, and a fan. Mark the picture of the fan.*

visual discrimination, auditory discrimination, letter-name and letter-sound knowledge, and a few outliers such as spelling, syllable knowledge, and memory. Knowledge of letters and sounds is assessed in a variety of ways, including visual matching
of letters, auditory discrimination of words with similar parts, matching letters with
pictures containing the sound of the letter, recognition of letters or sounds, identification of letters or sounds, and production of letters or sounds. For the purposes of
illustration, the letter *b* will be used to exemplify these different types of item formats
(see Figure 2).

The area of *literacy and language concepts* includes items that assess children's
knowledge of how to use language, reading strategies and conventions of printed
language, word recognition, and the language of instruction. Language usage was

**FIGURE 2**   Items Testing Knowledge of Sound and Symbol Concepts

1. Visual Matching

**What the child sees:**

# b | f d b g

**What the child hears:**   *Find the letter that is exactly the same as the first letter.*

2. Auditory Discrimination of Words with Similar Parts

**What the child sees:**

**What the child hears:**   *The pictures are book, drill, and pencil. Find the picture that
begins with the same sound that you hear at the beginning of bottle.*

3. Letter-Sound Correspondence

**What the child sees:**

→ i
→ b
→ q

**What the child hears:**   *Find the letter that stands for the sound you hear at the beginning
of bus.*

**FIGURE 2**    (Cont.)

---

4. Letter Recognition

   **What the child sees:**

   # p  b  q  o

   **What the child hears:**    *Find the b.*

5. Letter Identification

   **What the child sees:**

   # z  x  c  v  b  n  m

   **What the child hears:**    *Name these letters.*

6. Letter Production

   **What the child sees:**    Nothing

   **What the child hears:**    *Write the letter b.*

---

assessed using items that tapped the child's knowledge of syntax and grammar (see Figure 3). The assessment of children's understanding of reading strategies and the conventions of printed language included items that asked children to demonstrate their ability to do tasks such as identifying where to begin reading a book; demonstrating left to right and top to bottom progression, identifying the difference between letters, words, punctuation, and pictures; as well as knowing that the print carries the message. The third area in this major skill category was the child's knowledge of school language. Items of this type looked at the child's knowledge of relationships such as over, under, inside, around, first, next, last, and so on. Mainly because we could not find a more appropriate major skill slot in which to place them, we included a fourth type of subtest in this category—word recognition. Most often, this skill was tested by providing children with a set of four words, one of which is to be circled when the teacher gives a directive like, "circle the word that says GO." Occasionally, the children were asked to "read" the words. In all cases, the words on these tests were high-frequency words, the kind that dominate most basal preprimers.

The fourth major area that was included on readiness tests was *comprehension*. The assessment of comprehension took various forms. The most common was one in which the examiner read a short story of a few sentences to the children, who were then to choose the picture that best represented what had been read (see Figure 4a). A similar form was one in which the examiner again read a short story to the children

**FIGURE 3**   Item Testing Language Usage

**What the child sees:**

**What the child hears:** *Listen to what I say. The bird are flying. Mark the happy face if I said it right. Mark the sad face if I said it wrong.*

and then asked a question about what had been read. The children were then to choose the picture that best answered the question (see Figure 4b). A less common form was one in which the child was asked actually to read a sentence or short story himself and to fill in a missing word or answer a question about what had been read (see Figure 4c).

**FIGURE 4**   Comprehension

Example a.

**What the child sees:**

**What the child hears:** *Everyone on the block was standing outside the apartment building when the fire trucks came. All of the people were out of the burning building except a woman on the third floor. The firefighters were able to bring the woman down safely. Everyone cheered when they got to the ground. Mark the picture that shows what people cheered about.*

**FIGURE 4**    (Cont.)

Example b.

**What the child sees:**

**What the child hears:**   *The three pictures show some roller skates, an umbrella, and a snowsuit. When the Jones children cleaned out their drawers and closets for the garage sale, they found many things they didn't need any more. Sarah sold some stuffed toys and a snowsuit. Lisa sold a pair of roller skates with a broken strap and some pants that no longer fit. Mike sold an old umbrella and some comic books. Mark the picture of something Lisa sold.*

Example c.

**What the child sees:**

# The cat came _____ .

## home        can        house        boat

**What the child hears:**   *Read the sentence and the four words under the sentence. Mark the word that goes best in the blank in the sentence.*

The final category of classification of skills tested, labeled *other,* consisted of miscellaneous areas that did not fit into any of the other areas. Included in this category were items that assessed the child's knowledge of shapes, colors, mathematics, and quantitative language (see Figure 5). These types of items were excluded from the other major skill categories because they are not directly related to reading readiness even though they may be related to school readiness in general.

### Presentation

In this category we looked at the ways the items were presented to the students. Two subcategories of the presentation of items were considered:  mode and unit. In the *mode* of presentation, each item was classified in terms of the primary mode of presentation used by the examiner. The modes of presentation used on readiness tests

**FIGURE 5**   Other Types of Items

Example 1: Mathematics

**What the child sees:**

**What the child hears:**   *Mark the box that has four apples in it.*

Example 2: Quantitative Language

**What the child sees:**

**What the child hears:**   *Look at the three butterflies.  Mark the picture of the largest butterfly.*

were auditory, visual, and writing. An item that was presented using an *auditory* mode was one in which the child was to respond to something that the examiner *said*. For example, "Mark the picture of the leaf." Items that were presented using a *visual* mode required that the child respond to something that was *printed* in the test book—usually a letter, word, or picture. The final mode, *writing*, required the child to respond to something that the examiner *wrote* on the spot, such as asking the child to copy his name after the examiner had written it.

The *unit* of presentation refers to the type of stimulus that the child was asked to respond to—graphemic, phonemic, syllabic, word, phrase, sentence, connected discourse, patterns, numerical, picture, or book. Most of these categories are transparent in that the label defines each; however, there is potential overlap among some of them.  For example, often the teacher *said* "words" in both the phonemic and word categories. However in the phonemic category, the focus would have been on finding a picture that starts with the same sound as, for example, candle, while in the word category, the focus would have been on the lexical item itself as, for example, in finding the picture of the candle.  See Figure 6 for examples of these various levels of unit of presentation.

**FIGURE 6**   Units of Presentation and Units of Response

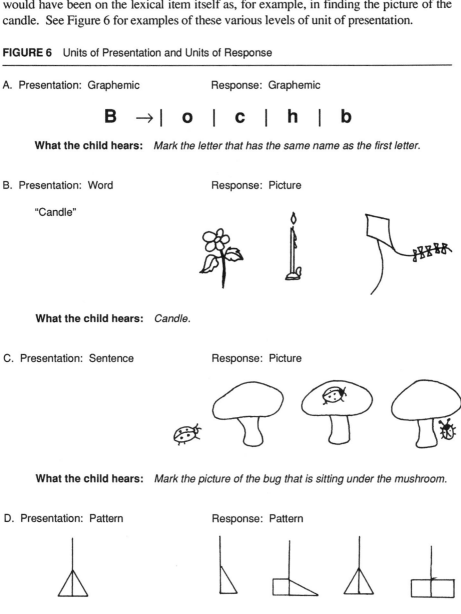

A. Presentation: Graphemic                   Response: Graphemic

**B**  →|  **o**  |  **c**  |  **h**  |  **b**

**What the child hears:**  *Mark the letter that has the same name as the first letter.*

B. Presentation: Word                         Response: Picture

   "Candle"

**What the child hears:**  *Candle.*

C. Presentation: Sentence                     Response: Picture

**What the child hears:**  *Mark the picture of the bug that is sitting under the mushroom.*

D. Presentation: Pattern                       Response: Pattern

**What the child hears:**  *Mark the pattern that is exactly the same as the first pattern.*

### Response

This category of children's responses has three subcategories: level of processing, stimulus type, and student response mode. The *level of processing* required of the student to respond correctly to an item ranged from recognition to identification to production. A *recognition* item was one that required the child to select the correct response from a list of alternatives such as "find the letter *a*" when the child is looking at the group of letters "*d o a p.*" In an *identification* item, the child would be required to name the letter her/himself, and in a *production* item, the child was asked to write the letter.

*Unit of response* looked at the stimulus that the child was to use to indicate the correct answer to the item. The units of response were picture, letter, word, nonsense word, phrase, sentence, connected discourse, book, numerical, or objects. See Figure 6 for examples of the levels of stimulus type.

The *student response mode* was simply a categorization of what the student had to do to respond to the item. The response modes were underlining, marking, pointing, filling in the circle (or bubble), writing, drawing, manipulating, and oral responses.

## RESULTS

Results are reported in two distinct sections and methodological traditions. First, we provide a set of short "case studies" for several of the tests in our corpus. For example, we review the *Metropolitan Readiness Test* in some detail because of its widespread use and its "representativeness" among group tests. But we also examine a few of the "outliers," such as Marie Clay's *Concepts About Print* assessment, to provide a sense of where the boundaries of our corpus of tests lay. Second, we provide a quantitative perspective on our corpus by examining the descriptive statistics generated from the analyses detailed in our methods section. We opted for descriptive rather than inferential statistics because we found that most effects worth discussing were obvious rather than subtle.

### *REPRESENTATIVE EXAMPLES*

### The Prototype

To get a feeling for the makeup of the readiness tests that are available, we decided to describe the test that seemed to exert the greatest impact on the field, the *Metropolitan Readiness Tests (MRT)*. It was chosen because it is the most widely used group test. The MRT has two levels. Level 1 is designed for use with children who are at the end of prekindergarten through the middle of the kindergarten year, and Level 2 is for children in the middle of kindergarten through the beginning of first grade.

Level 1 begins with a test called, "Auditory Memory." In this test the teacher first identifies all the pictures that will be used on the test (spoon, tree, chair, cat, house, ball, star, cup). Then the teacher says the names of three objects, such as *chair, house, tree,* and the child is to mark the box that contains a picture of those objects in the same order that the teacher read them (see Figure 7). There are 12 items of this type.

**FIGURE 7**    An Item Patterned after the Metropolitan Readiness Test: Memory Subtest

**What the child sees:**

**What the child hears:**    *(Find the box that has...)  Chair, house, tree.*

In the next section, labeled "Beginning Consonants," the children are to find a picture of the word that begins with the same sound as the two words the teacher says. It really represents an auditory discrimination task except that the focus is always on matching the target sound. Perhaps auditory matching would be the best label. No association with letters is required at all. For example, the child looks at pictures of a cat, a sock, milk, and an arm and is to choose the one that begins with the same sound as *miss* and *mine* (see Figure 8). There are 14 items like this.

**FIGURE 8**    An Item Patterned after the Metropolitan Readiness Test: Auditory Discrimination of Beginning Consonant Sounds

**What the child sees:**

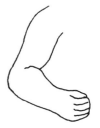

**What the child hears:**    *The pictures are: cat, sock, milk, and arm. Find the one that begins with the same sound as miss and mine.*

The third section of the test involves "Letter Recognition." The children look at four letters and are to mark the one that the teacher names. Four of the items use uppercase letters and six use lowercase letters (see Figure 9).

**FIGURE 9**   An Item Patterned after the Metropolitan Readiness Test: Letter Recognition

**What the child sees:**

# M | N | V | W

**What the child hears:**   *Mark the m.*

In the fourth section, "Visual Matching," the children look at a target pattern, letter, group of letters, or numbers and then mark the box that has the same thing as the first (i.e., target) box (see Figure 10). In the actual student booklet, the target box is highlighted in a different color. The test has 14 visual matching items.

**FIGURE 10**   An Item Patterned after the Metropolitan Readiness Test: Visual Matching

**What the child sees:**

# TX ▌ XL | TX | YT | XT

**What the child hears:**   *Nothing, but the general direction is to mark under the one that is just like what you see in the first (actually they give the color) box.*

The "School Language and Listening" section of the test has 15 items that test the children's knowledge of concepts and language used in school (no, between, center, cut, some, carrying, laughing, giving, flying, next to, from, indoors, larger, bigger, smaller, exactly the same). The children are to mark the picture that represents what the teacher says (see Figure 11).

**FIGURE 11**   An Item Patterned after the Metropolitan Readiness Test: School Language

**What the child sees:**

**What the child hears:**   *Mark the picture that shows the dog between the children.*

The last part, labeled "Quantitative Language," has 11 items that are related to math, such as counting, numerals, ordinal position, and so on. Again, the children are to mark the picture that represents what the teacher says, "Mark the second duck" (see Figure 12).

**FIGURE 12**    An Item Patterned after the Metropolitan Readiness Test:  Quantitative

**What the child sees:**

**What the child hears:**    *Mark the second duck.*

The Level 2 test is similar to the Level 1 test in many ways.  The same basic categories are represented, but the items are considerably more difficult.  Also, some of the types of behaviors tested on a single test in Level 1 are broken out into two tests in Level 2.  For example, there are separate tests for "School Language and Listening" in Level 2, and the quantitative section is broken out into "Quantitative Concepts" and "Quantitative Operations."  "Visual Matching" from Level 1 is augmented by a new variation called "Finding Patterns," in which a student now has to find the target pattern within a visually more complex array (e.g., find the it in visit).  The entire section on auditory memory is dropped and a completely new section is added— "Sound-Letter Correspondences"—in which the children are to choose the letter, from among four letters, that has the sound heard at the beginning of the word represented by the picture at the beginning of the row.  For example, the children look at a picture of a seal and are then to mark the *s* (see Figure 13).

As we suggested, the other sections of the Level 2 test differ from the Level 1 test in the difficulty of the items.  For example, on the Level 1 test, the children are asked to match patterns that are up to three letters long, and on the Level 2 test, they must match patterns that are up to six letters long; further, on the "Finding Patterns" test, the patterns are embedded in another, more complex, pattern.

Our examination of the other tests within our corpus leads us to the conclusion that the MRT is typical—wholly representative of items that are found on the other group-administered readiness test.  The other tests provide more variations on a theme than they do completely different "compositions."

**FIGURE 13**   An Item Patterned after the Metropolitan Readiness Test:  Letter-Sound Correspondences

---

**What the child sees:**

---

**What the child hears:**   *Listen to the sound at the beginning of seal. Mark under that letter.*

---

When used in conjunction with the ancillary materials that either accompany or can be purchased with the MRT, it is apparently designed to be used for two purposes: (1) diagnosing students' strengths and weaknesses in the areas tested and (2) helping teachers decide how to group children for instruction. We use the qualifier apparently because we could find no passage in the examiners' manual in which possible uses of the test were laid out unambiguously. But, by virtue of the fact that the class record sheet provides subtest scores for individuals and suggests placing students into one of three groups (plus, check, or minus) based upon subtest scores, we inferred that the authors intend it to be used for diagnosis and for grouping. The MRT also provides a form to be given to parents that explains the tests, shows how their child performed on the tests, and makes suggestions about things the parents can do to help their child improve.

### Outliers

If the MRT represents the center of our distribution of readiness tests, then the three we describe in this section represent the mavericks, the outliers that account for the variability within our data set.

*Developmental checklists.*   One type of readiness test that does not fit into a classification system with the tests already described is the developmental checklists which may either accompany the standard group test or stand on its own. These checklists are designed to be used with individual children. They look at the child's development in areas such as social-emotional development, physical development, cognitive development, and language development (see Table 2 for a more complete list).

To use one of these checklists, the parent or teacher simply observes the child and checks off the behaviors or characteristics that the child exhibits. When the checklist accompanies a standardized group test, as in the case of the MRT, it is recommended that the information from the checklist be used as an additional source

**TABLE 2    A Composite List of Skills/Behaviors/Traits Typically Found on Developmental Checklists**

I. Physical Development
   A. Large muscle development
      1. Climbs on climbing equipment
      2. Hops on one foot
      3. Bounces a ball
      4. Catches a ball
      5. Throws a ball
      6. Walks on tip toes
      7. Walks on a balance beam
      8. Jumps from a stool
      9. Skips
      10. Gallops
      11. Claps in time to music
   B. Fine muscle development
      1. Fastens buttons
      2. Ties shoelaces
      3. Strings beads
      4. Puts puzzles together
      5. Colors in the lines
      6. Cuts with scissors
      7. Copies letters and shapes
   C. Sensory development
      1. Recognizes objects drawn on board from across room
      2. Holds book at appropriate distance for reading
      3. Follows pictures in sequence across page with eyes
      4. Responds to oral directions from across the room
   D. General health
      1. Appears to be well nourished
      2. Remains awake and alert throughout the day
      3. Enters into outdoor play energetically
      4. Attendance records indicate adequate health
II. Language development
   A. Speech development
      1. Speaks clearly
      2. Expresses needs adequately
      3. Speaks language of school fluently
      4. Talks about everyday experiences
      5. Answers willingly when spoken to
      6. Modulates voice
      7. Asks questions
   B. Vocabulary development
      1. Asks about meanings of unfamiliar words
      2. Labels objects and actions correctly
      3. Describes objects in terms of size, shape, color
      4. Uses relationship words appropriately
      5. Uses appropriate category labels
   C. Language development
      1. Understands language of school
      2. Follows three part oral directions correctly
      3. Completes sentences with a logical ending
      4. Completes story with a logical ending
      5. Retells a familiar story
      6. Discriminates between words
   D. Written language
      1. Shows an interest in reading
      2. Attempts to read
      3. Asks about words written around the room
      4. Recognizes own name when written
      5. Attempts to write own name
      6. Dictates a phrase or sentence about an experience
      7. Knows reading progression
         a. Left to right
         b. Top to bottom
III. Cognitive development
   A. Information
      1. Names colors
      2. Names shapes
      3. Names sizes
      4. Knows the five senses
      5. Names body parts
      6. Gives own name
      7. Gives own address
      8. Gives own telephone number
   B. Awareness of details
      1. Recognizes likenesses and differences of objects
      2. Recognizes likenesses and differences of people
      3. Includes details when drawing a person

**TABLE 2   (Cont.)**

C. Memory
1. Memorizes names of other children
2. Memorizes songs and rhymes
3. Recites the alphabet
4. Counts to 20
D. Temporal and spatial concepts
1. Names days of the week
2. Names seasons of the year
3. Uses today, tomorrow, yesterday correctly
4. Tells time to the hour
5. Tells time to the half-hour
6. Identifies right and left on own body
7. Identifies right and left in space
IV. Social-emotional development
A. Intrapersonal skills
1. Recognizes own property
2. Keeps track of own property
3. Tries new activities
4. Tolerates a reasonable amount of frustration
5. Shows pride
6. Demonstrates responsibility
7. Shows creativity
8. Listens to a story for at least 15 minutes
9. Listens to directions before responding

10. Perseveres for at least 10 minutes on a single task
11. Completes tasks
12. Works alone without distraction
13. Responds positively to change in routine
14. Finds way from school to bus, carpool, or home
B. Interpersonal skills
1. Plays cooperatively/competitively as appropriate
2. Takes turns
3. Helps children and adults spontaneously
4. Follows adult direction without complaint
5. Leaves parents with little or no reluctance
6. Seeks help when needed
7. Responds appropriately to the emotions of others
8. Shows feelings
9. Protects self
10. Takes lead in playing with younger children
11. Participates in conversations
C. Hygiene/self-help
1. Toilet trained
2. Dresses self
3. Tries new food

of information to aid in the interpretation of the results of the group test. The stand-alone checklists (e.g., *Humanics National Child Assessment Form*) are designed to chart individual growth and development over time and as an aid in planning educational experiences for the child. In a sense, such checklists become convenient "reminders" for teachers; however, the basic responsibility for making judgments about student progress rests squarely on the shoulders of the teacher.

*The Gesell School Readiness Test.* Another test that did not fit into our original classification scheme was *The Gesell School Readiness Test.* We discuss it only because it has such a long history of use as a device for helping school personnel make decisions such as early kindergarten entry and referral to special programs. The primary emphases of this test are conceptual knowledge and perceptual-motor performance. Conceptual knowledge items involve tasks like identifying body parts, or talking about the world in which he lives (e.g., "What do you like to do best at home?"). The perceptual-motor tasks involve copying shapes, writing letters and numbers, and the Cube Test. The examiner also notes physical characteristics and behaviors. The Gesell Test is intended to measure the child's "developmental age," a construct purposely designed to differ from chronological age or experience. In this regard it is recommended for use as a screening device for placement in special programs or for delayed entry into ordinary programs (Gesell Institute, 1987); other evidence (e.g. Shepard & Smith, 1986) confirms its use in exactly these ways.

It has been criticized on a number of grounds: an outdated theory of child development (Meisels, 1987), lack of reliability and validity evidence (Carlson, 1985; Meisels, 1987), lack of a usable scoring system (Carlson, 1985), an unverified construct for developmental age (Meisels, 1987), and wholescale misapplication in school settings (Meisels, 1987; Shepard & Smith, 1986). One can only conclude that its use is fraught with controversy and that anyone considering its adoption should be prepared to enter the fray.

*The Concepts About Print (CAP) Tests.*    Another outlier we ended up including in our corpus, even though it was not reviewed in Buros, was Marie Clay's CAP Test. The CAP is really part of a larger battery of observational devices known as the *Diagnostic Survey* (Clay, 1985), which includes other "reading" assessments, such as letter identification, word identification, writing vocabulary, and running records of the child's oral reading of connected text. In New Zealand, the CAP tests are not used as readiness tests, instead they are used as a "progress check" one year after instruction has begun only for those children identified as potential "problem" readers. In the United States, however, the CAP tests have tended to be used in kindergarten in much the same way the readiness tests are often used; hence we have included them in our corpus.

What distinguishes the CAP from other readiness tests is that it is administered in the context of "reading" a real book. Each 5-year-old sits with the examiner and is asked to help by pointing to certain features as the book is read by the examiner. For example, the examiner would ask, "Where do I start reading?" or "Find a little letter like this (the child is shown uppercase T) or "Show me a word," and the like. The CAP is used in the United States as an aid to the teacher about one aspect of learning during the early stages of reading acquisition—knowledge of significant concepts about printed language. It should be noted, in passing, that in New Zealand, where the CAP is used as a part of a progress check, *no* systematic assessment of children is done prior to the onset of reading instruction.

## ANALYSIS OF THE CORPUS

Results are reported for all the types of categories that were used to analyze the tests we examined. Typically, one of two dependent measures is used—either the *number of subtests* exhibiting a particular feature or the *number of items* in a certain category. To assist the reader, we have organized our data reporting and discussion around three broad questions,

- How are the tests administered (issues of administration, time, and format)
- What kinds of things are tested (issues of the type of major and minor skill categories assessed)
- How are students tested (issues of item presentation and student response)

### How Are the Tests Administered?

Of the 20 tests in our corpus of currently available reading readiness tests, 16 (80 percent) were group tests and 4 were individual tests. Aggregated at the level of subtest, of the 208 subtests we examined, 170 (82 percent) were in group tests while 38 were in individual tests (18 percent). So, individual and group tests tend to assess just about the same number ($n = 10$) of subtests per test.

All group tests use a multiple-choice format and all individual tests use a checklist format. By checklist format, we mean that the test authors provide a checklist for each child, with spaces to record a test score and anecdotal comments for each subtest or, in some cases, for each item. Additionally, we found that three of the "tests" we ordered were not really tests. Instead they were developmental checklists that provided a long list of student behaviors and strategies that ought to be observed and judged; however, no explicit strategies were offered for conducting the observations. We decided not to include these three developmental checklists in our analysis.

The recommended ages for use of readiness tests ranged from prekindergarten through the beginning of fourth grade; however, 87 percent of the tests were recommended for use between the beginning of kindergarten through the middle of first grade.

While one-third of the tests did not come with recommended time guidelines, the time needed for administration of the remaining two-thirds of the tests ranged from 2 minutes to 225 minutes, with an average test time of 127.38 minutes (sd = 75.52). However this overall mean is misleading because of the huge difference between group and individual tests. Group tests averaged 162.4 minutes (sd = 45.67), while individual tests average 10.67 (sd = 7.36). These huge discrepancies bring into question the widespread assumption that group tests are necessarily more efficient than individual tests. Notice that a teacher could test 16 children individually in the time necessary to administer one group test. And this figure does not take into account either practice time or scoring time! One might argue that the teacher who gives a group test is getting lots more information on *more* subskills or aspects of reading readiness, thus weakening our argument against the inefficiency of group measures. But such an argument is invalid on several counts. First, the information from the group tests is rarely very curriculum specific. So a teacher learns that Georgette knows half the alphabet, but not which specific letters; and the 50 percent inference will likely be based upon a sample of four to ten letters. Second, many of the skills tested on group tests, while they may have reasonable predictive validity (they'll sort out the good readers from the poor), they will not necessarily ever become part of a curriculum. Auditory memory tests are a good case in point; short of helping students learn more about their world, there is nothing to teach. Third, for very young children, knowledge of directions and task requirements have to play a major role in group test performance; the tasks are simply too novel for too many young children to permit any other inferences.

## What Kinds of Things Are Tested?

There are several ways to answer the question about what is tested—by individual skill, by major skill category, for each test, for each type of test. We will try to balance all these perspectives in reporting these results. In Table 3, we report the average number of items per subtest and the number of subtests by major skill category for each of the 20 tests included in our corpus. The first conclusion to draw is that variability characterizes the data set. Most tests test a little bit of everything, but some, such as the Boehm R or the tests developed by Marie Clay (Concepts About Print and Ready to Read), are very specialized. Variability notwithstanding, the summary data

**TABLE 3    Average Number of Items per Subtest (and number of subtests) by Test and Major Skill Category**

| Test | World Knowledge | Sounds and Symbols | Literacy and Language Concepts | Comprehension | Other Skills |
|------|-----------------|--------------------|-------------------------------|---------------|--------------|
| CTBS A | 8.00 (1) | 20.50 (6) | 14.00 (2) | 2.00 (1) | 26.00 (1) |
| CTBS B | | 5.75 (4) | 6.25 (4) | 16.00 (2) | 20.00 (1) |
| Metropolitan 2 | | 11.20 (5) | 9.00 (1) | 9.00 (1) | 12.00 (2) |
| Metropolitan 1 | | 8.67 (6) | 15.00 (1) | | 11.00 (1) |
| Roswell/Chall | | 9.71 (14) | 35.00 (1) | | |
| MAT 6 | | 13.50 (4) | 24.00 (1) | | 24.00 (1) |
| SESAT 1 | 27.50 (2) | 6.00 (8) | | 37.50 (2) | 42.00 (1) |
| SESAT 2 | 27.50 (2) | 8.00 (5) | | 25.00 (4) | 44.00 (1) |
| Lollipop | | 4.33 (3) | 9.00 (1) | 1.00 (1) | 4.14 (7) |
| Boehm R | | | 50.00 (1) | | |
| PRI a | 5.33 (3) | 2.67 (3) | 4.00 (5) | 8.00 (1) | |
| ConcAbPrnt | | 1.00 (1) | 2.22 (9) | | |
| ReadyToRead | | | 45.00 (1) | | |
| GRTR Survey | | | 13.00 (2) | | |
| GRTR Diag | 9.00 (1) | 16.75 (4) | 9.00 (1) | | |
| Circus Batt | 35.50 (2) | 8.67 (15) | 26.67 (3) | 15.00 (4) | 20.00 (3) |
| CAT 11 | | 8.50 (4) | 14.00 (4) | 11.67 (3) | 54.00 (1) |
| CAT 12 | 10.00 (2) | 9.20 (5) | 10.00 (2) | 11.00 (2) | 20.00 (1) |
| ITBS 6 | 29.00 (1) | 4.56 (9) | 22.67 (3) | 16.00 (4) | 33.00 (1) |
| ITBS 5 | 29.00 (1) | 7.00 (5) | 29.00 (1) | 31.00 (1) | 33.00 (1) |
| **TOTALS** | | | | | |
| Number of subtests | 15 | 100 | 44 | 26 | 22 |
| Mean number of items | 19.46 | 8.95 | 13.39 | 16.88 | 19.09 |
| (St. dev) | 13.42 | 6.17 | 12.46 | 12.23 | 15.86 |
| Percentage of total items | 11.03 | 34.27 | 22.25 | 16.58 | 15.87 |

are of interest.  The last line in Table 3 (percentage of total items) is a simple calculation of the percentage of items from the entire corpus of items (n = 2,652) that assess that type of knowledge.  One-third of the items (but 48 percent of the subtests and, therefore, 48 percent of the judgments) are devoted to symbol-sound knowledge, with the second largest chunk devoted to literacy and language concepts (22 percent of the items and 21 percent of the subtests).  The mean number of items by major skill category data merit the interpretation that, on average, test constructors devote fewer items per subtest (presumably the unit from which diagnostic judgments would be made) to symbol-sound tests than they do to other types of tests.

There is, of course, much variability within each of these five major skill categories.  Table 4 depicts that variability by reporting the number and percentage of subtests devoted to each of the specific skills from the entire corpus.  For example, the 48 percent of the corpus figure for symbol-sound knowledge covers a multitude of sins, ranging from simple visual discrimination tasks to more difficult auditory tasks to letter knowledge to knowledge of specific letter-sound correspondences; most of these "sins" are well represented in the corpus.

**TABLE 4   Frequency of Skills Tested and Percentage of Total**

|  | Frequency | Percentage |
|---|---|---|
| A. World Knowledge |  |  |
| 1. Vocabulary/Picture Identification | 14 | 6.7% |
| 2. Sequencing | 1 | 0.5 |
| B. Sound and Symbol Concepts |  |  |
| 1. Visual Matching | 9 | 4.3 |
| a. Embedded Patterns | 1 | 0.5 |
| 2. Uppercase letters | 11 | 5.3 |
| 3. Lowercase letters | 9 | 4.3 |
| 4. Matching upper- and lowercase letters | 3 | 1.4 |
| 5. Upper and lowercase letters, mixed | 3 | 1.4 |
| 6. Letter-Sound Correspondences | 10 | 4.8 |
| 7. Initial Consonant Sounds | 18 | 8.7 |
| 8. Final Consonant Sounds | 7 | 3.4 |
| 9. Consonant Digraphs | 1 | 0.5 |
| 10. Consonant Blends | 2 | 1.0 |
| 11. Short Vowel Sounds | 6 | 2.9 |
| 12. Long Vowel Sounds | 3 | 1.4 |
| 13. Vowel Digraphs | 2 | 1.0 |
| 14. Dipthongs | 1 | 0.5 |
| 15. Phonetic Rules | 1 | 0.5 |
| 16. Syllables | 1 | 0.5 |
| 17. Spelling | 1 | 0.5 |
| 18. Rhyming | 5 | 2.4 |
| 19. Auditory Discrimination | 2 | 1.0 |
| 20. Memory | 2 | 1.0 |
| 21. Printing | 2 | 1.0 |

**TABLE 4    (Cont.)**

|  | Frequency | Percentage |
|---|---|---|
| C. Literacy and Language Concepts |  |  |
| 1. School Language | 11 | 5.3 |
| 2. Syntax | 9 | 4.3 |
| a. Negatives | 1 | 0.5 |
| 3. Compound Words | 1 | 0.5 |
| 4. High-Frequency Words | 11 | 5.3 |
| 5. Word Recognition (Auditory) | 2 | 1.0 |
| 6. Decoding Printed Words in Spoken Context | 1 | 0.5 |
| 7. Orientation | 1 | 0.5 |
| 9. Directionality | 2 | 1.0 |
| 10. Concept of a Letter | 1 | 0.5 |
| 11. Concept of a Word | 1 | 0.5 |
| 12. Message | 1 | 0.5 |
| 13. Alphabetical Order | 1 | 0.5 |
| D. Comprehension |  |  |
| 1. Auditory Comprehension | 19 | 9.1 |
| 2. Reading | 7 | 3.4 |
| E. Others |  |  |
| 1. Colors | 2 | 1.0 |
| 2. Shapes | 4 | 1.9 |
| 3. Mathematics | 14 | 6.7 |
| 4. Quantitative Language | 2 | 1.0 |

## How Are Students Tested?

The answer to this question can be either simple or complex. To get a broad picture of how students are tested, we first examine each of the relevant variables individually.

For example, we can say with some confidence that, in terms of level of processing, students are rarely asked to produce or construct answers to test items. We know that of the 208 subtests in our sample, 148 (72 percent) require students to recognize a response (e.g., find the letter *A* in this group), 49 (23 percent) require identification (e.g., what is this letter I am pointing to), and only 11 (5 percent) invite production (e.g., write the letter *A*). Teachers, or test administrators, are very clearly in control of the situation.

In Table 5 we look at the issue of level of processing from a slightly different slant. The data in Table 5 are the average number of items per subtest and the number of subtests broken down by major skill category, type of administration, and level of processing. These data suggest that the heavy reliance on recognition activities is primarily due to the preponderance of group tests in the readiness marketplace. Notice that identification and production are much more common in individual tests.

**TABLE 5    Average Number of Items (and Number of Subtests) by Type of Administration, Major Skill Area, and Level of Processing Required of Students**

| Level of Processing | World Knowledge | Sounds and Symbols | Literacy and Language | Comprehension | Other Skills | Total |
|---|---|---|---|---|---|---|
| | | | **Major Skills Area** | | | |
| | | | *Group Tests* | | | |
| Recognition | 19 (16) | 9.71 (72) | 14.48 (23) | 22.8 (15) | 25.58 (12) | |
| Identification | — | 5.5 (8) | 13.29 (7) | 11.75 (8) | 34.5 (2) | |
| Production | — | 1.0 (2) | 27.0 (2) | 1.0 (2) | 15.0 (1) | |
| | | | *Individual Tests* | | | |
| Recognition | — | 5.0 (1) | 2.5 (6) | — | 3.0 (3) | |
| Identification | — | 8.7 (14) | 15.67 (6) | 1.0 (1) | 5.67 (3) | |
| Production | — | 7.33 (3) | — | — | 3.0 (1) | |
| | | | *Total (Group + Individual)* | | | |
| Recognition | 19 (16) | 9.64 (73) | 12.0 (29) | 22.8 (15) | 21.07 (15) | 13.61 (148) |
| Identification | — | 7.59 (22) | 14.38 (13) | 10.55 (9) | 17.2 (5) | 10.92 (49) |
| Production | — | 4.8 (5) | 27.0 (2) | 1.00 (2) | 9.0 (2) | 8.91 (11) |
| Total | 19 (16) | 8.95 (100) | 13.39 (44) | 16.88 (26) | 19.09 (22) | |

The data for unit of presentation and unit of response are reported jointly in Table 6. The row and column frequencies and percentages provide data for each measure independently; the cell totals provide an interesting picture of the natural covariation between units of presentation and units of response. The summary data for the last two columns (frequency and percentage for units of presentation) corroborate what every novice, let alone experienced, kindergarten teacher knows: Students respond to a lot of pictures—marking them, circling them, or filling in the bubble next to them. Test makers (and workbook makers) rely heavily on pictures in creating their materials. Looking down those two columns, it is clear that students also respond to letters and words—marking them, circling them, or filling in the bubble next to them. In fact, those three stimuli— pictures, letters, and words—account for 81 percent of all the units of response in our corpus. Units of presentation tend to be somewhat more varied than units of response, with graphemic units, phonemic units, words, and sentences represented about equally in the corpus.

One note of explanation about the *phonemic* unit of presentation category is necessary. In over half of the *phonemic* cases, the test administrator actually said a "word"; we decided to classify these cases as phonemic rather than word because the clear intent of the item was to focus on a sound, as the auditory discrimination task, "find the picture that starts like ball," or the letter-sound task, "find the word that starts like ball." Those "word" units of presentation that were classified as *word* tended to be vocabulary items, as in "Find the picture of the dog."

TABLE 6  Frequency of Subtests by Units of Presentation and Units of Response

| Unit of Response | Unit of Presentation | | | | | | | | | | Sum | % |
|---|---|---|---|---|---|---|---|---|---|---|---|---|
|  | A | B | C | D | E | F | G | H | I | J |  |  |
| Picture | — | 26 | 21 | — | 26 | 12 | — | 3 | 1 | 5 | 94 | 45.2 |
| Letter | 28 | 11 | — | — | — | — | — | — | — | — | 39 | 18.8 |
| Word | 1 | 8 | 21 | — | 3 | — | — | — | — | — | 33 | 15.9 |
| Phrase | — | — | — | 1 | — | — | — | — | — | — | 1 | 0.5 |
| Sentence | — | — | 1 | — | 7 | 1 | — | — | — | — | 9 | 4.3 |
| Connected discourse | 2 | — | 1 | — | — | 4 | — | — | — | — | 7 | 3.4 |
| Book | — | — | — | — | — | — | 4 | — | — | — | 4 | 1.9 |
| Numerical | — | — | — | — | — | — | — | — | — | 8 | 8 | 3.8 |
| Patterns/ shapes | 1 | — | — | — | — | — | — | — | 8 | — | 9 | 4.3 |
| Objects | — | — | — | — | 1 | — | — | — | — | — | 1 | 0.5 |
| not classified | 1 | — | 1 | — | — | — | — | 1 | — | — | 3 | 1.4 |
| Total | 33 | 45 | 45 | 1 | 37 | 17 | 4 | 4 | 9 | 13 | 208 |  |
| % of total | 15.9 | 21.6 | 21.6 | 0.5 | 17.8 | 8.2 | 1.9 | 1.9 | 4.3 | 6.3 |  |  |

| | |
|---|---|
| A graphemic | F connected discourse |
| B phonemic | G book |
| C word | H picture |
| D phrase | I patterns/shapes |
| E sentence | J numerical |

It is interesting to note the natural covariation between units of response and units of presentation. For example, almost all *graphemic* units of presentation are associated with *letter* units of response. *Sentence* units of presentation are followed by *picture* responses about two-thirds of the time; typically, these are picture comprehension items in which the administrator says something like, "Find the picture of mother ironing Mary's dress." *Phonemic* stimuli were most often followed by pictures (mostly auditory discrimination) but sometimes by either letters or words (in both cases, letter-sound knowledge is normally being tested).

Table 7 contains mundane, but interesting data on how children are supposed to indicate their answers to test items. What is most notable about these data is the dominance of the fill-in-the-circle (or bubble or oval) activity. As with the data on level of cognitive processing, it appears that these data result from the heavy reliance on machine-scorable, group-administered tests. Equally remarkable is how seldom children are asked to do anything resembling an active mode of responding, such as saying something (11.5 percent) or writing something (3.4 percent).

Finally, Table 8 presents data on the mode of presentation of the stimuli for test items. Almost 75 percent of the time, children are directed to listen to something a teacher or test administrator says. Occasionally, they respond directly to something

TABLE 7    Frequency of Subtests Using Different Response Activities

| Response Activity | Frequency | Percent |
|---|---|---|
| Fill in circle | 131 | 63.0 |
| Mark | 24 | 11.5 |
| Oral | 24 | 11.5 |
| Point | 12 | 5.8 |
| Underline | 8 | 3.8 |
| Write | 7 | 3.4 |
| Manipulate | 1 | .5 |
| Draw | 1 | .5 |
| Total | 208 | 100 |

TABLE 8    Frequency of Subtests Using Different Modes of Presentation

| Mode of presentation | Frequency | Percent |
|---|---|---|
| Auditory | 154 | 74.0 |
| Visual | 52 | 25.0 |
| Writing | 2 | 1.0 |
| Total | 208 | 100 |

they see (these are almost all letter- or pattern-matching activities). Only twice in our entire sample were they to respond to something a teacher was supposed to write on the spot.

### Summary of Results

In summary, then, we can say that readiness tests, on the whole, have these prototypic characteristics:

1. They are typically administered to a group of children rather than to an individual child.
2. The clear emphasis (almost half of the subtests) is on sound-symbol knowledge.
3. They take a long time to give (a little over two hours spread out over a few days).
4. They rely a lot on students filling in bubbles based upon what the teacher says or what they see in a picture.
5. Recognition, not identification and production (the staples of reading), is the dominant level of cognitive processing involved; the group testing situation seems to be responsible for the dominance of recognition activities.

## DISCUSSION

### Portrait of a Kindergartner

One way of getting a handle on the operational definition of early reading emanating from readiness tests is to look at what happens during one from the point of view of a 5-year-old child. What does the world of reading look like to a typical kindergartner, Sam, taking a reading readiness test? First, he is told to go to bed early the night before the test and eat a good breakfast before coming to school on the day of the test. On the first day of testing, Sam sits at his place at his table with books set up all around him to make sure that no one else can look at his paper. He is given a sharp new pencil along with the instructions that it is not to be used to write on the test except for filling in the bubbles when the teacher tells him to. Next, the children practice filling in bubbles. The bubble must be completely filled in using marks that are very dark, and they must not go into any other bubble. After learning how to fill in bubbles properly, Sam is told that he is to erase the marks he just made, you see he needs to practice erasing completely just in case he wants to change his mind about something he does on the test. The next thing to learn about is the marker—how to put it under the row with the picture of the star at the beginning. This, Sam learns, is how he is to know which pictures he should be looking at.

Now the class is ready to begin to take the test. The teacher tells them that everyone should work very hard and try to do their best because the test will tell their parents and the first grade teachers how much they have learned in kindergarten. They are also told not to talk or look at anyone else's test. Sam puts his marker under the picture of the star and is ready to begin, except Sara can't find the star and Jim dropped his pencil on the floor. Finally, everyone is ready to begin the reading test. They find pictures, listen to sentences, find letters, and count things in pictures. When they are all finished, the teacher explains that what they have just done is the practice reading test; the real one will begin tomorrow and will look just like the one they did today. The class will be working on the test all week. Over the next few days, Sam and his classmates fill in lots of bubbles. Bubbles that tell which group of letters and which shapes look like the thing in the box at the beginning of the line. Bubbles that tell which picture begins with the first sound in the word they hear, bubbles that tell which letter the teacher says, and bubbles that tell which picture goes with the word or sentence the teacher says. Sam wonders when they are going get to read.

While this scenario may seem a little harsh and overstated, it is more typical than we would like to think. In the name of objectivity and efficiency, children are receiving odd messages about the nature of literacy. It is important to look at the readiness tests in terms of their usefulness to school personnel, but it is equally, if not more, important to look at the inferences about the nature of reading that children and their parents will draw from these sorts of tests.

### What Have We Learned?

In looking at the data from the analysis of the readiness tests, we have uncovered several facts and generalizations about them, all equally unsurprising to us and to educators. Overall, readiness tests in our corpus look very much like those designed by Gates and others in the 1930s; furthermore, they look very much like one another. Most of these tests are group tests presumably because of the assumption that it is more efficient to test a group of children all at one time than it is to test them individually. As we pointed out, this practice may rest on a faulty assumption about efficiency; it takes an average of 162.4 minutes to administer a group test (not including practice or scoring time), while it only takes an average of 10.67 minutes to administer an individual test. Therefore, once you have taken into account the additional time it takes to administer the practice group tests and score them (not to mention practice time), it may be just as efficient to administer individual tests, and, as we have argued, the information obtained from individual tests is often more useful to the teacher than are scores from norm-referenced tests.

An equally unstartling finding was the heavy emphasis on sound-symbol knowledge. Almost half the subtests dealt with sounds and symbols. This over-whelming emphasis on sound-symbol knowledge sends a very clear message—knowledge of sounds and symbols is a primary goal of early reading.

In terms of the ways children are tested on formal measures of early literacy, most are, to say the least, disconcerting. Children are tested on isolated skills in decontextualized settings rather than on reading tasks in situations in which they are asked to behave like readers. This conclusion is supported by several pieces of data. First, the examples presented to illustrate skills tested portray a picture of isolated, not integrated, reading skills. Second, recognition, not production or even identification, dominates as the primary mode of cognitive processing. One wonders what happened to the theory of reading as a constructive process. Third, when they recognize things, children are usually asked to respond to either a picture or something the teacher says. At the very least, real reading involves identification of words in sentences. Finally, what dominates the whole enterprise when children actually take the test is test-taking behavior—filling in bubbles, moving the marker, making sure everyone is in the right place. These activities may be related to test taking, but they have nothing to do with reading.

An important final point to consider in regard to these formal measures of early literacy is the message they are sending about what really counts. If you take the tests to be a reflection of the field's priorities in early literacy instruction, then what matters most is the child's ability to recognize pictures, letters, and sounds so they will be ready, someday, for the real thing.

### Beyond Standardized Readiness Tests

We chose to focus our discussion of formal measures of early literacy on readiness tests that were available as stand-alone entities on the professional market.

We did not include some other candidate indices of early literacy, such as the tests accompanying readiness levels of basal reading programs or the levels of standardized reading tests intended for grade 1. Consequently, the question of whether we have fairly represented the range of early literacy measures can be raised. To answer this question we now turn to a brief review of some of these measures of early literacy to see if they paint a different picture of early literacy from the one we have painted thus far. We look at tests from basal readiness programs, some early levels (first grade) of standardized tests, and first grade basal tests.

*Basal readiness tests.* On the grounds that the tests that they provide for measuring mastery of the program provide powerful evidence of what they consider important at this level, we looked at several of the leading basal series—Holt, Rinehart and Winston; Houghton Mifflin; Laidlaw Brothers; Macmillan Publishing Company; and Silver Burdett & Ginn—to see how they assessed student mastery of their programs. In looking at these tests we were struck by two things. First, these tests are remarkably similar to one another. In all cases the children are tested on letter recognition, auditory discrimination, and visual discrimination (in the form of matching letters and/or words). While there are some differences between the tests—sight words appear on two of the tests and knowledge of vowel sounds and rhyming each appear once—these tests are more alike than they are different from one another. Second, the degree of similarity between the basal tests and standardized tests, such as the *Metropolitan Readiness Tests,* is as remarkable as their similarity to one another. Not only are the skills tested similar, but the format is nearly identical. For example, notice the similarity between the way letter-sound knowledge is assessed in Figure 14 (extrapolated from one of our basals) and the format in Figure 13 (extrapolated from the *Metropolitan*). In making these comparisons, we were tempted to conclude that

**FIGURE 14**   An Item Patterned after Basal Readiness Tests

**What the child sees:**

**What the child hears:**   *Listen to the sound at the beginning of seal. Mark that letter.*

the basal publishers had the standardized readiness tests in mind (if not in hand) when they constructed their own readiness tests. This is not surprising in view of the fact that many schools use standardized tests as an indicator of the effectiveness of their instructional programs; and one way to help the students do well on the standardized tests is to give them practice on similar activities, which the basal tests provide. In sum, then, the first alternative picture of early literacy we have examined suggests that our first picture was representative.

*First grade standardized tests.* Next, we turn to standardized reading tests designed to be used with first grade children. These tests generally include subtests on vocabulary, word recognition, language usage, and reading comprehension. The vocabulary section is made up of items in which the student is to choose the word that best completes a sentence. For example, Mike _____ to school today. (went, likes, home, fast). In word recognition items the student is to select the word that begins or ends or has the same vowel sound as the word the teacher says—find the word that begins with the same sound as *boy* (the child looks at call, work, bat, my). Language usage items involve having the child choose the word that best completes a sentence. For example, The _____ are playing (girl, girls). The reading comprehension subtests are made up of two types of items. In the first, the child reads a sentence and chooses the picture that shows what the sentence is saying. In the second type of reading comprehension item, the child reads a short story of a few sentences and then answers a question or two about it.

*First grade basal tests.* Like the readiness tests, the first grade basal tests are remarkably similar to comparable levels of the standardized tests. Typically, they include tests of word recognition, letter-sound correspondences, and reading comprehension. In word recognition items, the student is to mark the word the teacher says. For example, the student looks at three words—*with, you, in*—and is told to mark the word *with.* For letter-sound correspondence items, the student is to mark the letter or word that has the same beginning, ending, or vowel sound as the word the teacher says. Among basal tests can be found the same two types of comprehension items that we described for the standardized tests.

While the first grade tests, both basal and standardized tests, paint a somewhat different picture of early literacy than the readiness tests, there is still a considerable amount of overlap between them. They all subscribe to the same philosophy—a subskills approach to reading instruction. In one sense, the first grade tests simply represent the next logical step following the readiness tests.

In answer to the question of fairness in representation we raised earlier, we feel confident that the similarity we have noted between formal readiness measures and those measures found in basals and on standardized reading tests permits the conclusion that we have provided a fair representation of early literacy assessment in our discussion of the data.

### Working Toward Alternatives

Why do we have these types of tests? How did we get into a situation in which important judgments about readiness for reading are based upon data from tests that, at best, only predict reading success? What are the alternatives we could consider? These are the questions with which we conclude our discussion of early literacy measures.

It is our conclusion that the measures of early literacy that dominate our field result from the same philosophy and traditions that undergird reading assessment generally. The assessment (and, no doubt, the instruction) of both early literacy and advanced literacy are beset by implicit, if not explicit, adherence to three related, counterproductive, and fallacious constructs: decomposition, decontextualization, and objectivity.

The subskills approach to reading instruction and assessment is based on the fallacy that the way to make a complex task, like reading, simple is to decompose it into smaller parts; then each part can be worked on until it is mastered; finally, the parts can be resynthesized into a working whole.

Once reading has been broken down into its "component parts," decontextualization takes over. Each of the "component parts" is then practiced in isolation until students achieve mastery. The assumption is that by isolating the skill in question, the student can focus directly on what needs to be done to master it. If the skill were practiced in a real reading context, so the argument goes, the extra contextual support would only divert the students' attention from the real task at hand—to learn the skill—and, hence, cloud the issue.

It is on these assumptions that most formal measures of early literacy are based. They test the "component parts" of reading in isolation from any natural, real reading context to see whether they have been mastered. These formal measures of early literacy provide schools with an added attraction nurtured, if not driven, by the accountability movement in educational politics. They give the illusion of being objective. Important decisions about children can be made on the basis of tests rather than, so the argument goes, on the basis of subjective judgments of fallible human beings. The irony here is that the tests are no more objective than teacher judgment; they simply move the subjectivity one level farther away from the student—to the fallible human beings who construct the tests in the first place.

What are the alternatives? Where, then, does the solution to the dilemma imposed by having formal measures of tasks few would label literacy lie? While we recognize all the problems attendant to individual assessment—most notably, administrator bias, inefficiency, lack of normative information, and subjectivity, we want to come down clearly on the side of what some (Collins, Brown, and Newman, in press; Valencia, Pearson, and McGinley, in press) have some to call "situated" assessments of individual students. We are convinced, based at least in part on our dissatisfaction with what is currently available, that the most productive methods of assessing early literacy lie in individual assessment of children while they are engaged in a literacy activity.  Situated assessments are desirable for two reasons.  The first is that they maximize the likelihood of optimal performance rather than typical performance since the child has more "data" and cueing systems available for rendering a task sensible.  Second, since situated assessments arise from the instructional setting, the issue of generalizability to real instructional situations disappears because there is no gap between assessment and instruction.  Of the tests we have reviewed, only those in Marie Clay's battery come close to meeting such a standard.  Clearly, we need more work in this area so that we can develop approaches that are even more situated than Clay's.  By the way, we would not go so far as to say that knowledge of specific skills, such as symbol-sound correspondences, are unimportant, but we would insist that they be dealt with in context, as needed and used by children engaged in the task of trying to render print sensible.

The major purpose of formal measures of early literacy is to help teachers make informed decisions about issues such as what materials to select, how to group students for instruction, and what students need to practice.  We acknowledge the fact that tentative initial decisions like these can be made (indeed are made) on the basis of standardized readiness tests or basal tests.  But, we all know that learning and teaching are processes that are too dynamic to rely upon single measures of anything, especially early literacy.  More than better tests, teachers need more knowledge.  They need the kind and depth of knowledge about reading that will permit them to develop the expertise to construct situated measures that match their needs and their students' needs very closely.  Some of these situated measures will have to be constructed "on the fly" while trying, for example, to answer such questions as, "Will Henry Smith be able to stand half a chance of reading the library book he has chosen?"  Others will be built for later reflection in trying to answer such questions as, "Are the students in my class becoming more reflective readers?"  But all will relate directly to students, tasks, and texts in a particular situation.

To prove that we can write with a forked tongue, we admit to a conviction that a second part of the solution lies in the construction of better commercially available tests.  We adhere to this conviction because we have difficulty envisioning a future in which politicians and administrators will have learned to trust our judgments completely; for better or worse, there will probably always be a place for wide-scale assessment of most things that matter to us.

But whatever new tests or procedures we build, we must insist that they reflect not only the traditions in emergent literacy, but also the fact that teachers are professionals who bear the ultimate responsibility for making informed decisions; it is our hope that those decisions will be based on the very best information we can gather.  Also, no matter how objective and detached we try to become in our assessment endeavors, they will always involve professional judgment, even if those judgments are moved out of the scoring and interpretation stages to the stages of conceptualization and item development.  Hence, the quality of the information we get from assessment activities will vary directly as a function of the knowledge that educators bring to those activities.  And it is increased awareness and knowledge through education that should be the focus of our efforts to reform literacy assessment.

# REFERENCES

AUSUBEL, D. P. (1959). Viewpoints from related disciplines: Human growth and development. *Teachers College Record, 60,* 245-254.

BETTS, E. A. (1946). *Foundations of reading instruction.* New York: America Book.

BLOOM, B. S. (1964). *Stability and change in human characteristics.* New York: John Wiley.

BRUNER, J. (1960). *The process of education.* Cambridge, MA: Harvard University Press.

CARLSON, R. D. (1985). Gesell school readiness test. In D. Keyser & R. C. Sweetland (Eds.), *Test critiques* Vol. II, pp. 314-318. Kansas City, MO: Test Corporation of America.

CLAY, M. M. (1966). *Emergent reading behavior.* Unpublished doctoral dissertation, University of Auckland, New Zealand.

CLAY M. (1985). *Early detection of reading difficulties* (3rd ed.). Portsmouth, NH: Heinemann.

COLLINS, A., BROWN, J. S. and NEWMAN, S. E. (in press). Cognitive Apprenticeship: Teaching the craft of reading, writing, and mathematics. In L. B. Resnick (ed.) *Cognition and Instruction: Issues and Agendas.* Hillsdale, N.J.: Lawrence Earlbaum Associates, Inc.

DICKSON, V. E. (1920). What first grade children can do in school as related to what is shown by mental tests. *Journal of Educational Research, 2,* 475-480.

DURKIN, D. (1989). *Teaching them to read* (5th ed.). Boston: Allyn & Bacon.

GATES, A. I. (1937). The necessary mental age for beginning reading. *Elementary School Journal, 37,* 497-508.

GATES, A. I., & BOND, G. L. (1936). Reading readiness: A study of factors determining success and failure in beginning reading. *Teachers College Record, 37,* 679-685.

GATES, A. I., BOND, G. L., & RUSSELL, D. H. (1939). *Methods of determining reading readiness.* New York: Bureau of Publications, Teachers College, Columbia University.

*Gates Reading Readiness Tests* (1939). Teachers College, Columbia University.

GESELL, A. (1925). *The mental growth of the preschool child.* New York: Macmillan.

GESELL, A. (1928). *Infancy and human growth.* New York: Macmillan.

GESELL, A. (1940). *The first five years of life.* New York: Harper & Bros.

Gesell Institute (1987). The Gesell Institute responds. *Young Children, 42*(2).

GOODMAN, K. S. (1967). Reading: A psycholinguistic guessing game. *Journal of the Reading Specialist, 4,* 126-135.

GOODMAN, K. S. (1968). *Study of children's behavior while reading orally* (Final Report, Project No. S425). Washington, DC: U.S. Department of Health, Education, and Welfare.

GOODMAN, K. S. & GOODMAN, Y. M. (1979). Learning to read is natural. In L. B. Resnick & P. Weaver (Eds.), *Theory and practice of early reading.* Hillsdale, NJ: Erlbaum.

GOODMAN, Y. M. (1967). *A psycholinguistic description of observed oral reading phenomena in selected young beginning readers.* Unpublished doctoral dissertation, Wayne State University, Detroit.

GOODMAN, Y. M. (1984). The development of initial literacy. In H. Goelman, A. Oberg, & F. Smith (Eds.), *Awakening to literacy.* Exeter, NH: Heinemann Educational.

GRAY, W. S. (1969). *The teaching of reading and writing* (2nd ed.). Glenview, IL: Unesco Scott, Foresman.

HALL, G. S. (1904). *The psychology of adolescence.* New York: D. Appleton.

HILDRETH, G. H., GRIFFITHS, N. L., & McGAUVRAN, M. E. (1964). *Metropolitan Readiness Tests.* New York: Harcourt Brace & World.

HILDRETH, G. H., GRIFFITHS, N. L., & McGAUVRAN, M. E. (1966). *Metropolitan Readiness Tests.* New York: Harcourt Brace & World.

HILDRETH, G. H., GRIFFITHS, N. L., & McGAUVRAN, M. E. (1969). *Metropolitan Readiness Tests.* New York: Harcourt Brace & World.

HOLMES, M. C. (1927). Investigation of reading readiness of first grade entrants. *Childhood Education, 3,* 215-221.

HUEY, E. B. (1908). *The psychology and pedagogy of reading.* New York: Macmillan.

MASON, J. M. (1984). Early reading from a developmental perspective. In P. D. Pearson (Ed.), *Handbook of reading research.* New York: Longman.

MEISELS, S. J. (1987). Uses and abuses of developmental screening and school readiness testing. *Young Children, 42*(2).

*Metropolitan Readiness Tests* (1933). New York: World Book.

MITCHELL, J.V. Jr. (Ed.) (1985). *The Ninth Mental Measurement Yearbook,* (Vols. 1-2). Lincoln, NB: University of Nebraska-Lincoln, Buros Institute of Mental Measurement.

MONROE, M. (1932). *Children who cannot read.* Chicago: University of Chicago Press.

MORPHETT, M. V., & WASHBURNE, C. (1931). When should children begin to read? *Elementary School Journal, 31,* 496-508.

MURPHY, H. A., & DURRELL, D. D. (1964). *Murphy-Durrell reading readiness analysis.* New York: Harcourt Brace & World.

PLATO (1892). *The Dialogues of Plato.* trans. B. Jowett, 2 vols. New York: Random House.

SHEPARD, L. A. & SMITH, M. L. (1986). School readiness and kindergarten retention: A policy analysis. *Educational Leadership, 44*(3), 78-86.

SMITH, N. B. (1928). Matching ability as a factor in first grade reading. *Journal of Educational Psychology, 19,* 560-571.

TEALE, W. H. & SULZBY, E. (Eds.) (1986). *Emergent literacy: Writing and reading.* Norwood, NJ: Ablex.

VALENCIA, S.W., PEARSON, P.D., McGINLEY, W. (in press). Assessing reading and writing in the middle school classroom. In G. Duffy (Ed.), *Reading in the Middle School* (second ed.). Newark, DE: International Reading Association.

VENEZKY, R. L. (1975). *Prereading skills: Theoretical foundations and practical applications.* (Theoretical Paper No. 54). Madison: The University of Wisconsin, Wisconsin Research and Development Center for Cognitive Learning.

## AUTHOR NOTES

The work upon which this publication was based was supported in part by the Office of Educational Research and Improvement under Cooperative Agreement No. OEG 0087-C1001. The publication does not necessarily reflect the views of the agency supporting the research.

We gratefully acknowledge the contributions of Judith K. Shelton who produced the artwork for this paper. The sample items in this chapter are similar to the items found on published tests in order to give the reader a sense of what the tests are like. However, the actual items on the test are not reproduced in order to preserve their security.

# 3

# THE PROMISE AND CHALLENGE OF INFORMAL ASSESSMENT IN EARLY LITERACY

*William H. Teale*

*The University of Texas at San Antonio*

## Abstract

William Teale argues for the development and incorporation of informal approaches to early literacy assessment that are compatible with an emergent literacy perspective. He advocates the use of measurement procedures that are conceptually and practically more proximal to the process of instruction. He concludes this chapter with a discussion of the challenges that face the field if this shift to informal assessment is to be successful.

Assessment is a process of gathering data and using those data to make decisions. It can be accomplished through a variety of instruments and measures. The purpose of any school assessment program is to improve services for children, thereby enhancing the quality of their education. There are a number of ways in which assessment can contribute to improved educational services. The one deserving perhaps the greatest attention is the subject of this volume: the link between assessment and classroom teaching. A carefully designed assessment program can significantly enhance learning because it provides the teacher with useful information about *what* needs to be taught to particular children and about the *when* and *how* of that teaching.

This chapter addresses the issue of assessment during the earliest phase of literacy development, the period up to the point when children read and write conventionally and fluently. It is typical for prekindergarten and kindergarten children and even many first graders to be in this phase of development. There are a variety of ways of measuring the literacy development of children of these ages in the school setting. Informal observations can be used to gather data in open and unobtrusive ways by noting what literacy knowledge, behaviors, and attitudes children exhibit in the course of ongoing classroom activities. Formal testing is a method at the opposite end of the spectrum from observation. The testing situation is usually somewhat artificial in comparison to the regular reading and writing activities of the classroom. Formal tests impose the greatest restrictions on performance since their items tend to be specific and the range of acceptable answers narrow. Performance samples occupy a middle ground between informal observations and formal testing. A performance sample does not occur spontaneously; the teacher sets it up with the intention of gathering specific kinds of data about a child's reading and writing. Performance samples resemble observations in that they yield a record of highly complex behavior on tasks that approximate the conditions and resources that children normally encounter in the classroom (or home and community settings). But performance samples are also testlike in that they center upon predefined tasks and activities that can be administered systematically.

If a school district chooses to assess the literacy development of its young children, it most often sanctions the use of a standardized group achievement test (Educational Research Service, 1986). Especially widely used are reading readiness tests like those described by Stallman and Pearson in Chapter 2 of this volume. Of course, classroom teachers may, and do, use other means of assessing student learning. But it is important to note that the results from standardized achievement tests are considered highly significant by school administrators, school and public policymakers, and the general public. Such tests also affect the way teachers teach (Frederiksen, 1984; Lerner, 1981).

Instead of standardized group measures like reading readiness tests, I advocate informal assessment—systematic classroom observations and performance samples of reading and writing—as the most appropriate means of assessing young children to obtain information that promotes good literacy instruction. This chapter explains theoretically why informal assessment should be preferred to the formal group measures, and it also presents some examples of promising informal assessment procedures that teachers can use. The arguments for informal assessment are based both upon current knowledge of early childhood literacy learning and upon an understanding of young children's developmental needs and social characteristics.

However, it must also be noted that there are problems associated with implementing programs for informal assessment of early literacy development. These issues are discussed in the chapter by presenting a series of challenges that must be met if informal assessment programs are to gain credibility and widespread use in our early childhood classrooms. An important purpose of the chapter is to offer a challenge for the 1990s: to suggest needed research and development that will produce for teachers of the twenty-first century valid and reliable tools for conducting informal assessment of early reading and writing. With such tools, early literacy instruction could be greatly enhanced.

## WHY INFORMAL ASSESSMENT?

I have already expressed the belief that informal literacy assessment yields the information most useful to teachers about how to teach the children in their classrooms. Why would teachers find results from such procedures more informative than results from formal standardized tests that are currently used in early literacy assessment? To answer this question, it is necessary to examine two things: (1) what young children are like and (2) what early literacy learning is like.

### Developmental and Social Characteristics of Young Children

Typically, 4-, 5-, and 6-year-olds have certain characteristics that make them less than desirable as participants in group standardized testing (National Association for the Education of Young Children, 1988). Although homes often provide young children with considerable experience in reading and writing, they rarely involve children in test-taking situations (Heath, 1983; Taylor, 1983; Taylor & Dorsey-Gaines, 1988; Teale, 1986). Lack of experience with test taking means that many children fail to respond appropriately to a standardized test because they cannot interpret the sociolinguistic demands of the situation.

Furthermore, children in the prekindergarten through grade 1 age range are also easily distracted when they participate in a group testing situation. The same child who will look at books for 30 minutes straight can be off task in 90 seconds in a test situation. Why? Because standardized tests are not designed to hold children's interest. Thus, especially with children at these age levels the tests in part measure how well the children sustain their attention to a task rather than simply indicating ability in the content and skills being tested.

The problem of high distractibility can be mitigated by one-to-one attention. Individually administered instruments keep young children "on task" more. Without one-to-one contact the likelihood of ending up with an inaccurate picture of the child's capabilities in literacy is high. Especially likely is the possibility of "false negatives," children whose abilities are seriously underestimated by the test simply because they didn't stay on task, they didn't really understand the nature and purpose of the task in the first place, or both.

One may be tempted at this point to say, "Well, then, the answer to our dilemma of how to assess early literacy development is simply to acculturate children into testing and to employ one-to-one testing situations. Then we can get useful results that inform day-to-day teaching." However, even if it were possible to make the testing situation more familiar to children (and I suspect this would be a misguided effort) or even if state legislatures appropriated enough money to run a one-to-one testing program for young children (and it is highly unlikely that any state or school district would use that amount of money in such a way), there is still a problem with reading readiness tests and related formal tests of early literacy that is even more fundamental: they do not measure all the right things.

*The content of early literacy assessment.*    What we measure should be determined by our knowledge of early literacy learning.  Research of the past decade has prompted a reconceptualization of the beginnings of literacy in young children.  It is now common to speak of *emergent literacy* (Teale & Sulzby, 1986).  Emergent literacy emphasizes that legitimate literacy learning begins very early in life for virtually all children in a literate society like that of the United States, with listening, speaking, reading, and writing abilities developing concurrently and interrelatedly. Long before children can read and write conventionally, they develop knowledge about literacy and engage in literate behaviors.  These behaviors and conceptualizations develop in predictable ways toward conventional literacy.  Thus, emergent literacy should not be regarded as merely precursor to real reading and writing or simply as a pseudoform of reading and writing that will be replaced by real reading and writing later on.  Rather, emergent literacy is legitimate reading and writing even though it is, in several respects, unlike the reading and writing of adults or even of older children who are conventionally literate.

Two points about emergent literacy must be discussed to explain why current standardized group measures of emergent literacy are not, from a content point of view, adequate for assessing early reading and writing development.  One relates to the overall nature of the literacy learning process.  The second has to do with the actual concepts that young children develop about written language and the strategies they use in their attempts to read and write.

First, let us examine the overall nature of the literacy learning process for young children.  As early literacy research has been conducted through ethnographic and naturalistic methodologies and through conventional experimentation, it has become clear that an adequate description of early literacy development must take into account the fact that, in the process of becoming literate, children are learning what reading and writing are for, they are learning how to read and write, and they are learning about reading and writing.  In other words, becoming literate is a multifaceted process involving attitudes, knowledge, skill, and self-monitoring.

Such a comprehensive perspective on literacy learning is perhaps best captured in the learning theory framework espoused by psychologists like Leont'ev (1981). Called activity theory, this way of conceptualizing learning argues that motives and goals, as well as psychological operations (e.g., pattern identification, prediction, inferencing), are all intrinsic parts of a process such as reading or writing.  From this perspective the fundamental unit of learning for a person is the activity, not a component skill or some knowledge that is part of the activity.

Leont'ev (1981) discusses three levels of the concept of activity: operations, actions, and the activity itself. As an example that involves literacy, let us take the case of baking a cake while using a recipe. The *activity* is "baking a cake." The *action* involving literacy is "reading the recipe." The operations related to reading include comprehending ideas, phrases, and words; recognizing words; perhaps even decoding or analyzing words structurally.

Actions are associated with particular goals. Operations are associated with the conditions under which an action is carried out. Thus, the action "reading the recipe" has as its goal understanding the processes by which certain ingredients can be combined so that a cake will result. The operations in this example are conducted under conditions like being able to refer to the recipe and having to deal with a particular type of text.

A perspective like activity theory provides a useful framework for understanding emergent literacy as well as conventional literacy. As young children observe and participate in reading and writing, they experience literacy as simultaneously involving motives, goals, and psychological processes performed under certain conditions. This experience helps them learn the *whys, whats,* and *hows* of reading and writing. All these dimensions are necessary in order to understand what it means to become literate.

Activity theory does not deny the importance of what are called skills in the scope and sequence of the typical reading program. However, these traditional skills are reconceptualized in activity theory because they are situated within a holistic context, intimately linked with goals and conditions. Operations are involved, but they are part of a larger skill (rather than an accretion of skills).

Such a perspective is extremely important for understanding the literacy learning of young children. In becoming literate, young children work from whole to part as well as from part to whole. They internalize activities and actions—"whole contexts"—at first. Only as they build their store of literacy experiences, and these experiences (contexts) resemble each other in some ways and differ in other ways, do children come to the point where they begin to focus on the operations. For example, it is not uncommon for young children to recognize *stop* on a stop sign but not in another context where the word is written. They may also recognize a word (point to it and say it) in one storybook but fail to identify that same word in another book or in the newspaper. This phenomenon is part of a perennial issue of concern in educational psychology—transfer of training. I believe that children do not learn skills (operations) and then apply them in a wide variety of situations. Rather, children learn situations (contexts), and as the situations become familiar and begin to repeat themselves and have constancies and variations, the familiarity with the situation enables the children to explore what makes them similar and what makes them different. They get to the level of skills *after* they have become comfortable at a more holistic level. At this point they begin to develop strategies for encoding speech in print, for recognizing words, for analyzing word structures. But these strategies do not develop in isolation from (or as precursors to) complete reading and writing activities.

Note that an activity theory perspective on early childhood literacy curriculum and teaching has profound implications for assessment. Most often, early literacy tests are organized around skills like letter-sound knowledge, visual and auditory discrimination, listening comprehension, word recognition, and knowledge of relationship words like *over, under, first, next,* and so forth (see Chapter 2, Stallman and Pearson). When a child actually takes one of these tests, the child is no longer engaging in the activity that we want to measure. What is being measured is the child's ability to perform isolated skills rather than his or her skill at reading or writing. Although it may be the case that measures of isolated skills correlate with overall literacy development for groups of children, making instructional decisions based on isolated skills testing is problematic and especially problematic in the case of young children. Stripping away what some persons regard as "merely context" actually ends up changing the activity for many 4-, 5-, and 6-year-olds. In a group testing situation we are not seeing what the children do in emergent reading and writing. Therefore, the conclusions about a young child generated from a test often say little about that child's actual performance or knowledge as displayed in reading and writing activities in the classroom. It is not surprising, then, that classroom teachers, concerned with making good instructional for individual children, find the results from such tests not particularly useful (Stiggins, 1985). Early childhood teachers need to understand how children comprehend, compose, decode, and encode in meaningful reading and writing activities like those that occur in the classroom. The key to obtaining such information is gathering assessment data in ecologically valid settings and interpreting the results in ways that attend to the why, what, and the how involved in children's reading and writing.

Now let us address the second point that explains why the content of current standardized group measures is not adequate for assessing early literacy development. To do so, let us selectively review some recent research on early literacy development to see what new insights they have provided. When we examine studies of home and community settings, for example, we see that young children's concepts of the functions and uses of literacy are of fundamental importance to literacy learning. Heath (1983), Schieffelin and Cochran-Smith (1984), Taylor (1983), Taylor and Dorsey-Gaines (1988), and Teale (1986) have all shown that basic to literacy learning are concepts of how reading and writing are used to mediate the activities in everyday life. When children understand that written language can, among other things, be used as a memory aid or a substitute for oral messages and for reasons ranging from financial and religious to instrumental and social interactional, they are able to integrate the knowledge and strategies they are learning into a coherent whole. Thus, the understanding of the functionality of literacy promotes long-term development.

Another example of how recent research has given substantial insight into young children's literacy processes and concepts is in the area of storybook reading. Analyses of actual parent-child and classroom storybook readings (e.g., Cochran-Smith, 1984; DeLoache & DeMendoza, 1987; Heath, 1982; Martinez & Teale, 1989a; Ninio & Bruner, 1978; Snow & Goldfield, 1982; Sulzby & Teale, 1987) have shown that storybook reading is a socially created activity and an activity that can be characterized by the metaphor of scaffolding (Bruner, 1978). Adult and child both contribute to the making of meaning in storybook reading events, with the adult usually taking primary responsibility for shaping the interaction in particular ways at first and the child gradually internalizing more and more of the storybook reading routine. For example, in repeated readings of particular books, we see the child becoming increasingly able to "read" the book by herself in the way that she and her parent or she, her classmates, and her teacher read it in interaction (Snow, 1983; Sulzby & Teale, 1987).

In fact, research has shown that children's independent rereadings of familiar books prior to the time they can read conventionally play a key role in young children's literacy development. Evidence indicates that all children who are regularly read to at home engage in these emergent storybook readings (Sulzby & Teale, 1987), and classroom studies show such readings to be a common phenomenon among kindergarten children (Martinez & Teale, 1989b; Sulzby & Teale, 1987). Nor are these emergent storybook reading behaviors mere correlates of development; microanalyses suggest that they actually contribute to learning about written language (Eller, Pappas, & Brown, 1988; Sulzby, 1985a). Thus, recent research has certainly helped to show more about what children learn from storybook reading as well as how they learn it.

In the area of early childhood writing, significant strides have also been made. For example, research on invented spelling (e.g., Henderson & Beers, 1981; Read, 1975), studies by Ferreiro on children's developing concepts of how written symbols encode language (Ferreiro, 1984, 1985, 1986; Ferreiro & Teberosky, 1982), Dyson's work on the relations between drawing and writing (e.g., Dyson, 1986) and how young children negotiate among multiple worlds to compose texts (Dyson, 1988), and research on the forms of writing used by young children (e.g., Sulzby, 1985b; Sulzby, Barnhart, & Hieshima, 1989) have all given new insight into different strategies children use to symbolize and to encode ideas and speech in print. Work like this has also suggested developmental patterns in children's writing knowledge and strategies.

The discussion of recent insights into young children's literacy concepts and strategies has been deliberately selective and brief; more extensive reviews can be found elsewhere (e.g., McGee, Richgels, & Charlesworth, 1986; Sulzby & Teale, in press). My purpose here was simply to indicate that the field today knows considerably more than was known a decade and a half ago about the processes and knowledge involved in early literacy development.

It is interesting to note that the impact of this enlarged and enriched conception of early childhood literacy development on instruction is already evident in the literature and in classrooms. In recent years articles have appeared on such topics as using environmental print (Hiebert, 1986; Schickedanz, 1986), predictable books (Bridge, 1986; Heald-Taylor, 1987), repeated readings of storybooks (Martinez & Roser, 1985; Sulzby, 1987), and writing (Martinez & Teale, 1987; Teale & Martinez, 1989) to foster literacy learning in early childhood programs. Methods books advocating an emergent literacy perspective on early reading and writing instruction have been published (e.g., Morrow, 1989; Salinger, 1988). Numerous individual teachers and several school districts across the United States are focusing their kindergarten programs on an emergent literacy perspective (e.g., Fairfax County Public Schools, 1986; Orange County Public Schools, 1986). It is as yet too early to determine the effects of these programs because the needed research is still in progress. However, there is reason to believe that such an emphasis will enhance the literacy education of young children.

Our current understandings of the various facets of early literacy learning and teaching just discussed are not, however, reflected in the assessment procedures currently sanctioned by states and by the majority of school districts in the United States. Reading readiness tests and related instruments assess very few of the concepts and strategies just reviewed, and they pay relatively little attention to the activities being widely implemented in early childhood programs. A review of the skills typically tested on the standardized group instruments shows, for example, almost no attention to emergent storybook reading, to children's not-yet-conventional spelling strategies, or to children's understanding of the functions and purposes of literacy. Thus, although educators have substantial insight into what the content of developmentally appropriate early childhood literacy instruction (and therefore assessment) should be, assessment methods currently in use in schools are largely not congruent with that knowledge.

By the same token the content of the tests does affect instruction. Because teachers tend to "teach to" the tests sanctioned by school districts or states, there is a tendency to fragment reading and writing in the curriculum, overemphasizing isolated skills, overusing drills and rote memorization, and not engaging children in enough reading and writing of whole texts and thinking through literacy. In short, many of the activities that foster early literacy learning are not promoted by the assessment program. The content of assessment and the content of exemplary instruction must come together if we are to build good early childhood literacy programs, but they cannot until the content of assessment changes to reflect what we know.

Small wonder then, that several states—North Carolina and Arizona, for example—and many individual school districts in the United States have moved to eliminate or seriously curtail group testing of reading in the early grades. And small wonder that many countries have never bought into widespread standardized testing of literacy in the first place, particularly testing of young children. The down side of such testing far outweighs the benefits, especially the benefits to the classroom teacher.

When we consider the content of the standardized measures themselves and when we consider the developmental and social characteristics of young children, we find the dominant approach to early childhood literacy assessment lacking in several respects. As an alternative to these measures, let us examine how informal assessment might better serve the needs of teachers of young children and, ultimately, of the children themselves.

## THE PROMISE OF INFORMAL ASSESSMENT

Informal methodologies such as systematic observation and recording of children's behaviors in classroom activities, keeping collections of work samples, and periodic performance samples of children's reading and writing gathered in one-to-one or small group settings that maintain ecological validity of literacy activities hold great promise for providing teachers with information that informs their teaching of individual children. These methods can also serve to rectify the current situation in which there exists an almost pernicious relationship between schools' official procedures for assessing early literacy and the teaching practices that research suggests would be positive. It is possible to bring teaching and assessment together in the classroom. Through utilization of observation and performance samples, we can minimize the amount of time teaching must stop to do formal testing and still get valid, reliable assessment data that help to provide enhanced services to children. At the same time these methods can be used to provide to policymakers and the general public evidence of accountability in teaching and learning.

To indicate the potential of these informal assessment methods, I should like to give three examples of promising techniques that can provide information to the classroom teacher that is very valuable in helping him or her teach particular children. My purpose is not to produce an exhaustive list of the techniques available. More extensive discussions of methods and instruments can be found in sources like Clay (1979), Genishi and Dyson (1985), Jaggar and Smith-Burke (1986), Teale (1988b), and Teale, Hiebert and Chittenden (1987), and in the chapters in this volume by Juel (Chapter 8), Morrow (Chapter 7), and Sulzby (Chapter 6). Rather, my aim is to provide examples that suggest the potential of informal methods for helping teachers teach. The three examples relate to the insights into early literacy discussed in the preceding section of this chapter: children's concepts of the functions and uses of written language, early childhood writing, and young children's storybook reading.

The first example of how assessment can be made to fit with early childhood literacy instruction relates to the issue of *children's understandings of the functions and uses of written language*. It has been argued that these conceptions represent the starting point of literacy in young children (Smith, 1976; Teale, 1988a). A widely recommended instructional means for promoting these understandings is to set up the dramatic play area in any number of ways—for example, a restaurant, a dinosaur museum, a doctor's office, a travel agency/airport, a newspaper office, a supermarket—and include in these settings as many forms of written language that are natural to them as possible. For example, the travel agency/airport could have large charts with manipulable flight numbers, times of day, city or country names, and words like *delayed, on time,* or *canceled.* Also included could be forms for airline tickets, boarding passes, travel brochures, appointment calendars, and maps. Of course, writing instruments and blank paper and note pads would also be placed there so that children could create other products that they might need (money, checks, directional signs indicating where to stand in line, and so forth). The purpose is to have the children incorporate written language into their dramatic play when they go there. Having set up the dramatic play area with the materials and also having discussed the subject of travel with the children and modeled certain uses of written language in the travel agency/airport setting, the teacher can assess children by observing them as they play. To what extent does each child incorporate the written language props into his or her play? In what ways does a child create written language that is used in the play? Such observations help the teacher to determine the child's overall understanding of the range of ways in which written language can function in everyday activities. Records for progress in this aspect of literacy development could take the form of anecdotal notes or be kept as a checklist. In either case assessment goes hand-in-hand with instructional practice.

A second example involves assessing *children's developing writing concepts and strategies*. A primary means of gathering data on this aspect of literacy development is analyzing processes and products that arise from what the children do in the classroom writing center. A writing center in an emergent literacy classroom is a place where children have daily opportunities to experiment with writing (Martinez & Teale, 1987). By examining the writing children produce there and the ways in which they reread what they have written, the teacher can obtain assessment information about a variety of facets of writing development: (1) the child's emerging familiarity with the features of written language (e.g., vocabulary, devices, rhythm, intonation) in comparison to those of oral language, (2) spelling and decoding strategies, and (3) composing strategies. For example, the child who writes IWTCAPDB for "I want to see a panda bear" is operating on different knowledge from the child who writes ALXOFELAYL for "Thank you for sending us all the books." Finding that Shawanda has, over the past week, moved from organizing her stories in unfocused chains to focused chains (Applebee, 1978) is informative. Listening to whether a child uses an oral language intonation or a written language intonation when rereading what he has written helps the teacher understand where the child is on the developmental path toward conventional literacy. The teacher can use data like these to provide appropriate instruction for each child. Perhaps the most valuable method of gathering such information is the writing folder, a collection of two or three pieces of writing from each week accompanied by, if necessary, a transcription of the way the child read the pieces. The writing folder enables the teacher to document development over time and provides an invaluable resource for parent conferences.

Storybook reading episodes also provide rich assessment information for the classroom teacher. Storybook reading is arguably the instructional activity most important to an early childhood classroom. As was mentioned previously, both adult-child interactions and children's independent, emergent storybook readings play a role in development. Typically occurring adult-child interactions like group storybook reading time can provide valuable assessment information. During group storybook time, the teacher can focus on one or two children per day, noting such factors as attention, the degree to which the children predict appropriately, their recall of key facets of the text, their participation in choral reading of predictable parts of the book, and their literary comprehension of stories.

One-to-one performance samples of teacher-child storybook reading can also be conducted for the purpose of gaining insight into facets of literacy development like knowledge of basic concepts of print (e.g., what part of the book is actually read, directionality), ability to match print to speech (i.e., to voice point), knowledge of concepts like *letter* and *word* and of conventions like punctuation, and even general comprehension strategies and abilities. During the one-to-one reading of a book, the teacher can informally question the child for assessment purposes. Such a procedure is similar in some ways to Clay's *Concepts about Print Test,* but it uses material more ecologically consistent with books typical of everyday instruction, and it can be geared to survey a broader range of knowledge and strategies. It also shares the goals of Morrow's procedures for analyzing children's participation in storybook readings and could be integrated with her procedures for retelling stories (see Chapter 7, Morrow).

A third type of storybook reading activity that provides valuable assessment data is a child's independent attempts to read stories, that is, the child's emergent storybook reading strategies. Sulzby's research has identified different developmental properties of children's emergent storybook reading strategies (Sulzby, 1985a). By reading a book three or four times to the class and then asking individual children who cannot yet read conventionally to read the story aloud in a one-to-one setting, the teacher can determine the ways in which the child attempts to construct meaning from text. Over time the teacher can chart the child's growth toward conventional reading. A five-point scale designed for classroom use in assessing such development has been described in Teale (1988b).

Techniques like these provide the teacher with theoretically based information about individual children's emerging knowledge of and strategies for reading and writing. The information relates directly to teaching practices and is therefore immediately applicable in the classroom setting. The methods of gathering data are, to a large degree, integral to instruction, and the record keeping techniques would not be too cumbersome. All these factors —validity, utility of the information gathered, and ease of use—are important to consider when it comes to assessment procedures for the classroom. Informal assessment techniques like the ones just described offer special promise for accomplishing all the factors. With proper development of the techniques, their results can have meaning to teachers, to researchers, and to measurement specialists alike.

## THE CHALLENGE FOR INFORMAL ASSESSMENT

Having investigated the promise that informal approaches hold for early literacy assessment, we turn now to the current state of the art in informal assessment and in the institution of school itself to indicate that there are obstacles to moving the field toward such an approach. I see four major challenges that must be met if we are to use informal early childhood literacy assessment and instruction on a large scale and in a productive manner in our schools.

First, there is a need to know more about early childhood literacy learning itself. To date we have made tremendous strides, but there is still much to be learned about why young children develop literacy, about what they actually learn, about how they become literate, and about when various concepts and strategies are developed. Especially pressing is information about children from outside the ethnic and cultural mainstream. Developmentally appropriate instruction arises from basic research findings and from carefully conducted classroom research studies. We still have a great deal to discover. That is not to say, however, that development of valid and reliable early childhood literacy assessment procedures must wait on additional research. Clearly we know enough to take decisive and productive action in this area. The chapters in this book and other publications cited throughout this chapter indicate that we have acquired the knowledge base to create developmentally appropriate measures of early childhood literacy learning that are valid and reliable. But we must continue to ensure that assessment procedures reflect what quality research indicates about young children and literacy development.

The second challenge relates to the techniques and instruments themselves. It is clear that there is currently a paucity of high-quality informal measures of early literacy. Large-scale efforts must be mounted to develop and field test informal assessment procedures like those discussed in this chapter. For example, Sulzby's (1985a) basic research on emergent storybook reading has provided a solid empirical base for the development of an assessment procedure. That procedure must now be tested under classroom conditions with representative samples of young children. A high-quality instrument sensitive to the range of children being assessed and to the needs of the classroom teacher can be created only with such rigorous development procedures. In other words, what is necessary is to commit money and effort to the development of informal measures in a manner analogous to what has been done with large-scale standardized tests of early literacy such as readiness tests and achievement tests of beginning reading.

For the reliability and validity of informal measures to be realized, however, a third challenge will have to be met. The power of informal early literacy assessment comes from being able to see how young children use their emerging knowledge and skill to accomplish a complex task. Their approach to the task is often not conventional, but it is almost always rational. The great insight for the teacher comes from understanding what the child has done and why the child has done that. Such a perspective is what helps in planning instruction. In other words, what informal measures facilitate is helping us see early literacy from the child's point of view. It must be recognized, though, that the quality of informal measures is highly dependent upon teacher knowledge. In order to implement the use of performance samples like emergent storybook readings as an assessment technique, to conduct observations in the dramatic play area, or to analyze five months' worth of samples in a child's writing folder, the teacher must know what to look for. To a larger degree than with a standardized test, the instrument for informal measures is the teacher.  Therefore, a successful informal assessment program will require an educational inservice component to help teachers develop their knowledge.  I would go so far as to say that efforts to establish informal assessment as a viable tool in the early childhood classroom are doomed to failure without such in-service.  School districts should plan carefully to help teachers understand why such assessment procedures are valuable, what they can learn about children by using them, and how they can use the techniques, interpret the results and apply the information gained.  An assessment program that makes extensive use of informal procedures is not as easy to establish as is one that relies only upon standardized tests, but the benefits that can be gained are worth the effort.

Finally, there is one challenge that must be met for the three previous ones even to be worth working on.  An integral part of the development of an informal assessment program necessarily involves political considerations.  If informal assessment is to be implemented in our early childhood classrooms, it must be legitimized.  Informal assessment carries considerably less weight in the school decision-making process than do standardized measures.  Informal assessment is also often viewed with suspicion by measurement personnel in school districts.  For the public and policy makers standardized tests are usually the *only* measure of accountability or effectiveness that is known or used.  Despite the fact they do not find the results from standardized tests very useful in daily classroom planning and instruction, even teachers themselves tend to hold standardized tests in considerable esteem.  There are no doubt numerous reasons why informal measures do not occupy the status of formal measures.  But a critical goal for early childhood education must be to reeducate the public, policymakers, and teachers to the fact that informal measures can be just as accurate, just as reliable, just as valid—and even more useful for instructional purposes.

For this to happen we must, of course, meet the challenges of the three previous points mentioned.  Thus, our four challenges are inextricably intertwined.  The challenges must be made part of an overall movement that is at once an issue of instruction, an issue of measurement, and an issue of politics.


## CONCLUSIONS

We stand at a crossroads in early childhood education.  The last few years have brought increasing pressures to start children in school on the road to academics earlier and earlier.  Perhaps more than any other area, literacy (at least reading) is stressed as the key component of early academics.  Unfortunately, in many instances, academics has been equated solely with formal and direct teaching.  Accompanying this thrust has been an increasing tendency toward formal testing of young children.  Partly in response to such trends, the National Association for the Education of Young Children recently issued its "Position Statement on Standardized Testing of Young Children 3

Through 8 Years of Age" (National Association for the Education of Young Children, 1988). The NAEYC lists seven guidelines for the use of standardized tests with young children. The statement also concludes that although standardized testing can play an important role in "ensuring that children's achievement or special needs are objectively and accurately assessed and that appropriate instructional services are implemented,...standardized tests are only one of multiple sources that should be used when decisions are made about what is best for young children" (p. 46).

This conclusion is especially important to emphasize when considering the classroom teacher. Good literacy instruction is based on decisions about children's abilities in relation to their behaviors in legitimate reading and writing activities. Good literacy instruction stems from what the teacher knows about a child's literacy knowledge, a child's literacy skill, and a child's affective responses to the processes and content being taught. Especially significant in the effort to develop assessment measures is the idea of trustworthiness. If measures are to succeed in accomplishing the goals outlined in this chapter, teachers must regard them as trustworthy. That is, teachers should recognize that what is being measured is like what is being taught in the classroom and that what is being measured has relevance to the literacy activities of the children themselves. It has been my contention in this chapter that young children's literacy learning cannot be adequately assessed without making informal practices an integral part of the overall assessment program of the school. Observation and performance samples must become a legitimized part of the assessment process in our early childhood classrooms if we can ever succeed in the goal of providing developmentally appropriate literacy instruction to our 4-, 5-, and 6-year olds. Early childhood literacy assessment must be recontextualized to bring it more in line with positive literacy instruction. Under such circumstances assessment can speak more directly and more powerfully to teachers and thereby result in better literacy learning environments for young children.

But as the previous section of this chapter indicated, we must also be careful with informal assessment. We must work hard to develop procedures and ways of interpreting information that result in valid, reliable measures of early literacy. We must take steps to help early childhood teachers recognize children's early literacy knowledge and strategies. Otherwise, we shall find that the direction of early childhood education increasingly determined by group standardized testing as we move into the 1990s and beyond. It will not be simple, but it is certainly possible to bring literacy assessment and literacy instruction together in developmentally appropriate ways. In this way assessment could make its greatest contribution to improved services for children.

# REFERENCES

APPLEBEE, A. N. (1978). *The child's concept of story: Ages two to seventeen.* Chicago: University of Chicago Press.

BRIDGE, C. (1986). Predictable books for beginning readers and writers. In M. R. Sampson

(Ed.), *The pursuit of literacy: Early reading and writing*, pp. 81–97. Dubuque, IA: Kendall/Hunt.

BRUNER, J. S. (1978). Learning how to do things with words. In J. S. Bruner & R. A. Garton (Eds.), *Human growth and development*. Oxford: Oxford University Press.

CLAY, M. M. (1979). *The early detection of reading difficulties*. Auckland, NZ: Heinemann.

COCHRAN-SMITH, M. (1984). *The making of a reader*. Norwood, NJ: Ablex.

DELOACH, J., & DEMENDOZA, O. (1987). Joint picturebook interactions of mothers and one-year-old children. *British Journal of Developmental Psychology, 5,* 111–123.

DYSON, A. H. (1986). Transitions and tensions: Interrelationships between the drawing, talking, and dictating of young children. *Research in the Teaching of English, 20,* 379–409.

DYSON, A. H. (1988). Negotiating among multiple worlds: The space/time dimension of young children's composing. *Research in the Teaching of English, 22,* 355–390.

Educational Research Service. (1986). *Kindergarten programs and practices in public schools*. Arlington, VA: Educational Research Service.

ELLER, R. G., PAPPAS, C. C., & BROWN, E. (1988). The lexical development of kindergartners: Learning from written context. *Journal of Reading Behavior, 20,* 5–24.

Fairfax County Public Schools (Elementary Language Arts Department). (1986). *The kindergarten language arts strategies*. Fairfax, VA: Fairfax County Public Schools.

FERREIRO, E. (1984). The underlying logic of literacy development. In H. Goelman, A. Oberg, & F. Smith (Eds.), *Awakening to literacy*, pp. 154–173. Exeter, NH: Heinemann.

FERREIRO, E. (1985). Literacy development: A psychogenetic perspective. In D. Olson, N. Torrance, & A. Hildyard (Eds.), *Literacy, language and learning: The nature and consequences of reading and writing*, pp. 217–228. Cambridge: Cambridge University Press.

FERREIRO, E. (1986). The interplay between information & assimilation in beginning literacy. In W. H. Teale & E. Sulzby (Eds.), *Emergent literacy: Writing and reading*, pp. 15–49. Norwood, NJ: Ablex.

FERREIRO, E., & TEBEROSKY, A. (1982). *Literacy before schooling*. Exeter, NH: Heinemann.

FREDERICKSEN, N. (1984). The real test bias. *American Psychologist, 39,* 193–202.

GENISHI, C., & DYSON, A. H. (1985). *Language assessment in the early years*. Norwood, NJ: Ablex.

HEALD-TAYLOR, G. (1987). How to use predictable books for K-2 language arts instruction. *The Reading Teacher, 40,* 656–663.

HEATH, S. B. (1982). What no bedtime story means: Narrative skills at home and school. *Language in Society, 11,* 40–76.

HEATH, S. B. (1983). *Ways with words: Language, life and work in communities and classrooms*. Cambridge: Cambridge University Press.

HENDERSON, E. H., & BEERS, J. (Eds.). (1981). *Developmental and cognitive aspects of learning to spell*. Newark, DE: International Reading Association.

HIEBERT, E. H. (1986). Using environmental print in beginning reading instruction. In M. R. Sampson (Ed.), *The pursuit of literacy: Early reading and writing*, pp. 73–80. Dubuque, IA: Kendall/Hunt.

JAGGAR, A., & SMITH-BURKE, M. T. (1986). *Observing the language learner*. Urbana, IL: National Council of Teachers of English.

LEONT'EV, A. N. (1981). The problem of activity in psychology. In J. V. Wertsch (Ed.), *The concept of activity in Soviet psychology*, pp. 37–71. White Plains, NY: M. E. Sharpe.

LERNER, B. (1981). The minimum competency testing movement: Social, scientific, and legal implications. *American Psychologist, 36,* 1057–1066.

MARTINEZ, M., & ROSER, N. (1985). Read it again: The value of repeated readings during storytime. *The Reading Teacher, 38,* 782–786.

MARTINEZ, M., & TEALE, W. H. (1987). The ins and outs of a kindergarten writing program. *The Reading Teacher, 40,* 444–451.

MARTINEZ, M. G., & TEALE, W. H. (1989a). Classroom storybook reading: The creation of texts and learning opportunities. *Theory into Practice, 28,* 126–135.

MARTINEZ, M. G., & TEALE, W. H. (1989b). [The effects of structured classroom library activities on kindergarten children's emergent reading abilities]. Unpublished raw data.

MCGEE, L., RICHGELS, D., & CHARLESWORTH, R. (1986). Emerging knowledge of written language: Learning to read and write. In S. Kilmer (Ed.) *Advances in early education and day care,* Vol. 4. Greenwich, CT: JAI Press.

MORROW, L. M. (1989). *Literacy development in the early years: Helping Children Read and Write.* Englewood Cliffs, NJ: Prentice Hall.

National Association for the Education of Young Children. (1988). NAEYC position statement on standardized testing of young children, three through eight years of age. *Young Children, 43,* 42–47.

NINIO, A., & BRUNER, J. S. (1978). The achievement and antecedents of labelling. *Journal of Child Language, 5,* 5–15.

Orange County Public Schools. (1986). *Weaving literature into writing.* Orlando, FL: Orange County Public Schools.

READ, C. (1975). *Children's categorization of speech sounds.* Urbana, IL: National Council of Teachers of English.

SALINGER, T. (1988). *Language arts and literacy for young children.* Columbus, OH: Charles E. Merrill.

SCHIEFFELIN, B., & COCHRAN-SMITH, M. (1984). Learning to read culturally: Literacy before schooling. In H. Goelman, A. Oberg, & F. Smith (Eds.), *Awakening to literacy,* pp. 3–23. Exeter, NH: Heinemann.

SCHICKEDANZ, J. A. (1986). *More than the ABCs: The early stages of reading and writing.* Washington, DC: National Association for the Education of Young Children.

SMITH, F. (1976). Learning to read by reading. *Language Arts, 53,* 297–299, 322.

SNOW, C. (1983). Literacy and language: Relationships during the preschool years. *Harvard Educational Review, 53,* 165–189.

SNOW, C. E., & GOLDFIELD, B. A. (1982). Building stories: The emergence of information structures from conversation. In D. Tannen (Ed.), *Analyzing discourse: Text and talk,* pp. 127–141. Washington, DC: Georgetown University Press.

STIGGINS, R. J. (1985). Improving assessment where it means the most: In the classroom. *Educational Leadership, 43,* 69–74.

SULZBY, E. (1985a). Children's emergent reading of favorite storybooks: A developmental study. *Reading Research Quarterly, 20,* 458–481.

SULZBY, E. (1985b). Kindergartners as writers and readers. In M. Farr (Ed.), *Advances in writing research, Vol. 1: Children's early writing development,* pp. 127–199. Norwood, NJ: Ablex.

SULZBY, E. (1986a). Writing and reading: Signs of oral and written language organization in the young child. In W. H. Teale & E. Sulzby (Eds.), *Emergent literacy: Writing and reading,* pp. 50–89. Norwood, NJ: Ablex.

SULZBY, E. (1986b). Young children's concepts for oral and written text. In K. Durkin (Ed.), *Language development during the school years,* pp. 95–116. London: Croom Helm.

SULZBY, E. (1987, April). *Teaching for literacy in the kindergarten: The impact of emergent literacy.* Paper presented at the Annual Meeting of the American Educational Research Association, Washington, DC.

SULZBY, E., BARNHART, J., & HIESHIMA, J. (1989). Forms of writing and rereading from writing: A preliminary report. In J. Mason (Ed.), *Reading and writing connections.* Newton, MA: Allyn & Bacon.

SULZBY, E., & TEALE, W. H. (1987). *Young children's storybook reading: Longitudinal study of parent-child interaction and children's independent functioning.* Final Report to the Spencer Foundation. Ann Arbor: The University of Michigan.

SULZBY, E., & TEALE, W. H. (in press). Emergent literacy. In P. D. Pearson, R. Barr, M. L. Kamil, & P. Mosenthal (Eds.), *Handbook of reading research,* 2nd ed. New York: Longman.

TAYLOR, D. (1983). *Family literacy: Young children learning to read and write.* Exeter, NH: Heinemann.

TAYLOR, D., & DORSEY-GAINES, C. (1988). *Growing up literate: Learning from inner-city families.* Portsmouth, NH: Heinemann.

TEALE, W. H. (1986). Home background and young children's literacy development. In W. H. Teale & E. Sulzby (Eds.), *Emergent literacy: Writing and reading,* pp. 173–206. Norwood, NJ: Ablex.

TEALE, W. H. (1988a, November). *Becoming literate: The first step in learning to read and write.* Paper presented at the 22nd Annual California Reading Association Conference, San Diego, CA.

TEALE, W. H. (1988b). Developmentally appropriate assessment of reading and writing in the early childhood classroom. *Elementary School Journal, 89,* 173–183.

TEALE, W. H., HIEBERT, E., & CHITTENDEN, E. (1987). Assessing young children's literacy development. *The Reading Teacher, 40,* 772–777.

TEALE, W. H., & MARTINEZ, M. G. (1989). Connecting writing: Fostering emergent literacy in kindergarten children. In J. M. Mason (Ed.), *Reading and writing connections.* Newton, MA: Allyn & Bacon.

TEALE, W. H., & SULZBY, E. (Eds.). (1986). *Emergent literacy: Writing and reading.* Norwood, NJ: Ablex.

# 4

# MEASUREMENT ISSUES IN EARLY LITERACY ASSESSMENT

*Jeffrey K. Smith*

*Rutgers, The State University of New Jersey*

### Abstract

In this chapter, Jeffrey K. Smith looks at early literacy assessment from the point of view of a measurement specialist. He argues that the principles that guide measurement in general need to be applied irrespective of whether one takes a reading readiness or emergent literacy approach.

> *They cared passionately for the truth, but their*
> *sense of evidence was different from ours.*

Jacob Bronowski on the Spanish Inquisition

The beginnings of literacy are undergoing dramatic changes in America, if not in the minds of young children, then surely in the ideas of those who research the topic. The concept of reading readiness is being replaced by the notion of emergent literacy. Among the researchers leading this reformulation are Clay (1966, 1979); Teale (1982), Sulzby (1985), Genishi and Dyson (1984), and Mason (1980). Although it would be inappropriate for a measurement specialist to attempt to describe a reading theory, the essence of the difference between the idea of reading readiness and the idea of emergent literacy seems to revolve around the difference between education and development. Reading readiness suggests that there is a time when it is appropriate to begin reading instruction with a child and, as an implied corollary, a time when it is inappropriate. Emergent literacy suggests that reading is a developmental phenomenon much more akin to language development than, say, learning the states and their capitals. Thus, from the emergent literacy perspective, the seeds of reading ability are resident at birth, needing nurturance and occasional weeding; the reading readiness model in contrast might liken learning how to read as an adult building a reading ship in the bottle of a child's brain. A more complete, and no doubt more accurate description of emergent literacy can be found in Chapter 2 (Stallman and Pearson).

Concomitant with this shift toward a more developmental perspective is a call for a change in the types of measures used to assess reading. The call for change includes requests for a shift away from product-oriented measures toward measures assessing the process of reading (Valencia and Pearson, 1987; Royer and Cunningham, 1981) as well as recommendations for a shift from formal measures to informal measures of reading (Johnston, 1987; Teale, Hiebert, & Chittenden, 1987).

The purpose of this chapter is to examine these issues not from the perspective of a reading specialist interested in measurement, but from that of a measurement specialist interested in reading. The focus then, of this chapter is the measurement issues and concerns of early literacy assessment. Formal and informal approaches will be examined as well as the reading readiness and emergent literacy perspectives on the growth of reading ability.

## IS THIS TRIP NECESSARY?

It is often useful to begin deliberations about assessment with the assumption that none is necessary. This is the psychometric equivalent of zero-based budgeting. The need for assessment is not justified until there is a need for information that will assist us (at some level) in instruction.

A basic premise in engaging in any measurement activity is the notion that the information to be gained from the measurement is to be used in some fashion. The information might benefit the teacher in determining what instruction to present to the student, in determining placement for a student, in grading the student (although let's hope not for 3- and 4-year-olds), or in evaluating the efficacy of the instructional program that the student has received. These are all legitimate information needs in traditional instruction. The problem with early literacy is that it does not always fit into the category of traditional instruction. If we are talking about a first grade reading program in a traditional elementary school, then the information needs listed above are probably appropriate. If we are talking about a mother at home with her 3- or 4-year-old child, then there probably are no information needs beyond what the mother will pick up through the natural interaction with her child. Kindergarten poses a different set of issues, since kindergarten may be similar to traditional first grade, or it may be more similar to the story reading of mother and child. Finally, it should be noted that early reading does not necessarily mean early age. Lack of reading ability is not confined to early childhood. Much of the difficulty encountered in measuring early reading can be attributed to the difficulties of measuring anything with young children. Many of these problems are eliminated if we considered illiterate adults. However, to invoke adult illiterates would nearly hopelessly confound this effort, so the discussion will be limited to *young* early readers.

The point of this discussion is to emphasize that measurement should follow an information need and that information needs vary according to the instructional setting under consideration. A useful criterion for deciding whether to engage in a measurement activity is to ask the question, "What am I going to do with this information once I have it?" The answer to this question can then be compared to the difficulty of obtaining the information. Obviously, we would always like the benefits to outweigh the costs.


## STARTING POINTS

Before beginning a measurement endeavor, it is important to understand what the situation is and why one is engaging in the activity. Let us examine three settings. The first might be a typical first grade setting. The teacher is planning on dividing the class into three reading groups and is going to use a basal reading series and perhaps a phonics workbook with the students. She needs a basis for dividing the pupils into the groups, and she needs to know what level to begin instruction for each of the groups. Furthermore, it would be useful if she knew if there were any children whose ability with respect to reading is either exceptionally high or exceptionally low. Beyond that, she probably does not need too much more information to begin. If she does not intend to individualize instruction or focus on specific weaknesses with children, her information needs at the beginning of the school year will probably be met if she can accomplish the tasks just listed.

The second setting might be a half-day kindergarten. The teacher will not be splitting the class into three groups; no basal reader or phonics program will be used; and noting exceptionalities is not critical to the instructional goals of the teacher. The reading program will focus on learning the alphabet and on reading stories to the pupils. Socialization and adjustment to school take priority over direct instruction, and so the information needs are dramatically different. It might be noted that this model of kindergarten appears to be growing less typical each year. It is being replaced by the first grade model just described being moved down a year.

The third setting might involve a reading resource teacher who is working with a half-dozen first grade pupils who are experiencing difficulty with reading in one fashion or another. This teacher wants to individualize instruction and wants to focus on the exact nature of the difficulties that the pupils are encountering. Her goal is to return these pupils to regular instruction.

Now that we have the settings, let's look at the measurement consequences of some of the needs described. The first grade setting described suggests an instructional approach which is probably typical of most systems. The teacher needs information for grouping, starting points, and exceptional students. The necessary information can be gathered in several fashions: through the use of a standardized reading measure, through an informal assessment of reading ability by the teacher, or through a discussion with the pupils' kindergarten teachers or parents. All three methods have strengths and weaknesses, and it is best to use at least two of the methods before reaching any decisions.

The kindergarten setting described involves no need for information about children's reading abilities whatsoever. All children will be working together on reading-related activities and no direct instruction will take place except for learning the alphabet. The only rationale for testing to take place here (whether formal or informal) would involve needs that the district may have for evaluating programs or for identifying children who are likely to exhibit learning difficulties later in their programs. If there is no benefit to be gained from testing, there is no reason to engage in it.

The third setting is the one where a need for explicit information about individuals is the most extensive. This is also the situation where teachers are often the most insecure about what or how to test and are most likely to rely too heavily on the results of standardized measures. There are myriad tests to choose from and new ones being developed on a monthly basis. Ninety-seven reading tests are reviewed in the *Ninth Mental Measurement Yearbook* (Mitchell, 1985), which contains mostly instruments developed since the eighth edition of the series. Theories of reading and reading instruction are also developed on a fairly regular basis. There are 61 different subheadings under reading in *Mental Measurement Yearbook*. When a teacher gets to the point of looking at test results from a particular test, the confusion can grow even more rapidly. Now, in addition to trying to comprehend the terms that describe the variables being measured on the test in use, the teacher also has to tackle measurement concepts. Since measurement specialists are not noted for being interested in communicating with anyone except other measurement specialists, the classroom teacher can find standardized test results bordering on the Kafkaesque. This is, of course, something of a parody, but it is true that most teachers are not able to make good use of standardized test results, particularly at the elementary level. This often causes them to discount the results, which is unfortunate because they are throwing away useful information, or they overuse the results, which may be dangerous if the results are not well understood.

In all three situations, all we have done is to begin the school year. What happens, say, three months into the year as far as the information needs of the teachers are concerned? Let's examine the three settings in December of the school year before moving on. In the traditional first grade classroom, most pupils ought to be doing fairly well. They are probably appropriately placed and making good progress within their groups. But this almost certainly won't be true for all pupils. It will become apparent to the teacher that the strongest pupils in the middle group are probably somewhat better readers than the weakest readers in the top group. She may also find that one or two readers in the top group are somewhat bored by the pace in that group.

Finally, she is likely to discover that the low group isn't a group at all, but a collection of individuals with very different strengths and weaknesses.

The kindergarten teacher may be discovering that several of the pupils can read the storybooks on their own and enjoy doing so while other pupils are restless during story reading or are encountering difficulty in learning the alphabet. This teacher may want to begin to tailor activities to the abilities and interests of the students in the class.

The reading resource teacher is developing a good feel for what works and what doesn't work with most of her small class, but may feel that she isn't being successful at all with one or two of the children. She is looking for the key to unlocking the problems that the pupils are having.

In all three settings, the use of standardized measures has disappeared almost completely. The knowledge gained from the administration of such a measure is dated; the students who the teachers are working with now are no longer the students who took those tests. The information that the teachers may have gained from the formal measures has been incorporated into the teacher's overall perspective of the child and has been tempered, or even more dramatically altered, through the daily one-on-one experiences that the teacher has with the child.

Now, let us move on to the end of the school year. The traditional first grade teacher needs to summarize the progress of each of her students to report to parents and to make recommendations for placement for second grade. The kindergarten teacher may or may not be faced with this demand, but some information is likely to be necessary for constructing next year's classes for her students. The reading resource teacher needs to make fairly specific recommendations about the placement and instructional programs she feels are most appropriate for her students.

Finally, in most school districts, administrators need to have an idea of the overall progress levels of students in the various schools in the district. This type of assessment is typically conducted at the end of the year. We move then, fairly quickly, from no assessment to a constellation of information needs that imply assessment procedures. Some of these needs can be met more efficiently with formal procedures; others most assuredly require informal approaches. The debate between formal and informal procedures is, in some respects, a straw man. Obtaining the necessary information to meet the need is the issue: sometimes this can be accomplished in 30 seconds in an interaction between a teacher and a child; other times it will require a fairly standard set of procedures to be applied.

## ISSUES IN CONCEPTUALIZING EARLY MEASUREMENT

Once there is determined a need for information and therefore some assessment, it is important to establish what concepts are to be measured and how we think these concepts behave. This is where there are important differences between those who promote an emergent literacy perspective on early reading and those who promote a reading readiness perspective. Although it may seem strange, it would be useful at this point to spend some time considering the field of mathematics. In assessing early math achievement, one is usually interested in such things as the child's ability to count, to do simple additions and subtractions, to understand the number line, and so on. There is a fairly close correspondence between the instructional methods and the instructional outcomes. Thus, matching assessment to outcome is not too difficult. In reading, there are fairly substantial differences among various approaches to teaching reading. Often, we find ourselves in the position of measuring the instructional process as opposed to the instructional outcome. For example, as a mature, adult reader, you haven't had to sound out any of the words in this article with the possible exception of some of the names of authors cited. You certainly did not need to employ any of the "word attack" skills you may have learned as a child. That is because almost all the words you encounter are in your sight word vocabulary. But for children, especially beginning readers, turning strings of letters into words is much of the game of reading. One can readily become a great reader without ever realizing that this sentence contains "ea" words with four different pronunciations. Thus, there is more than one route to competent reading. If a measure is designed to provide information about the instructional process, it must be related to that process. In arithmetic, this is not usually too difficult. In reading, the mismatch may be substantial.

In a reading readiness model, the focus is almost solely on reading, and within reading, priority is given to decoding skills. There is a strong emphasis on reading as the ability to turn written language into spoken language (whether the spoken language is audible or internal). There is also an emphasis on determining the appropriate time to commence instruction in decoding skills. In emergent literacy, the idea of literacy is seen as involving reading *and* writing skills (and often speaking and thinking skills) (Teale, Hiebert, & Chittenden, 1987). These are viewed as being inextricably related to another and not useful to disentangle for purposes of instruction. There is also the view that reading begins well before children can decode words (Mason, 1981). This can be seen in children's mimicking of reading and in their telling of stories. A philosophical difference between reading readiness and emergent literacy might be captured in the view each takes of the child and the curriculum. Emergent literacy seems more respectful of the child and his or her naturally occurring efforts. Reading readiness focuses more on the importance of getting the child into the instructional sequence.

We can see the implications for assessment that these views would hold. From a reading readiness perspective, the information need for the first grade teacher would be a determination of where the pupil stood in relation to a continuum that would start at being unready to learn to sound out words and continue on until all decoding rules were learned. There would probably also be a need to know about the child's grasp of concepts such as left to right, and so on. From an emergent literacy perspective, such information would be considered to be a fairly small portion of the information necessary to have a complete picture of the learner with respect to literacy development. There may be a pupil who has a fairly sophisticated notion of what stories and books are, but is limited with respect to sounding out words. Another pupil may have a decent sight word vocabulary, but no sounding skills, and no notion of what stories are.  Yet another pupil may have strong sounding skills and the ability to write out thoughts using his or her own spelling system, but may not have much experience with being read stories.

Thus, in the two models, we will be interested in looking at different things that children can do.  Our conceptualizations of the processes involved in learning to read are different.  The teacher in the first grade classroom described is probably going to find a reading readiness measure more useful in making grouping decisions than a measure based on the emergent literacy perspective.  Why?  Because it appears that her instructional program is based on the same conceptualization of reading that reading readiness measures are.  This is not to say that if she took a seminar on emergent literacy that she might not find that a far more exciting and useful way to teach reading (nor is it to say that she necessarily would), but rather that the measures that we employ ought to be consistent with our information needs which are based (in large part) on our instructional intentions.  Now let's turn to the kindergarten teacher.

Here we might reasonably argue that the emergent literacy perspective on reading is operational.  With the possible exception of a strong emphasis on learning the alphabet, most "instruction" in reading would consist of story reading and other more naturalistic activities.  The measurement implications are not very strong here, however, since the teacher does not have great information needs.  It is interesting to note that when this group moves to first grade instruction, the information needs will in all likelihood flow from a somewhat different instructional perspective.

Next, let us consider the reading resource teacher.  This teacher works with pupils for whom the regular system of instruction does not seem to be functioning appropriately.  Her instructional approach may be very much oriented toward an objective-based, diagnostic system of instruction.  This is the very system that proponents of emergent literacy have so much difficulty with (Valencia & Pearson, 1987).  While there is no question that if one is going to use such a system for instruction, that it should be coupled to an assessment system with which it is compatible, there is undoubtedly an inertia associated with the fact that reading readiness instructional programs and diagnostic measures are extant and have a long history of use.

To summarize the preceding briefly, it has been argued that:

1. Measurement ought to follow and complement instruction.
2. Without a clear information need, there is no justification for measurement.
3. Different instructional approaches will call for different concepts to be measured.
4. Current instructional practices tend to be more oriented toward a reading readiness perspective.

There is a final measurement need that has been hinted at, but not fully explored. This is systemwide testing that is used to assess the overall progress of students at the class, school, or district level.  A recent addition to this testing is mandated state testing, which exists in 44 states.  This type of testing tends to be highly influential in the curricular decisions that school districts make, and it is this influence that critics of standardized testing point to.  At the upper elementary and high school levels, the criticisms of the nature of the end-of-year testing is not particularly convincing.  That is, most reading tests at these levels involve passages and questions.  While there may be disagreements about the length of the passages and the nature of multiple choice questions (e.g., Valencia & Pearson, 1987), it is difficult to argue successfully that for the most part, students who get higher scores do not possess more reading ability than people who get lower scores.

At the kindergarten and early primary levels, there is much more room for disagreement as to what is or is not legitimate to put on a test and how those traits should be measured.  Since most pupils are far less than fully proficient readers at these ages, it becomes problematical as to what should be included on such measures.  Part of the problem involves the difference between the two perspectives mentioned earlier in this chapter.  An emergent literacy perspective would argue for certain concepts to be included, while a reading readiness perspective would argue for different concepts.  The decisions on these issues are critical at this level since they will influence the subsequent curricular decisions.

This is not simply an issue of whether to use test A or test B.  If a state or a district adopts a certain testing program because of desirable characteristics at the high school level, it will in all likelihood adopt the same program K-12.  If at the elementary level, there is an emphasis on decoding skills, the district (or state) is locked into an instructional model with a strong decoding component.  This is a paradigm case of testing leading instruction.  Even though there are scholars who advocate "measurement-driven instruction" (e.g., Shoemaker, 1975; Popham, 1987), few would advocate letting decisions for testing high school students preclude reasoned discussion over the nature of the elementary school curriculum.  Yet, too often, this is a de facto consequence of such decisions.

## TECHNICAL STRENGTHS AND WEAKNESSES
## OF FORMAL AND INFORMAL MEASURES

To discuss the technical strengths and weaknesses of formal and informal measures, it is necessary to understand what they are.  There are basically four concerns here: objectivity, reliability, validity, and bias.  It should be pointed out at the outset that objectivity, reliability and bias can be considered to be special cases of validity (Messick, 1980).  Given that they are almost always treated separately, we will do so here.

The first issue to consider is objectivity.  There have been several definitions given to this term over the years, but the most common definition is that objectivity is the degree to which the scores derived from the measure being given mean the same thing for all individuals being tested.  If student A gets a 34 and student B gets a 34, then we ought to be able to draw the same conclusions about these two students with respect to concept being measured.  Of course, if the students differ on other concepts of interest, then our overall assessments of them may be quite distinct.  It is with respect to objectivity that the most serious and substantial criticism of formal testing occur, even though many people think of standardized measures as being objective, if nothing else. The problem lies with the artificiality of the setting and tasks of many formal procedures, and the potential for young children to misinterpret directions, become distracted, or just generally decide not to participate fully in the measurement activity. Whereas we are usually fairly confident that a student trying to get into a good college has given us his or her best effort on a college entrance exam, we are not so sanguine that the lack of performance on the part of a 5-year-old truly reflects lack of ability or simply lack of interest.

There is a second problem with objectivity. If we are interested in a child's ability to follow words in a storybook in an appropriate order, it would probably be best to do so with a storybook with which the child was familiar. If we want to know if children understand the relationship between written words and spoken words, we may want to tap into each child's world specifically. This is not possible with most standardized techniques available today. It is important to note that some of these issues could be made amenable to a formal, even norm-referenced, approach. It would require some substantial rethinking of what went on a test, but some of these ideas can already be found in Chapter 9, by Mason and Stewart.

Objectivity is also a problem for informal measures. Here the problem lies not so much with the materials and content of the measure as with the presentation of tasks and the interpretation of results. When a measure has a strong personal, clinical component to it, the resultant scores are often as much a function of the person giving the measure as the person taking the measure. If we move most of the responsibility for testing young children to classroom teachers, we are making strong assumptions about the ability of such teachers to make very important instructional and placement decisions. The original impetus for the Binet scales was the inability of medical doctors to make reasonable decisions about the intellectual capacities of pupils in Paris (Binet, 1905). Will two teachers reach the same conclusions about progress and placement decisions on a given child? Should teacher judgment be the sole determining factor in assessing the success of curricular innovations, special education classifications, and so on? Few individuals are confident enough about their abilities to take on such a burden. A critical problem with informal measurement techniques is that the tester (usually the teacher) becomes the measuring device. Some will be outstanding, some will not.

The next issue to consider is reliability. Reliability is the ability of an instrument or procedure to measure concepts consistently. That is, a reliable measure will reproduce its results if the measure is repeated. Various factors can influence the reliability of a measure. Among these are the questions or procedures used, the administration of the measure, the scoring of the measure, the stability of the trait, and the degree to which the measure or procedure is capable of engendering consistent behavior in the individuals tested. In trying to assess early reading, each of these issues turns out to be something of a problem for both formal and informal approaches. Of particular concern, though, are the last two items: the stability of the trait and the ability of the instrument to produce consistent behavior in the individuals tested. The stability of the trait has to do with children more than measurement approaches with one important exception. An emergent literacy perspective calls for different concepts to be assessed than a reading readiness perspective. The question that arises is: Which set of concepts is likely to be evidenced in a consistent fashion over a short period of time? This is a concern since traits that change rapidly in either direction are not particularly useful for making curricular or placement decisions. Even more interesting is the stability of the individuals being tested. Here is where the real question arises, particularly with respect to young children and formal measures: How likely is a set of scores for a kindergarten child to be a reflection of the ability to sit still and work on problems as opposed to reading ability? The answer here is basically twofold. First, the question can be addressed in an empirical fashion. Test-retest reliabilities provide some evidence. But for the issue to be addressed directly, the results of a standardized procedure would have to be compared to indicators whose validity was fairly well accepted. Juel (Chapter 8) provides the model for such a study in her work, showing that students who show early difficulties on a standardized measure tend also to show reading problems several years later. The second part of the answer has to do with considering high-scoring and low-scoring students separately. With the exception of cheating, it is very difficult for a student of low ability to get a high score on a test. On the other hand, there are many ways for students of high ability to get low scores. Thus, our confidence is typically greater in high scores than in low scores. Informal measures can often avoid problems of low scores due to inattentiveness, since the examiner typically knows the student and can judge whether he or she is truly engaged in the task.

As mentioned, the key issue is not reliability as much as validity. This is because reliability is a form of validity. They are related in much the same way as "antique" and "old" are related. For something to be antique (valid), it has to be old (reliable). But validity is far more than reliability. Validity is the degree to which the results of the measure coincide with reality. Does the measure or procedure produce the information that we need? It is difficult to make direct comparisons of formal and informal procedures here, since, when used properly, both can be valid. When stretched beyond their intended utility, neither are particularly valid. Let's look at informal procedures first. These include story retellings, oral readings, pupil response to being read to, and sometimes merely the close observation of pupils engaged in literacy behaviors in nonassessment settings. The strength of these measures are their immediacy, their relevance to instruction, and their ecological validity. Informal measures can be given at any time, can be as extensive or brief as the setting calls for, and can be tied directly to, or even be part of, instruction. The weaknesses are their lack of accuracy, uniformity, and the degree to which the assessment can be influenced by factors unrelated to the concepts being measured. In most settings, informal measures are very useful in gathering information "inflight." A teacher can make assessments of students' progress as she teaches them. The danger is lack of accuracy. Research on the grading of the same essay written with good or poor handwriting ought to be sufficient warning to us concerning the validity of informal measures. The validity of such approaches for end-of-year testing would be insufficient for almost any purpose. Formal measures of early reading pose a different set of problems with validity. First, for what they are generally intended to do, they are fairly valid. Their intent is to provide a measure of what a child can do at a given point in time with respect to early reading. There is evidence that they are fairly effective at doing this, especially for identifying pupils with reading difficulties (see Chapter 8, Juel). What they are not good at is providing up-to-the-minute progress or at providing information consistent with an emergent literacy perspective, although there is movement in that direction (see Mason and Stewart, Chapter 9).

The final issue is bias. Bias is often thought of as something necessarily involving race or sex (see, e.g., Jensen, 1980). But bias can occur also against pupils who dress poorly, or who act out in class, or who are simply quiet. Whenever an individual plays a large role in the administration or scoring of a measure, bias can come into play. Here, then, with informal measures that rely on administration and scoring by a teacher, the potential for bias is increased. Bias in formal measures is more typically a function of terms, pictures, or stories being used for which groups are differentially familiar. At the level of the individual item, this can be examined statistically; for the measure as a whole, more often than not, there is little evidence as to the presence or absence of bias.

## RECOMMENDATIONS

Measurement and assessment exist to facilitate learning. Although there are some remarkably technical aspects to measurement, it should not be difficult to keep it in perspective. The challenge to measurement posed by the emergent literacy perspective is an exciting one. The reactions of the measurement community to this challenge may seem to be slow from the perspective of the advocates of emergent literacy, but for measurement people, they are occurring at nearly breakneck speed. For emergent literacy advocates, standardized tests represent a tremendous obstacle in the way of getting schools to use an emergent literacy perspective in instruction. If it isn't on the test, the schools won't use it. Measurement specialists interested in standardized testing take an equally rational, yet contradictory, position. If it isn't in the schools, it shouldn't be on the test. The test is intended to measure instruction as it occurs. This should produce a deadlock, but it hasn't. Within the next two to three years, there will be a variety of formal measures available with an emergent literacy perspective. What about the issue that emergent literacy and formal assessment are inherently incompatible? In terms of providing up-to-the-minute, instructionally relevant information, formal assessment is not feasible without a computer. It's probably also not desirable. In terms of obtaining information about what a child does when engaged in naturally occurring reading settings, again formal assessment is not a consideration.

In terms of providing information on other aspects of early literacy consonant with an emergent literacy perspective, they are not only possible, they exist.

To sum up, just as early reading is in a period of great flux, so is the field of measurement. Performance assessment, computer simulation, portfolio evaluation, and the general broadening of the traits of individuals that might be assessed are all part of the field of measurement today. These changes are taking place after a long period of relying heavily on the multiple-choice format and tightly defined test specifications. The field of measurement is characterized by caution perhaps more than anything else, and with good reason. If important decisions are to be made about people, they deserve serious and thoughtful attention and deliberation. An example of such thinking can be found in Haertel and Calfee's (1983) examination about what should be tested in school achievement measures.

Measurement and reading specialists are not the only players in the game of determining what gets measured in reading or how it gets measured. Publishers, politicians, teachers, parents, and school administrators are all important contributors, often more important than they realize. If we are to make progress toward a more productive relationship between assessment and instruction in early literacy, we must include all constituencies in our discussions and debates, not only informing the others, but learning from them as well.

## REFERENCES

BINET, A. (1905). A propos de la mesure de l'intelligence. *Annee Psychologique, 11*, 69–82.

CLAY, M. (1979). *Reading: The patterning of complex behavior.* Exeter, NH: Heinemann.

CLAY, M. (1966). *Emergent Reading Behavior.* Unpublished doctoral dissertation, University of Auckland, New Zealand.

GENISHI, C. & DYSON, A. (1984). *Language assessment in the early years.* Norwood, NJ: Ablex.

HAERTEL, E., & CALFEE, R. (1983). School achievement: Thinking about what to test. *Journal of Educational Measurement, 20*, 119–132.

JENSEN, A. (1980). *Bias in mental tests.* New York: Free Press.

JOHNSTON, P. H. (1987). *Reading comprehension assessment.* Newark, DE: International Reading Association.

MASON, J. (1980). When do children begin to read? An exploration of four-year-old children's letter and word reading competencies. *Reading Research Quarterly, 15*, 203–227.

MASON, J. (1981). Prereading: A developmental perspective. Technical Report No. 198, Center for the Study of Reading. Urbana: University of Illinois.

MESSICK, S. (1980). Test validity and the ethics of assessment. *American Psychologist, 35*, 1012–1027.

MITCHELL, J. V. (1985). *The Ninth Mental Measurements Yearbook.* Lincoln, NE: University of Nebraska Press.

POPHAM, W. J. (1987). The merits of measurement-driven instruction. *Phi Delta Kappan, 68*, 679–682.

ROYER, J. M., and CUNNINGHAM, D. J. (1981). On the theory and measurement of reading comprehension. *Contemporary Educational Psychology, 6,* 187–216.

SHOEMAKER, D. M. (1975). Toward a framework for achievement testing. *Review of Educational, 45,* 127–147.

SULZBY, E. (1985). Children's emergent reading of favorite storybooks: A developmental study. *Reading Research Quarterly, 20,* 458–481.

TEALE, W. H. (1982). Toward a theory of how children learn to read naturally. *Language Arts, 59,* 555–570.

TEALE, W. H., & SULZBY E. (Eds.). (1986). *Emergent literacy: Writing and reading.* Norwood, NJ: Ablex.

TEALE, W. H., HIEBERT, E., & CHITTENDEN, E. (1987). Assessing young children's literacy development. *The Reading Teacher, 40,* 772–777.

VALENCIA, S. & PEARSON, P. D. (1987). Reading assessment: Time for a change. *The Reading Teacher, 40,* 729–733.

# 5

# POINTS OF DEVELOPMENT,
# NOT POINTS OF FAILURE

*Robert P. Parker*

*Rutgers, The State University of New Jersey*

### Abstract

A reflection on the chapters in this part is presented by Robert Parker. He comments on the positions of Stallman and Pearson, Teale, and Smith, pointing out the ways in which their work provides both history and critique for the two competing perspectives on literacy assessment. He then presents a different philosophical perspective for viewing early literary assessment specifically and the measurement of literacy ability generally.

The three chapters in this section provide historical background on, criticisms of, and suggestions for the conduct of early literacy assessment. Included in these discussions are helpful descriptions of the two major competing perspectives on early literacy development, as well as analyses of salient issues in the field.

In chapter 2 (Stallman and Pearson) formal measures of early literacy are described and evaluated in relation to changing perspectives on how young children learn to read and write. First, they trace the relation of such measures to the child development theories that prevailed during their construction. Then, against this historical backdrop, they analyze and report findings about 20 formal literacy measures.

In the historical workup, they examine particularly the development of the concept of reading readiness. In various forms, this concept has dominated the field of reading for 60 years, including reading measurement, reading curriculum materials, and reading instruction. The reading readiness perspective is based on a "componential assumption" about the nature of the reading process. More popularly called the subskills approach, this componential assumption underlies most measures of reading readiness, basal reading programs, and conventional reading pedagogy. Not until the late 1960s did an alternative perspective on beginning reading appear.

This new perspective, called emergent literacy, "takes into account all of the child's interactions with books, print, reading, and writing as important" events in the process of "becoming an independent reader" (p. 7). Children, thus, are viewed as being "in the process of becoming literate through their active engagement" in daily situations involving reading and writing. They literally take the process of learning to write and read in hand for themselves (Spencer & McKenzie, 1975).

Smith's chapter further clarifies differences between these two perspectives from an assessment point of view. (Chapter 4, p. 67, Smith)

> In a reading readiness model, the focus is almost solely on reading, and within reading, priority is given to decoding skills. There is a strong emphasis on reading as the ability to turn written language into spoken language (whether the spoken language is audible or internal). There is also an emphasis on determining the appropriate time to commence instruction in decoding skills. In emergent literacy, the idea of literacy is seen as involving reading *and* writing skills (and often speaking and thinking skills) (Teale, Hiebert, & Chittenden, 1987). These are viewed as being inextricably related to another and not useful to disentangle for purposes of instruction. There is also the view that reading begins well before children can decode words (Mason, 1981).

In fact, information about children's understanding of decoding rules and of concepts like left to right would be considered a fairly small portion of the information necessary to have a complete picture of the learner with respect to literacy development (Chapter 4, Smith).

Teale (Chapter 3) adds to this emergent literacy perspective. Acknowledging that "legitimate literacy learning begins very early in life for virtually all children" in highly literate societies, he claims also that "listening, speaking, reading, and writing abilities [develop] concurrently and interrelatedly." (This idea, in fact, is not new. Participants in the "Language Across the Curriculum" movement have made this claim since the mid-1960s, though it is just now becoming widely accepted in North America (Parker & Goodkin, 1987)). Moreover, children's "behaviors and conceptualizations" in regard to writing and reading, "though unlike those of adults or even older children who can read and write conventionally, develop in predictable ways toward conventional literacy."

The situation is this: a 60-year-old reading readiness perspective, deeply entrenched economically, politically, and educationally, is being vigorously challenged by advocates of a newer, emergent literacy perspective. What, then, seem to be the current realities and possibilities for those wishing to assess children's literacy abilities? And, further, what might be some important guidelines for teachers and measurement people to follow in assessing children's literacy learning? Stallman and Pearson's chapter (Chapter 2), plus Smith's (Chapter 4), can help answer the first question. To answer the second fully, we can begin with Teale's chapter (Chapter 3) and then turn to another document that provides a comprehensive perspective on this question: *Ways of Looking at Children's Writing,* a report prepared by the SCDC/National Writing Project in England (1987). (SCDC stands for School Curriculum Development Committee, formerly the Schools Council, a government agency in Great Britain that funds and monitors a variety of school-based curriculum development projects. One project funded by the SCDC is the National Writing Project, an extension of the National Writing Project in the United States.)

After reviewing 20 formal reading readiness measures commercially available to educators, Stallman and Pearson found very few differences among the tests. The *Metropolitan Reading Test* (MRT), which they reviewed "in some detail because of its widespread use and its 'representativeness' among group test" is

> typical—wholly representative of items that are found on the other group-administered readiness tests. The other tests provide more variations on a theme than they do completely different "compositions." (Chapter 2, p. 25, Stallman and Pearson)

Basal series readiness tests present a virtually identical picture. They are remarkably similar to one another and to the commercial tests. "Not only are the skills tested similar, but the format is nearly identical" (Chapter 2, p. 39, Stallman and Pearson). Only the two tests developed by Marie Clay (*Concepts About Print* and *Readiness to Read*), which they call "outliers," are very different.

The 20 tests reviewed comprised a total of 2,656 test items:

> One-third of the items (but 48 percent of the subtests and, therefore, 48 percent of the judgments) are devoted to sound-symbol knowledge, with the second largest chunk devoted to literacy and language concepts (22 percent of the items and 21 percent of the subtests). (Chapter 2, p. 32, Stallman and Pearson)

The tests clearly emphasize children's sound-symbol knowledge above any other kind they might have.

This finding underscores, first, the unvarying subskills approach of these tests (unvarying since the 1930s!), and, second, the emphasis within this approach on one of the most limited and mechanical of the identified "components" (see Chapter 2). So, testmakers, in adopting the subskills perspective that emergent literacy advocates claim reduces the reading process, further reduce the subskills approach by focusing a large portion of their subtests on a limited "component," sound-symbol knowledge.

The situation is grimmer, however. As Stallman and Pearson note, "students are rarely asked to produce or construct answers to test items" (Chapter 2, p. 33, Stallman and Pearson). And "equally remarkable is how seldom children are asked to do anything resembling an active mode of responding such as saying something (11.5 percent) or writing something (3.4 percent)." Seldom do testers ask children actually to read. Instead, they test children "on isolated skills in decontextualized settings." Not surprisingly, critics claim that the tests measure testtaking, not reading ability. Claiming to test children's *reading* abilities when reading is not what the instruments require children to do seems suspect.

According to Stallman and Pearson, educators using an emergent literacy approach in teaching reading have had little choice if they wanted to do formal group assessment of reading. Only a few instruments have offered a genuine alternative to the subskills approach found in most existing formal measures. So, to this point in time, emergent literacy advocates have had to use informal methods of assessment. However, at this writing both instructional materials and tests which reflect more directly an emergent literacy perspective are under development.

Perhaps there is no measurement issue in a technical, psychometric sense, but there is a measurement issue from economic and political perspectives. Because few formal measures have used an emergent literacy perspective, the debate between the two approaches to beginning reading has been, ipso facto, an assessment debate as well.

On this issue, Teale offers some assistance. He advocates "informal assessment—classroom observations and performance samples of reading and writing—as the most appropriate means of assessing young children to provide good literacy instruction" (Chapter 3, p. 46, Teale). Informal assessment procedures, he claims, yield more "useful information to teachers about how to teach the children in their classrooms." Children's literacy learning involves motives, goals, and other psychological processes, and none of these processes is assessed through most existing formal measures.

From existing research, Teale discusses some categories for informal assessments, as examples:

1. *Knowledge of the functions of written language.* Children learn the functions of print before they learn its forms (Halliday, 1975; Parker, with Morrow, 1989).

2. *Varied storybook reading experiences.* Varied experiences with storybooks such as pretend readings as a prelude to "actual" story reading play "an important role in helping children become literate."

3. *Writing strategies.* Because young children's writing and reading abilities develop concurrently and interrelatedly, it makes sense for teachers to provide daily opportunities for composing a variety of types of written language, just as they provide time for daily reading instruction. Teale especially wants teachers to attend to the children's strategies, unconventional as they often look, for it is [their] insight into what the children are actually doing that can best inform instruction (Chapter 3, Teale).

*Ways of Looking at Children's Writing* (1987) offers a comprehensive framework for linking assessment with teaching. This report, which represents an official response to the governmental Task Group on Assessment and Testing in the United

Kingdom, reflects the efforts of many of the 1,500 teachers participating in the 23 local branches of the SCDC National Writing Project.

The report's "overriding conclusion" is worth quoting: "writing is a highly complex, social practice which cannot be reduced to any simple list of terms or criteria, and...writers cannot be assessed by one off tests at particular ages." If testers and educators were to accept this conclusion, it would eliminate one-shot, decontextualized writing assessment by declaring it inappropriate. Though the conclusion refers to writing, I think it applies *equally to reading,* as do other conclusions presented in the report.

For example, the report suggests additional "emphases," presented as questions, that future writing assessments might reflect. The first question, "What can the child write?" emphasizes what children *can* do rather than what they can't. Because the effect of most group assessments is to focus attention on weaknesses or low points in the profiles resulting from children's responses, educators have tended to emphasize their failures more than their successes. In this report, children's failed experiments in their writing attempts are given a different emphasis. They are "noted as points of development not as points of failure."

The second question is: "What conditions promote the best writing?" Assessment of children "cannot be considered in a vacuum; rather it forms an integral part of critical reflection" on the curriculum processes of classrooms (Burgess, 1984). Because writing and reading arise within, and are influenced by, the nature of the classroom curriculum process, the forms children's products take result from the nature of particular classroom contexts. Any assessment of children's literacy abilities is simultaneously an assessment of the classroom contexts within which they have developed. Many educators, however, continue to use formal measures, assuming they are "objective," context-free. In reality, though, like listening and speaking, writing and reading are *social* practices (Bakhtin, 1981), and children learn them in social contexts through social processes (Gundlach, 1985) as part of their overall development in the "social semiotic" (Halliday, 1975, 1978). Because writing and reading are, always, social practices inserted into larger sociohistorical processes (Burgess, 1985), any context and/or history-stripping forms of assessment must inevitably yield a distorted picture of what children *can* actually *do* when their intentions are engaged (Ferguson & Slobin, 1973).

Third, the report asks "What types of writing need to be considered?": the answer given is that there is "no one type of writing which can represent a writer's abilities." Assessments of individuals and groups, "therefore, must include a wide range of writing tasks," not just a single task or form. And the assessment must make "explicit the applicability of any assessment on one task to other types of writing." Portfolio assessments would, for example, be more legitimate than one-shot, holistic assessments.

And, fourth, the report asks "What expectations are there for a writer's development?" Though researchers of young children's writing agree that there is little evidence to support a stage theory view of children's writing development, many curriculum and measurement specialists, especially in large urban areas where group testing of children is a major activity, are attempting to develop benchmarks for children's writing at various ages or grades. The writers of this report, in contrast, say,

> we do not feel that it is possible or desirable to provide a series of developmental markers which will differentiate a 5-year old's writing from that of a 11-year old. Development is too complex to be reduced to milestones and benchmarks showing where one is and certainly too related to the task to be reduced to a single score.

The writers are not saying that, in most cases, we can't tell the writing of an 11-year-old from that of a 5-year old. Obviously, most of the time we can, and we can specify what features of the writing lead us to make such judgments, at least to some extent. That is not the issue. If we do, however, specify certain features of the writing of 11- and 5-year-olds that characterize them *in general,* we then tend to take this list of features to represent the whole of writing skill at those ages. Further, we tend to categorize and label children, often in terms of "deficits," based on the application of these lists of features to their writing performances. These features are *not the whole of the writing, ever!* They are a reduced version, and we tend to forget this reality. We also use these reductive judgements about children to place them in categories, often pejorative, which are difficult to escape from because the categories become the way that teachers view the children.

The assessment "policy guidelines" in this report offer educators a broad framework to use in devising assessment procedures for use with individual children in single classrooms or for groups of children in school districts or states. Regardless, these guidelines tie assessment considerations to current knowledge about how children actually learn to read and write and to the ways that this learning is actually affected by classroom curriculum contexts. We might call this *grounded* assessment, assessment that is grounded in literacy learning and curriculum process knowledge. Because of this grounding, the assessment will be linked to instruction—the theme of this volume.

This conclusion about grounded assessment seems to end matters, but it doesn't, because it leads us back to *technological* solutions to psychometrically defined problems. We are left where we began, a situation which invites a fresh starting point. That fresh starting point, I propose, is to be found in philosophy. We need to discuss literacy assessment philosophically, and we need to choose our philosopher(s) carefully, looking away from our traditional positivist paradigm, with its resulting behaviorist orientation, toward a constructivist paradigm with its resulting transactionalist orientation. Otherwise, our discussions will represent business as usual, and we will end up not only posing problems in the same terms, but also proposing the same solutions to them.

By using a constructivist philosophical paradigm, we can develop a genuine *criticism* of current beliefs and practices. Only when we develop a genuinely new critical consciousness about assessment will we be able to envision truly different ways of assessing children's literacy learning.

Philosophers like John Dewey, Michael Polanyi, and Richard Rorty, individually and collectively, offer a truly alternative philosophical perspective on education, including assessment. In addition to recommending that we build a new discourse about assessment on the work of these philosophers, I want to recommend Bernard Lonergan's philosophy of the cognitional process as offering an even more powerful framework for shifting the grounds of our discourse about literacy assessment (1977, 1981). Lonergan (1981) suggests that we might examine our own cognitional processes when assessing children's literacy, thus putting at issue what *we* are doing rather than the technology of our doing it. He suggests that we begin by asking "What are we doing when we are assessing children's literacy learning?" rather than the more traditional "How do we do assessment (so that certain psychologically derived criteria are met)?"

If our process of answering that question proves exhilarating and provides useful knowledge, we might then ask a further question of ourselves: "What are we knowing when we are doing it?" These are *philosophical* questions, and they mark a philosophical inquiry into the psychological process(es) of assessment—our own psychological processes. Because they are philosophical questions, the answers we construct will constitute a new grounds for understanding assessment and making assessment judgments about children. It will also help us to understand what we are doing when we use these judgements to make decisions about curriculum and teaching. Through this process, we will learn how to appropriate and take responsibility for our assessment processes, our judgments about children, and the decisions we make as a result of these judgments. We will understand, further, that assessment is, inherently, a subjective process because it involves persons, as *subjects,* making and using judgement about other persons—in this instance, children. Perhaps, it will even result in our developing a new moral stance toward this activity of assessing and judging children.

## REFERENCES

BAKHTIN, M. (1981). *The dialogic imagination.* Austin: University of Texas Presss

BURGESS, T. (1984). The role of writing in the curriculum process. In M. Chorny (Ed.), *Teachers as learners.* Calgary, Alberta: University of Calgary Faculty of Education.

BURGESS, T. (1985). The question of English. In M. Meek & J. Miller (Eds.), *Changing English.* London: Ward Lock.

FERGUSON, C. A., & SLOBIN, D. (1973). *Studies of child language development.* New York: Harper & Row.

GUNDLACH, R., STOTT, F. M., & MCNAMEE, G. D. (1985). The social foundations of children's early writing development. In M. Farr (Ed.), *Advances in writing research, Vol. I: Children's early writing development.* Norwood, NJ: Ablex.

HALLIDAY, M. A. K. (1978). *Language as a social semiotic: The social interpretation of language and meaning.* London: Edward Arnold.

HALLIDAY, M. A. K. (1975). *Learning how to mean.* London: Edward Arnold.

LONERGAN, B. (1977). *Insight: A study of human understanding.* New York: Harper & Row.

LONERGAN, B. (1981). *Understanding and being: An introduction and companion to insight,* M. Morelli & E. Morelli (Eds.). Toronto: Edwin Mellen.

PARKER, R., & GOODKIN, V. (1987). *The consequences of writing: Enhancing learning in the disciplines.* Portsmouth, NH: Boynton/Cook.

PARKER, R., with MORROW, L. M. (1989). Writing as a vehicle for developing literacy. In L. M. Morrow, *Literacy development in the early years: Helping children read and write.* Englewood Cliffs, NJ: Prentice Hall.

School Curriculum Development Committee/National Writing Project (1987). *Ways of looking at children's writing,* London: SCDC Publication.

SPENCER, M., & MCKENZIE, M. (1975). Learning how to read and the reading process. In H. Rosen (Ed.), *Language and literacy in our schools: Some appraisals of the Bullock Report.* London: University of London Institute of Education.

# 6

# ASSESSMENT OF EMERGENT WRITING AND CHILDREN'S LANGUAGE WHILE WRITING

*Elizabeth Sulzby*

*The University of Michigan*

### Abstract

Elizabeth Sulzby moves the discussion of emergent literacy to the examination of emergent writing. She describes in depth children's forms of writing as children add new understandings about writing to their already existing repertoire. She argues that children can and will produce emergent writing if exposed to a literate environment and that this writing activity can be assessed by teachers. She presents the theoretical background and concrete examples necessary for such assessment.

If a group of visitors were to tour a number of kindergarten classrooms across school districts in the United States[1] to see how young children are taught to write, they would probably be amazed at the diversity. In some cases, writing means composition of text; in others, it means imitating the writing of adults. In some classrooms, children are writing away, using emergent forms (scribble, drawing, etc.) of writing, with a sprinkling of conventionally written words or phrases, to compose stories, invitations, poems, or even jokes. In other classrooms, children's only writing instruction involves copying conventionally spelled words from the board or ditto sheets and practicing forming their letters conventionally. In others, children copy from experience charts which they have dictated to the teacher and the teacher has written in conventional forms. Still other variations appear, but it would soon be clear that different assumptions were abroad in these differing classrooms concerning young children's abilities in writing and about what a teacher should ask or provide for young children to do. First grades provide similar variations, but the contrast is the most dramatic in kindergartens.[2]

This chapter addresses assessment of emergent writing (including the transition into conventional writing); *writing here refers to written composition and not just the mechanics of letter formation and word copying.* The argument is made, based upon convincing empirical evidence, that (1) all young children exposed to a literate environment can and will write emergently long before they understand and regularly produce conventional writing and (2) teachers and researchers can assess children's writing development. Additionally, the language that children use surrounding writing activities gives crucial evidence of their developing concepts. I provide some examples from the assessment instruments I have been developing but pose problems either that others are working on or that need attention. But first some definitions.

## DEFINITIONS

### Assessment

This chapter is based upon the assumption that all school instruction depends upon assessment in some manner, no matter how formal or informal each is or how old or young the students are. That is, within the child's performance of any assignment or self-selected activity, the teacher can assess some part of the child's knowledge in that domain. *Taking the time to observe and analyze the child's performance in the situation comprises an act of assessment.* This kind of assessment should be part of all teaching activities. Most of what we think of as assessment, however, consists of tasks and observations with the particular purpose of focusing upon the status of child's performance and underlying the understandings within a domain.

Assessment allows teachers to gain perspective on the development of the individual child, through comparisons with the developmental patterns seen in other children. Through such comparative analyses, assessment can illuminate teachers' understanding of the individual child. Better understanding of the individual child should then lead to better guidance of children by the teacher.

Definition of the domain being examined is crucial. Even when the goal of assessment was to see how well children could learn to compose connected discourse, outdated depictions of writing portrayed it as stagelike, with young children having to learn the mechanics of letter formation and word copying before they, as older students, eventually could compose simple sentences and, much later, compose connected discourse such as stories, poems, and letters. Comparison of children across letter formation is a quite different assessment than is comparison of children across emergent writing of stories or letters. Comparison of children's performance with the mechanics of writing can be made from within an emergent writing point of view, but it yields somewhat different comparisons, as we will see later. In this chapter, I focus upon composition of written discourse primarily and mention mechanics from an emergent standpoint.

The status of research on the assessment in young children's writing currently is thriving but only just beginning. This is similar to the status of classroom- and child-relevant assessment in general (Brown, 1989; Shepard, 1989; Stallman & Pearson, this volume; Valencia, Pearson, Peters, & Wixson, 1989). As a background for examining assessment of emergent writing, we are developing pictures of individual development and of comparative development simultaneously from disparate studies, done with different groups, under different conditions, with different tasks, and from different research methodologies. From this disparity, however, a broader picture of children's writing is emerging. Before we look at this research base, let us consider what we mean by emergent and conventional writing.

## Emergent Writing

Emergent writing is part of a broader domain of emergent literacy. By *emergent literacy,* I mean the reading and writing behaviors of young children that precede and develop into conventional literacy. By behaviors, I mean both the external behaviors and the underlying concepts that the behaviors signify. From looking at how young children write and read (Sulzby, 1983), I have concluded that emergent writing is a legitimate construct. Even though children's emergent writing does not look like the orthography in published books and articles, it functions as a record of a composition or intention. This writing is produced at a request to "write" or with the announced intention to "write." The forms in which it appears display parts of the concepts that children are inferring about writing; hence, emergent writing is conceptual and not just the results of faulty imitations of adult behavior.

The definition for emergent writing begins with the assumption that writing is a *developmental phenomenon;* that is, children's ideas are qualitatively different from those of literate adults, and they change over time in qualitative ways. Emergence, as it has been used in developmental psychology particularly, connotes both continuity of development and discontinuity (Teale & Sulzby, 1986), in which a new phenomenon in the child's development can indeed be said to appear. The transition of emergent writing into conventional writing illustrates both continuity and discontinuity.

I do not think, however, that writing can be described as invariant, hierarchically ordered stages, in which children move from one underlying conceptualization to another. Rather, children appear to be adding new understandings about writing, somewhat as a repertoire of understandings in the sociolinguistic sense. As children develop as emergent writers, they reorganize the repertoire, and this reorganization represents what are often depicted as developmental stages. It is certainly clear that children change and become conventional writers, but their development does not appear to follow one invariant, hierarchical order. We see a number of patterns of development, with a general progressive track. We have far to go definitionally in this domain, but exploring the limits of definitions such as these can act as a stimulus to better theory, research, and assessment.

A second important feature of emergent writing, and writing in general, is that reading is integrally tied to writing. Conventional writers compose and reread their own writing and so do emergent writers; the nature and degree of compositional and rereading behaviors can be traced developmentally to help us understand how young children become conventionally literate.

On the surface, however, emergent writing is often described by the external forms of writing (Sulzby, 1985; Sulzby, Barnhart, & Hieshima, 1989). Examples 1 and 2 show two rather well-known forms, scribbling and invented spelling, classified

**EXAMPLE 1\*** Scribble with Rereading (Written Monologue)

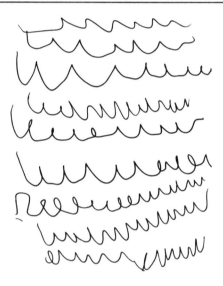

Transcription:

The Golden Swan
By "Katherine"†

Once there was a swan
And she was beautiful
But she was not like the other swans
So she went to the Crystal of Light
And she made a wish.
When she came back
The other swans saw the swan.
She was like them.
They loved her like a sister
And she lived happily ever after.
The end.

\*All examples are from kindergarten children.
†Pseudonyms are shown within quotation marks. For some studies, we had permission to use children's first names and for others we did not.

**EXAMPLE 2**   Invented Spelling, Mixed With Conventional (without Spaces)

Transcription:

There once was a little girl
and she wanted a friend.
One day a little boy
came by.
Hi, I want a friend.
Well, I want a friend, too.
Well, let's be friends, okay?

by outward appearance. The child's rereading language is shown with each example. The terms used to classify the forms of writing and rereading from writing are explained in more detail later in the chapter (Tables 1 and 2).

### Conventional Writing

One way to define conventional writing, or conventional orthography, is to refer to writing in the form that is codified in dictionaries. However, this definition seems inaccurate as a description of children's writing development. As we will see shortly, many children begin to produce a few conventional forms quite early, at ages 3-4, and yet do not hold conventional understandings of these forms (Ferreiro & Teberosky, 1982). Based upon our research findings (Barnhart, 1986; Kamberelis & Sulzby, 1988; Sulzby, 1985b, 1986; Sulzby, Barnhart, & Hieshima, 1989), I think that the onset of conventional writing is quite gradual, but the following operational definition is useful.

*Conventional writing* is defined by the child's production of text that (1) another conventional literate person can read conventionally *and* that (2) the child himself or herself reads conventionally. Example 2 would be classified as conventional writing, by this definition, only if the child read from it conventionally. *Conventional reading* (see Sulzby, 1985a) indicates that the child is reading by using print (rather than picture or solely memory) cues and is moving flexibly and in a coordinated fashion across a number of aspects or strategies to construct a meaningful interpretation of the text. The three key aspects are (1) some knowledge of letter-sound relationships, (2) some understanding that the word is a stable, memorable unit, and (3) some indication of comprehension of written text. Briefly put in more traditional language, we can say that children need simultaneous access to some knowledge of letter-sound relationships, sight vocabulary, and comprehension strategies. In each case, "some" indicates that exhaustive knowledge of these aspects is not what's needed to "get the child reading conventionally"; rather, each child seems to need varying amounts of knowledge, but it is the strategic coordination that is crucial. Being able to produce texts that others can read and that you can yourself read in the same manner is an important developmental step—one that has continuity with the child's past history as a writer/reader and that has discontinuity in that the child can now do something qualitatively different. Thus, tracing the child's progress from emergent to conventional writing becomes a key assessment task for kindergarten-first grade teachers.

Once a child is writing conventionally, a host of assessment techniques are available. A text can be assessed holistically. Syntactic structures can be counted and evaluated. The presence or absence of cohesive elements can be noted. Length of total composition can be measured by number of clauses, T-units, or other elements. Elements of a given genre can be documented. The intended relationship between the writer and intended audience can be inferred. A full taxonomy of characteristics and vocabulary to name them are readily available with a fairly long research history. The elements of importance in emergent writing, however, are still being discovered, related, and named. In this chapter, much discussion will be given to what the relevant elements are, how they may be related, and how they can be named.

Assessment of both emergent and conventional writing are coming to share similar characteristics, however (Raphael, Englert, & Kirschner 1989; Teale, 1988; Wolf, 1989). The focus is being put more and more upon *process* and upon the *writer* rather than solely upon the product. Portfolios or collections of writing samples over time are viewed as more relevant than single-shot assessments. Children's language about and during writing is considered crucial information about their growth as writers.

## RESEARCH ON YOUNG CHILDREN'S WRITING

Research in homes (Anderson & Stokes, 1984: Gundlach, McLane, Stott, & McNamee, 1985; Sulzby & Teale, 1985; Taylor, 1983; Taylor & Dorsey-Gaines, 1988; Teale, 1986) and in schools (Allen, 1989; Dyson, 1984; Ferreiro & Teberosky, 1982;

Goodman, 1986; Martinez & Teale, 1987; Mason, Peterman, Powell, & Kerr, 1989; Schickedanz, 1986; Sulzby, 1985c; Sulzby & Teale, 1985) has documented amply that children from infancy through school entry take part in writing activities. They "play around" with writing. During this time, their writing takes many different forms (e.g., scribble, drawing, nonphonetic letterstrings, copying of conventional print, invented spelling, producing conventional print, rebus, abbreviations, pseudoletters, and idiosyncratic forms) long before it is conventional. Children's access to implements to write with and opportunities to take part in functional "literacy events" varies across homes, but some generalizations seem to be warranted.

### Time of Onset

One way of looking at writing development is to consider the "time of onset" or first appearance of the use of various writing and reading forms (see Sulzby & Teale, 1985). Time of onset is fairly easy to trace for the forms of writing since the graphic traces are easily observable; children's speech during composition is less well documented.

*Forms of writing.* Children who have writing models available in their environment (parents, teachers, or siblings who write in front of them) tend to begin marking in a repetitive way that could be called scribble during the period between 12 and 18 months. This scribble can be considered undifferentiated scribble. Then the scribble becomes differentiated into scribble for writing and scribble for drawing, even before there is objective evidence of representational drawing. Soon the child begins to produce graphics that can be called representational drawing (in the sense that an adult could recognize a common form, such as a doggie or tadpole-looking person). Even after the child can differentiate these forms, the child continues to show an ambivalence between whether drawing is or is not writing. The child will also mix conditions under which drawing is treated as writing or as drawing. But by late in the second year or during the third year, most children have at least two writing forms: scribble and drawing. Children may also begin dictating during this time or during the third year, asking adults to "Write *doggie.*"

Writing with letters covers a large number of categories of writing forms: imitating conventional words, using nonphonetic letterstrings, invented spelling, and conventional orthography. Writing with letters usually begins late in year 2 but more typically in year 3. Learning letter names and forms has a long developmental trajectory with letter formation looking amazingly common across children (multilegged E's, reversed letters, and R's constructed of unconnected lines and circles). The child's signature carries an important significance in development (see especially Ferreiro, 1986), usually begins as scribble, and often becomes the first "stable string" of conventional print that the child produces.

During this time, children may begin to compose stories or messages using long strings of letters that seem to have no phonetic relationship with the composition. These are called nonphonetic letterstrings and can be classified into at least three subcategories: random letterstrings, patterned letterstrings (reoccurring patterns, particularly in alternating vowels and consonants), and "name elements" in which the letters of a name are recombined in numerous ways. By the end of age 3 or during age 4, children often produce compositions which mix scribble, drawing, and strings of letters. Only rarely is there any evidence of phonetic relationships or "invented spelling."

While invented spelling rarely appears in the composition of very young children, a few children produce or dictate the first letter or a few letters of single words during year 3.[3] Throughout the period of ages 3 through 7, for most children, invented spelling appears slowly, usually first in isolated words rather than connected discourse. Invented spelling can be subcategorized a number of ways. The two most fully documented types are syllabic invented spelling, in which the child uses one letter per syllable and full invented spelling, in which the child uses one letter per phoneme. Between the two types is a range of development which researchers have divided a number of ways, depending upon the number and position of letters within syllables and words (e.g., Allen, 1989; Sulzby, 1985b). I use the term *intermediate invented spelling* to cover all the development between syllabic and full invented spelling, simply as a convenience and because I have not yet found any theoretically important and/or empirically convincing way of ordering the "intermediate" steps. Full invented spelling is slow in appearing and coming under the child's fluent control. It usually appears with a mix of conventional appearing spellings. For most children, it appears as a phenomenon in later kindergarten or in first grade, although it appears earlier for some children.

Conventional orthography occupies a position of production before competence, in the linguists' sense. As mentioned earlier, children begin to produce conventionally spelled words (or stable strings, to use Ferreiro's, 1986, term) in the third or fourth year but conventional understanding *appears* to develop after invented spelling. Invented spelling seems to be an important part of development that logically precedes a conceptional understanding of English orthography. Invented spelling is phonemic in nature; that is, there is some graphic way of depicting every distinctive speech sound (or sound that makes a difference in telling words apart). The spellings that have become codified as "dictionary" or "correct" spellings of English often have silent letters ("sign" or "knight"), multiple spellings for the same sound (the O sound in "so," "slow," "thorough"), or even reversed sounds (/hw/ in "what"). Additionally, some pronunciations are shortened or elided from their spellings ("runnin'," "Jumpin'," and the articles "a" and "the"). The same spelling system is used across quite different dialects, across the many nations that use English.

English spelling has been depicted as being morphophonemic (Chomsky & Halle, 1968), indicating that clues to meaning through morphological units are preserved even at the expense of a purely "phonetic" translation from speech to print. As the work of Ferreiro & Teberosky (1982; see also Barnhart, 1986) indicates, transformations and modifications made with words that children appear to be producing or using conventionally can show that their understanding does not yet include the understanding that writing needs to include phonetic information. From a theoretical standpoint, I have argued that children learning English also need to learn eventually that words are written as stable units—the same word should be spelled the same way across instances—and that there is a standard spelling that does not coincide with pronunciation—"spelling the way it sounds" is not enough in English.

Other less common forms, such as pseudoletters, rebus, and abbreviations, appear later in development than might be expected. Each appears to be a simpler way of writing than time of onset would indicate. For instance, pseudoletters might seem to be imitations like letterlike scribble, yet both Ferreiro and Teberosky (1982) and I (Sulzby, 1985c; Sulzby, Barnhart, & Hieshima, 1989) have found that they appear *after* children know a number of conventional letters. Rebus has been suggested as an easy way to help children first build meaning-symbol understandings and then move to the idea that the sound can be separated from the referent (a picture of an eye used for the sound of long I). Children do not use rebus until quite late in development, after that notion has become clear in traditional orthography. Similarly, children's use of syllabic invented spelling is quite different from the idea of abbreviation which usually appears after children are using intermediate or full invented spelling quite fluently.

From examining time of onset we can infer reasons why a particular ordering of forms might be used in assessing children's development, but theoretical reasoning about how the forms operate in later development is also needed. A particular form of writing that appears early may not be abandoned early, but used in a reorganization of understandings. An example of this is the use of drawing. Children acquire drawing as a form of writing very early. They continue to use it quite tenaciously well into their sixth and seventh years, but with much ambivalence about its status. Eventually, we see them transforming drawing as writing into drawing as illustration—or so I used to think. Now, I think that drawing as illustration is too simple an idea for what happens. Consider Example 3, "The Three Bugs."

In "The Three Bugs," the illustration serves as an elaborate pun of Baby Buggy in his or her baby buggy. The printed text certainly stands alone as a "decontextualized" whole, but it is not the complete composition. Together, the words of the text and the drawing form the entire text, in which the words and picture interact with each other. It may be that when children hold onto drawing as a form of encoding meanings, they are learning how different symbol systems work—symbol systems that co-occur in the storybooks and picture books young children read and in the magazines, articles, and newspapers that adults read.

*Language during writing.* Much less is known about how children's language during writing develops. Most of the work has focused upon reading intonation. One exception is Scollon and Scollon (1981) who reported that their own daughter used reading intonation during dictating into a tape recorder at age 2. Doake (1981) and Holdaway (1979) report readinglike intonation in preschoolers. Sulzby (1985a) found 2- and 3-year-old children using reading intonation in storybook reading situations.

**EXAMPLE 3**   Invented and Conventional Spelling

---

# The Three Bugs

Once there was a bug and his name was harry, And he lived with his girl frienc marry. They wer a very happy cople. One day harry asked marry will you marry me? yes but when? tomouro ofcors dum dum. So the next day they got marred. Then one day marry siad, I have planed to have a baby. So Soon one day they had a boby. And

they named it bugy.

---

Sulzby and Teale (1987) report reading intonation as being among the speech behaviors of 4-year-old Spanish-English bilingual preschoolers and among the home reading reenactments of low and middle income English and Anglo children aged 2, 3, and older. Information from storybook reading behaviors is relevant, however, because children seem to use these same forms when they reread from their own writing at the kindergarten–first grade level (Sulzby, Barnhart, & Hieshima, 1989). From our home literacy observations (Sulzby & Teale, 1985, and unpublished observational notes), we have found that children use a special intonation for talk during composition, for dictating to adults, and for rereading children's own writing, as early as age 3, but we do not have detailed evidence about time of onset across a sufficiently large number of children. Much more information is needed in this area, particularly about the language of composition.[4]

At any rate, time of onset alone is only one clue about writing development. There might be times when a teacher or diagnostician might want to ask a parent approximately when a child began to use different forms of writing and reading. Such information, if there is some evidence that the memories might be dependable, could be useful to know how much time and what kind of interaction is needed in the classroom. Much more relevant and directly useful is information about the child's current repertoire of writing and reading behaviors.

### Distribution of Behaviors During Kindergarten

Writing in kindergarten seems to be a robust behavior—all the children that I have worked with have written in some recognizable form, and that's amazing. However, there are classroom situations in which children will not write, and I have witnessed those as well. As mentioned in the introduction and section on instructional contexts, children may either display their abilities to write and read emergently or hide them. Children respond readily, however, to simple requests for emergent reading and writing from a teacher who shows willingness to accept children's emergent behaviors. The conditions under which children respond readily to invitations to read and write are fairly simple but extremely important. First, teachers need to use unhedged language requesting reading and writing: "Write a story," "read your story," "read me your book." Second, they must let children know that they will accept whatever forms of reading and writing children use. For details on a simple routine for getting children started writing in classrooms, see Sulzby (1989; also see Sulzby, Barnhart, & Hieshima, 1989, and Sulzby, Teale, and Kamberelis, 1989).

*Forms of writing.* After a number of studies of children's writing (Sulzby, 1983, 1985c; Sulzby & Teale, 1985), I developed a checklist for indicating which forms of writing children were using. This checklist also included a list of the forms of rereading and some indications of where the child was looking during reading. This checklist was slightly revised after a two-year study (Sulzby, Barnhart, & Hieshima, 1989) of children's writing with monthly samples during kindergarten and quarterly samples during first grade. The categories for the revised system for assessing the Forms of Writing are listed in Table 1; a simplified form can be used for classroom assessments by dropping the subcategories of each form. The checklist for Forms of Reading is discussed later.

Children continue to use drawing, scribbling, and nonphonetic letterstrings abundantly in kindergarten; invented spelling is a relatively new and somewhat rare occurrence (Sulzby, 1983, 1985b; Sulzby, Barnhart, & Hieshima, 1989). Some children begin to show a conventional understanding of writing and to produce stories

**TABLE 1    Forms of Writing Checklist (Revised from Sulzby 1985b)***

| Research Checklist | Abbreviated Classroom Checklist |
| --- | --- |
| Drawing as Writing | Drawing |
| Drawing as Illustration | Scribble |
| Scribble, Wavy | Nonphonetic Letterstrings |
| Scribble, Letterlike | Invented Spelling |
| Letters, Random | Conventional |
| Letters, Patterned | —Copying |
| Letters, Name Elements | —Produced |
| Pseudoletters (Letterlike Units) | Other (List these by name)† |
| Copying from Environmental Print | |
| Invented Spelling, Syllabic | |
| Invented Spelling, Intermediate | |
| Invented Spelling, Full | |
| Name | |
| Conventional | |
| Other (List these by name)† | |

*The order of the list does not necessarily indicate the order of acquisition nor of subsequent development.

†Occasionally children invent or re-create idiosyncratic systems, such as one boy's description of Braille, which he kept calling *Siamese,* or use less common forms such as rebus or abbreviations.

and other pieces of writing in which they mix invented and conventional spellings. Invented spelling appears earlier for a given child in writing isolated words rather than in connected discourse. In fact, Barnhart (1986; Barnhart & Sulzby, 1986) found that children's use of forms varies systematically across requests to write isolated words, sentences, or stories, with invented and conventional spellings used more frequently with words, next with sentences, and least with stories. (Sulzby (1983; 1985c) found similar variations across requests for inventories ("write all you can write") and stories, as well as across audience situations (well-known adult; child and adult guests to the classroom), with children showing more variation in the complexity of the stories in motivating situations. In situations where children seem excited about the audience for their writing, a number of children reverted to less advanced-appearing forms of writing for a seemingly more advanced compositional purpose (multipage stories in scribble or drawing with complex story lines). Other researchers (Allen, 1989; Ferreiro & Teberosky, 1982) have reported similar kinds of nonrandom variation across classroom and research tasks.

A given child may use all five of the most common writing forms (scribble, drawing, letterstrings, invented spelling, or conventional orthography) at a given period of time, even adding a less common form such as pseudoletters; another may concentrate on only one or two forms. A child who has begun to use invented spelling may continue to show a strong preference for a form such as scribble. Assessment of the language surrounding the writing may nevertheless show quite advanced understandings about writing. Some children reread from scribble using the language and intonation of a written monologue; some even trace the scribble with their finger, making finger, voice, and scribble end simultaneously. In Example 4, we see a story in letterlike scribble. This child said the words of a composition while scribbling and then reread from the scribble. The only change in his rereading and composing language was a shift from nouns in composing to pronouns in rereading. He coordinated his pointing and speech to the print.

**EXAMPLE 4**  Letterlike Scribble

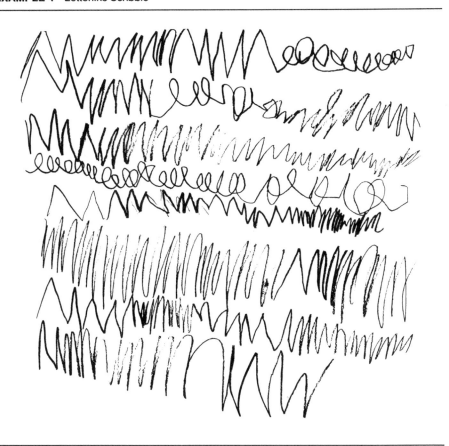

Rather than using one form exclusively in a composition, children often use multiple forms, mixing letterstrings and scribble, or scribble, drawing, and conventional spelling. Additionally, writing forms appear, disappear, and reappear cyclically; the sophistication of the forms of writing can only be assessed by examining other evidence, such as the language that children use surrounding the writing—particularly, by composing and rereading language. In Examples 5a and 5b, we see two

**EXAMPLE 5**   Invented Spelling Without Spaces and Written Monologue in Pseudoletters

---

WK DAI WS WAMiGiNePG
WWSII HRDKaePETHiN I list wooThe KaPETHN
WSGoeN To ET MiUP I WS SKARD
IMGINePG BM UP He STRTiTSkW EL

---

stories by a child just beginning first grade who wrote a fairly readable story in intermediate invented spelling one day and wrote a story in pseudoletters the next day, using the language (unrecorded) of a written monologue for both, although she tried to track the print briefly for the invented spelling story.

*Forms of reading.* There is a fairly extensive body of research on children's rereading language at the kindergarten-first grade level. Initially, I had hypothesized (Sulzby, 1983) that children's rereading language would not necessarily parallel the patterns of language in emergent storybook reading, but we have found that the parallel is quite strong (Sulzby, Barnhart, & Hieshima, 1989). Children's storybooks are quite lengthy in comparison with their written compositions. Length of composition affects the accuracy with which a listener can judge the nature of the child's rereading language.

Furthermore, storybooks are written in conventional orthography and allow for different possibilities in rereading. We have found a number of surprising contrasts, however. For example, it appears unlikely that the printed form of scribble would allow children to use their knowledge of letter-sound relationships.[5] With conventional orthography the child is afforded the possibility of regular decoding. We might, however, expect to find both oral and written monologue language used with any of the nonphonetic forms (scribble, drawing, letterstrings), and we do find them. But we also found children attending to print, pointing to these forms, and seeming to use language equivalent to forms which we thought were only possible with conventional orthography. Another surprise was the finding (Kamberelis & Sulzby, 1988) that when children first begin to write through encoding phonetically (invented spelling) they do not necessarily immediately use decoding to retrieve the text, nor even seem to think that it is an option.

The following discussion of the forms of rereading may make these claims clearer. In Sulzby (1985a), I argued that children's language during storybook reading could be classified by drawing upon the concepts of the relationships between oral and written language that young children are exposed to within a literate society in which parents read to their children. I claimed that categories based upon oral and written language relationships would not form a universal hierarchy but would vary according to the use of oral and written language conventions within a culture. Subsequently, we found evidence of culturally dependent effects in storybook reading language (Sulzby & Teale, 1987). In the discussion that follows, I have adapted the categories from the Sulzby Classification Scheme for Emergent Storybook Reading to apply to rereading from one's own writing. In some cases, the abbreviated length of most of children's written stories has led to the collapsing of subcategories from the storybook scheme. In two cases, "One Clause" and "Naming Letters," new categories were added. The forms of rereading are listed in Table 2, along with simplified checklist for classroom use.

Occasionally a child's writing sample was collected but he or she did not reread. Perhaps the child was taken out of class for a special lesson or appointment. For those instances, "not observed" was checked. The next two categories are more interesting and perhaps analogous to low- and high-level refusals in storybook reading (Sulzby, 1985a). Unexplained refusals are coded as refusals, but the special category of "I

**TABLE 2    Forms of Rereading From Emergent Writing (Revised from Sulzby 1985b)***

| Research Checklist | Abbreviated Classroom Checklist |
|---|---|
| Not Observed | Refusal |
| Refusal (Don't Know, No Response, "No") | Unexplained |
| "I didn't write"† | "I didn't write" |
| One Clause | Conversational |
| Labeling/Description | Oral Monologue |
| Dialogue | Oral/written mix |
| Oral Monologue | Written monologue |
| Oral/Written Mix | Attending to print (not yet conventional) |
| Written Monologue | Conventional |
| Naming Letters | Other (list these by name) |
| Aspectual/Strategic | |
| Conventional | |
| Other (List these by name) | |

*The order of list generally indicates order of development; length of composition affects categories, however, particularly "One Clause." Categories are based upon fuller explanations of emergent  storybook reading language in Sulzby (1985a).

†This may be analogous to "refusing to read based upon print awareness" from storybook scale.

*Source:* Revised from E. Sulzby, Forms of Writing and Rereading Example List, unpublished examiner's manual (Evanston, IL: Northwestern University, 1985).

didn't write" seems to be important. In this category, which can also include "I was just writing," the child seems to be indicating knowledge about the conditions under which conventional print works. We expect to have children say, "I didn't write," about scribble or drawing; however, we have had children proclaim that "I love you" on a self-designed Valentine is not writing or that the letters used to try to sound out "Count Dracula" were not writing (Sulzby, 1989). In these instances, assessment can become more sensitive if the teacher or researcher probes gently and nondirectively: "Tell me more about that."

The category "One Clause" is necessary in research on children's writing because when children produce texts that are only one clause long, we do not have connected discourse, the "unit" upon which the system is based. But length is not a linear variable in young children's writing. Children may reread a multiclause story from scribble, drawing, or nonphonetic letterstrings, yet when beginning to write in invented spelling, they may stop with one clause or even part of a clause. This often seems to be because of the effort that it takes to use this new form.[6] If their rereading of such a text involves making use of memory for text or actually making use of print cues, the rereadings would also be one clause. "One Clause" is a warning to give this sample of writing and rereading special consideration in assessment. A one-clause production precludes judgments such as whether or not the child is reading conventionally from print because the sample is insufficient to allow that judgment, but it can alert the assessor to take a look at other samples and instances of writing by this child.

In the categories from "Labeling/Describing" through "Written Monologue" the child is not tracking the print as if it is what one reads from. (We often ask children to read again, "And this time point as you read," but now I am talking about first readings when the adult does not call the child's attention to print.) In "Labeling/Describing" the child uses language such as, "This is my momma. This is my uncle. This is our house, and the grass," while pointing to parts of a picture or even printed text. "Dialogue" is conversational language used with the writing, often in dialogic interaction with the adult. Oral monologues are full stories, told in the intonation of interactive storytelling. They typically use wording more frequently expected in oral storytelling situations. Written monologues are also full stories, but the child's intonation is that of a reader. Often the wording shows signs of a written standard, including literary language, but occasionally the sample is too brief to make that judgment. Also, children may begin sentences with conjunctions such as "and" or "and then," yet they end the preceding sentence with sentence-final intonation, breathe in, and begin the new sentence with a new burst of air, clearly signaling breaks between the sentences. The distinction between oral and written monologues in storybook reading is much more clear, with both wording and intonation used distinctively (Sulzby, 1985a, "monologic storytelling" and "reading verbatimlike story"). This is probably due to the model of the original composition by a published author in contrast to the burden of having to compose the entire piece as a kindergartner.

The storybook reading classification scheme has a category called, "Reading and storytelling mixed." This category is theoretically similar to "oral/written mix" in rereading from one's own writing; yet many rereadings must be placed in this category not for theoretical but for practical reasons. For assessment, this would be considered a borderline case, or a case in which there is insufficient evidence to judge between oral and written monologue.

A new category, "Naming letters," had to be introduced into the Forms of Reading checklist that does not directly parallel categories in the storybook classification scheme. It appears, however, that there may be an indirect parallel, but we do not yet have sufficient samplings to conclude confidently that this is the case. Sometimes when asked to "read your story," a child will simply name all the letters, in or out of order. This kind of reading certainly shows attention to print and seems analogous to "reading aspectually," from the storybook scheme. In the storybook version of "reading aspectually," children attend to print, but focus alternatively upon one or more aspects of reading, either sounding out to nonsense, reciting known words randomly from the page, or reciting the story in a verbatimlike manner, but tracking the print highly inaccurately. In these cases, the child is breaking the reading activity up into parts; this type of reading appears to be a fairly brief transition into reading holistically from print.

Examples 6a, 6b, 6c, 6d, 6e, and 6f illustrate the variability in how children read from writing forms that look similar; this set shows different kindergartner's stories in the same writing form—nonphonetic letterstrings—and illustrates the forms just discussed. Examples 6a, 6b, and 6f were written monologues. Brian's was only two clauses long; his intonation rather than wording was the deciding factor in calling it a written monologue. In spite of the great difference in the number of letters used in their written forms, Pat's and Ulana's stories were each recited as four clauses long. Pat's clauses, one of which was a title, were short simple sentences with a clear drop in voice at the end of each. Ulana used more complex syntax—one compound sentence and others with modifying phrases, adjectives, and adverbs. In Example 6c, Bryan read by naming letters. Richard read 6d as an oral monologue, but Mark's reading of 6e had to be coded as oral and written mixed. Thus we can see how the forms of writing must be interpreted in light of the child's rereading behavior. While missing from this set of examples, reading letterstrings with more traditional "aspectual/strategic" reading has also been witnessed in our studies. In Table 2, I suggest combining "Naming Letters" and other forms of "Strategic/Aspectual" reading into one category, "Attending to print, but not yet conventional" for a classroom assessment checklist.

In the original Sulzby Classification Scheme for Emergent Storybook Reading (Sulzby, 1985a), I listed four subcategories once a child was attending to print as a source for reading: "Refusing to read based upon print awareness," "reading aspectually," "reading with strategies imbalanced," and "reading independently" (herein referred to as "reading conventionally").The first two have already been described. "I didn't write" and other such comments have been interpreted to be analogous to a print-based refusal. "Naming letters" was discussed as being similar to "reading aspectually." "Reading with strategies imbalanced" is a form of holistic reading in

**EXAMPLE 6**  Letter String Stories

---

STKPVSSPKVSS

Example 6a  Letterstrings by Brian

Bryan

L iVGSVS

BYoKOx

HUW

FLO

oi NO

Example 6c  Letterstrings by Bryan

MBWEEEB

GFEOF

DGB

Example 6b  Letterstrings by Pat

Example 6d  Letterstrings by Richard

TeHMINLOKER

HRAKLiLO

iMANiATQOiN

MiKLiUVY

OTLiUTLPMi

OTLOWMARP

TOLWMRP

OMLQOTFE

RTMRLPEFO

Example 6e  Letterstrings by Mark

NOLATXPXUARCDOSYOLKMN
ERMVOXOPYSMHGJXMONJMON
NLTXPORHATXOHGTMIVOMJOS
HTOXRPOHAXOH6MONJSJORD
ORTLXPORTHAOTAHSJORONX
OTLOXPRHRTEFGDFORTC
XTOXPRHTREGFDOFRSTNO
OXXHRHPTWSYOHHSTNO
XOTHAPHNWSOYHTNOH

Example 6f  Letterstrings by Ulana

which the child tracks the print accurately, in left-to-right order, matching words with speech, but when the child has difficulty identifying a word, he or she overrelies on one or more aspect, without switching strategically across aspects. When a child is "reading independently," now called "reading conventionally," he or she uses strategies in a flexible and coordinated manner, to interpret a text in a manner that seems to satisfy the child and is understandable to another conventionally literate person. In assessing children's rereading from their own writing, it is often difficult to distinguish between reading aspectually and strategically, hence the categories have been collapsed into "aspectual/strategic." Another large problem for assessment is the issue of length. Many times in research, when spot sampling is done, a child's reading will be placed by default into the "aspectual/strategic" category because the child's story is insufficiently long for a judge to see flexible and strategic uses of strategies. Hence, for accurate assessment a number of samples may be needed and inferences need to be drawn across many sources.

From examining the evidence from studies across infancy to first grade and from studies focusing on kindergarten, we can see that writing appears to have a long developmental track. The persistence of multiple forms of writing into kindergarten and first grade suggest that children's writing develops as a repertoire of forms that gradually develop into a conventional performance and understanding of the orthography. Many instructional contexts, however, appear to preclude children showing parts of their repertoire. Each of these issues is relevant to the kind and frequency of assessments that are relevant for writing.

### Instructional Contexts

If teachers want to assess writing, they need to know some of the ways in which contexts affect how children write. Let us reconsider some of the instructional contexts described earlier in which we find writing going on in kindergarten or first grade classrooms. In some classrooms, assignments and instructions to the children indicate that only one form of writing is considered to be legitimate: conventionally spelled orthography. Some of these classrooms may be using traditional readiness or textbook-guided techniques. Often, in these classrooms, writing is treated only as conventional orthography, and children's tasks are to learn to form the letters, memorize a few words (such as first and last names, color and number words, or preprimer sight vocabulary) and to copy correct forms.

An interesting contrast that nonetheless often may end up conveying to children that only standard orthography counts as writing is the Language Experience Approach, in which children dictate their speech to the teacher to write for them. The Language Experience Approach may communicate to children that their orally delivered language is honored and that their emergent reading is honored, but not that the *children's* forms of writing are honored.[7] It is best if dictation is treated as the teacher "writing for you in grownup writing" and if children are also expected and encouraged to "write for yourself, your own way."

Teachers in whole language and/or emergent literacy classrooms usually encourage and accept all forms of writing used by children. Occasionally, however, they may unconsciously discourage some forms. In some classroom situations in which children are encouraged to write, children nevertheless may be guided in ways that may reflect more traditional concerns about protecting children against tasks that are too difficult. In these situations, children may be asked to draw a picture and then label the picture.[8] Later, they might be asked to write a sentence or longer passage under the picture. By preempting drawing and using it through the teacher's directions as a *stimulus* for writing, teachers are indicating to children that drawing is not a form of writing at a time in which, in free-choice situations, children still use drawing. While they show some awareness that drawing "is not really writing," they nevertheless will use it and maintain, occasionally with ambivalent comments, that it *is* writing.

Process writing approaches are totally compatible with children's emergent literacy in principle, with group responding to writing given highest priority in kindergarten. Revision should be encouraged selectively, as the teacher finds that the child is fluent enough with invented and conventional writing. Proofreading is often considered too much for a very young child—a chore that may stifle creativity and fluency just as the child needs to be gaining confidence. For these reasons, often an adult offers to take dictation or to type the story "in grownup" for the child. This is fine so long as the message is not given to the child that his or her forms are unacceptable. In some cases, children may stop using any forms of writing except conventional forms, often becoming dependent upon the adult to "spell it for me."

Thus, from these considerations, we can see that the overall instructional messages around writing may affect children's choice of ways to write. Other aspects besides the forms of writing and reading may also be affected by the context. In a recent review of the literature, Sulzby, Teale, and Kamberelis (1989) compared situations in which children have been observed to write in the home with the school setting. They suggested that these themes which can be observed in literacy-rich homes may be neglected in school settings due to instructional constraints.

- Children's writing is often transient.
- Children's writing is a sign of their power and is negotiated with parents and other adults.
- Children's writing takes many forms [and they] move across these forms easily.
- Children can get engrossed in major multimedia construction that may take days to complete.
- Children use writing for aesthetic creation.

Dyson (1988) has called our attention to how children can and do negotiate their understandings and manipulations of multiple worlds in classroom settings, working with and around the constraints set up by classroom tasks, even when teachers set up barriers to the full range of writing forms. When teachers set up opportunities through classroom materials, arrangement, and instructional tasks, children may display far more power and creativity in writing—assessment needs to consider how supportive or constraining the context is.

The classroom situation which I think is most producive to assessing the full range of writing development for young children is one in which all the forms of writing are available to the children through assignments, free-choice activities, and the teacher's comments and attitudes. This would seem to be particularly important for kindergartners and preschoolers who use these forms publicly with little shame. First graders often make quite clear comments that forms such as scribble, drawing, and letterstrings are *not* writing, yet in a number of studies (Barnhart, 1986; Martinez & Teale, 1987; Sulzby, 1983; Sulzby, Barnhart, & Hieshima, 1989), first graders have been found to use these forms well into first grade.

We do not know the full impact of restricting writing forms upon children of different ages. By indicating to children that particular forms are not accepted, however, teachers also limit the kinds of language and nonverbal behaviors that accompany those forms. Limitations on acceptable forms may also prevent the teacher from seeing and making assessments based upon how children transform these forms during the process of becoming conventionally literate. One rather apparent example of this is the transformation of drawing from being a form of writing into becoming an illustration or carrying another function in relation to conventional orthography.

Another example is a speculation that I have extrapolated from Clay's (1975, 1979a) work: children may be transforming all these forms into a conventional understanding of orthography that results in a highly proficient and creative use of language in writing. We do not understand all this process yet, but here are a few suggestions about how this may work. Through scribble, children are exploring the linearity of written text and salient features of print. Over years of development, some children have been seen transforming scribble from unglanced at or untracked print to print that seems to be treated as an object of memory. Sulzby, Barnhart, and Hieshima (1989) report having observed three children saying speech during composition through scribble that they later used in rereading. Some videotaped examples have showed children pointing to oddly shaped pieces of scribble over repeated rereadings and saying the same words at the same points in the text. Through letterstrings, children may be exploring the allowable co-occurrence of letters in the English writing system. Children appear to move rather quickly from random letterstrings to strings in which frequently occurring patterns reoccur. The most important pattern, we speculate, is the alternation of vowels and consonants. The manner in which the author of "The Three Bugs" (Example 3) transformed drawing with print into an integral part of a more inclusive text offers provocation to consider other reorganizations and transformations that children may make with the forms of writing and reading. Understandings such as these, and the ever-present signs that children understand at some level that print is used to convey a codified, composed set of meanings, suggest to us that we need to assess the full range of writing behaviors through classroom situations that allow these forms to be honored.

## GENERAL METHODOLOGICAL ISSUES

Before we move on to summarize what we know and need to know about writing development and assessing it, let us consider some general methodological concerns. While not all the problems have yet been solved and some appear quite intractable, I raise these concerns to enlist help of teachers and researchers.

Even though my comments have indicated that the careful eyes and ears of a classroom teacher or other concerned adult are needed for good assessment, traditional issues of reliability and validity certainly must be addressed. When we assess writing, we want to know that two or more informed observers would look at a child's writing, hear the child's composing or metalinguistic speech, or listen to the child's rereading and come to the same conclusions in categorizing or interpreting it. Similarly, with any kind of assessment of creativity and motivation in writing. Needless to say, the more naturalistic the assessment, the more difficult it becomes to specify the criteria that observers are using or should be using. Developing common terminology and working definitions are critical, but should not become so codified as to hinder us from new insights.

In using the checklists that I have presented in this chapter, my colleagues and I have found that simple checklist comparisons of categorizations are not a sufficient basis for understanding whether or not judges agree when they are learning how to assess writing, particularly as new phenomena are being explored, but that judges' narrative descriptions backing up their categorizations are essential. Many times judges may check different categories, but the details in their narrative explanations are almost identical. Through working with our judgments together, we come to share a terminology that expresses the commonality of our judgments. Conversely, we learn when terminology may mask important differences in our interpretations.

Another key concern about assessing writing is that writing is a production task. That is, there is no way in which we can say students are responding to the same stimulus item, in any meaningful way that suggests that all have the same opportunity to respond in somewhat similar ways to any degree of helpful specificity. If we ask multiple-choice or true-false questions, we can argue that all readers have the same question and the same response options from which to choose. We might then have some justification in saying that "Children did not know X content," although that is also debatable. We have far, far less justification in using the terms "does not know" or "cannot do" based upon samples of writing. All we can say is that the child *did* create a piece of writing of this type under these circumstances. But we are encouraged by the robustness of behaviors that we see across children and within children using the techniques suggested here.

Admissions such as these about the methodological difficulties with writing would seem to have defeated any claim that we can assess writing. but we think that is not the case. While there is no way that we can claim that current emergent writing assessments "test the outer limits" of children's ability or carve out the full extent of a child's zone of proximal development (Vygotsky, 1978), there appear to be some commonalities of responses under certain contexts that are fairly predictable. For example, the commonality of my experience with phenomena reported by other researchers (such as Ferreiro, Dyson, and Clay) using diverse methodologies is encouraging.

## DESIGNING ASSESSMENTS OF EMERGENT WRITING

So, what do we have to think about to assess writing by young children who are not yet writing conventionally? We have to be concerned about how close children are to conventional writing and how they are developing toward it. We have to be concerned with what the tasks are that we are asking children to do. We have to be concerned with the context. We have to worry about the wording we use in assessment. We also need to take into account motivational aspects—Is the child trying? Is the teacher/assessor encouraging (or discouraging) the child? Writing is a production task, so assessment needs to consider the open-ended nature of the tasks. Writing is variable across contexts, so multiple assessments are crucial. We must keep in mind that we are always assessing the behavior of one child and thus multiple assessments, while making comparisons with other, usually anonymous children, have to be related back to this one child.

## NOTES

[1] The discussion in this chapter is primarily limited to children writing in English; however, the phenomena of emergent reading and writing are being reported from numerous countries and, theoretically, should be universal for literate populations.

[2] In a recent Special Report in *Newsweek*, April 17, 1989, developmentally appropriate practice for children aged 5 through 8 was discussed and illustrated. A first grade classroom was used as the illustration for writing. While children were actively responding to literature, writing was depicted as being first, requests to draw pictures, then encouragements to write labels, finally to use invented spelling which the teacher would transcribe into conventional orthography. This example was probably simplified in the reporting process, but it fits with many classroom implementations that I have witnessed.

[3] One child, almost age 4, made her first recognizable invented spelling, using only the consonants in her name while driving through an automatic car wash: "K, R, N, Mama, K, R, N—that's my name, huh, K, R, N?" Other words, such as "cat" and "dog," were only first letters.

[4] There are also times when the child says, "I was just writing." "Just writing" seems to mean without a compositional intent.

[5] We occasionally hear that children seem to sound out while reading from scribble, but this behavior seems to be auditory segmentation that would be part, but not the entire activity, of regular decoding. This voluntary display of phonemic awareness with scribble seems to be relatively rare.

[6]Contrast the unfinished character of Example 5a with Examples 1–3.

[7]This can be avoided if teachers carefully explain that dictation is being used as just another way to write, "the grownup way," and if the other forms of writing are elicited and accepted as "children's ways of writing." I recommend letting children know that the teacher recognizes the distinction between grownup and child forms of writing and has the expectation that children will become conventional writers.

[8]There may also be a reflection of Graves' (1983) report that first graders often begin writing through labeling, a topic which we will return to later.

## REFERENCES

ALLEN, J.B. (1989). Reading and writing development in whole language classrooms. In J. Mason (Ed.), *Reading and writing connections*, pp. 121–146. Needham Heights, MA: Allyn & Bacon.

ANDERSON, A.B., & STOKES, S.J. (1984). Social and institutional influences on the development and practice of literacy. In H. Goelman, A. Oberg, & F. Smith (Eds.), *Awakening to literacy*, pp. 24–37. Exeter, NH: Heinemann.

BARNHART, J.E. (1986). *Written language concepts and cognitive development in kindergarten children.* Unpublished doctoral dissertation, Northwestern University, Evanston, IL.

BARNHART, J.E., & SULZBY, E. (1986, April). *How Johnny can write: Kindergarten children's uses of emergent writing systems.* Paper presented at the annual meeting of the American Educational Research Association, San Francisco, CA.

BROWN, R. (1989). Testing and thoughtfulness. *Educational Leadership, 46,* 31–33.

CHOMSKY, N., & HALLE, M. (1968). *The sound pattern of English.* New York: Harper & Row.

CLAY, M.M. (1975). *What did I write?* Auckland, NZ: Heinemann.

CLAY, M.M. (1979a). *The early detection of reading difficulties* (2nd ed). Auckland, NZ: Heinemann.

CLAY, M.M. (1979b). *Reading: The patterning of complex behavior* (2nd ed). Auckland, NZ: Heinemann.

DOAKE, D. (1981). *Book experience and emergent reading behavior.* Unpublished doctoral dissertation, University of Alberta.

DYSON, A.H. (1984). Learning to write/learning to do school: Emergent writer's interpretations of school literacy tasks. *Research in the Teaching of English, 18,* 233–264.

DYSON, A.H. (1988). Negotiating among multiple worlds: The space/time dimensions of young children's composing. *Research in the Teaching of English, 22*(4), 355–390.

FERREIRO, E. (1986). The interplay between information and assimilation in beginning literacy. In W. Teale & E. Sulzby (Eds.), *Emergent literacy: Writing and reading.* Norwood, NJ: Ablex.

FERREIRO, E., & TEBEROSKY, A. (1982). *Literacy before schooling.* (K.G. Castro, Trans.) Exeter, NH: Heinemann. (Original work published in 1979.)

GOODMAN, Y.M. (1986). Children coming to know literacy. In W.H. Teale & E. Sulzby (Eds.), *Emergent literacy: Writing and reading.* Norwood, NJ: Ablex.

GRAVES, D. (1983). *Writing: Teachers and children at work.* Exeter, NH: Heinemann.

GUNDLACH, R., MCLANE, J.B., STOTT, F.M., & MCNAMEE, G.D. (1985). The social foundations of children's early writing development. In M. Farr (Ed.), *Advances in writing research, Vol. 1: Children's early writing development. Norwood, NJ: Ablex.*

HARSTE, J.E., WOODWARD, V.A. & BURKE, C.L. (1984). *Language stories and literacy lessons.* Portsmouth, NJ: Heinemann.

HIEBERT, E. H. (1981). Developmental patterns and interrelationships of preschool children's print awareness. *Reading Research Quarterly, 16*, 236–260.

HOLDAWAY, D. (1979). *The foundations of literacy.* Sydney, AUS: Ashton Scholastic.

KAMBERELIS, G. & SULZBY, E. (1988). Transitional knowledge in emergent literacy. In J.E. Readence and R.S. Baldwin, (Eds.), *Dialogue in literacy research,* Thirty-seventh Yearbook of the National Reading Conference. Rochester, NY: National Reading Conference, 95–106.

KING, M., & RENTEL, V. (1981a). *How children learn to write: A longitudinal study.* Final Report to the National Institute of Education (Vol. 1, NIE-G-79-0137 and NIE-G-79-0039, RF Project 761861/712383 and 765512/711748). Columbus, OH: Ohio State University Research Foundation.

MARTINEZ, M., & TEALE, W.H. (1987). The ins and outs of a kindergarten writing program. *The Reading Teacher, 40*, 444–451.

MARTLEW, M. (1986). The development of written language. In K. Durkin (Ed.), *Language development in the school years.* London: Croom Helm.

MASON, J.M., PETERMAN, C.L., POWELL, B.M., & KERR, M.K. (1989). In J. Mason, (Ed.) *Reading and writing connections,* pp. 105–120. Needham Heights, MA: Allyn & Bacon.

MASON, J.M., & STEWART, J.P. (this volume).

RAPHAEL, T.E., ENGLERT, C.S., & KIRSCHNER, B.W. (1989). Acquisition of expository writing skills. In J. Mason (Ed.), *Reading and writing connections,* pp. 261–290. Needham Heights, MA: Allyn & Bacon.

SCHICKEDANZ, J. (1986). *More than the ABC's: The early stages of reading and writing.* Washington. DC: National Association for the Education of Young Children.

SCOLLON, R., & SCOLLON, S.B.K. (1981). *Narrative, literacy, and face in interethnic communication.* Norwood, NJ: Ablex.

SHEPARD, L.A. (1989). Why we need better assessment. *Educational Leadership, 46*, 4–9.

STALLMAN, A., & PEARSON, P.D. (this volume).

SULZBY, E. (1983, September). *Beginning readers' developing knowledges about written language.* Final report to the National Institute of Education (NIE-G-80-0176). Evanston, IL: Northwestern University.

SULZBY, E. (1985a). Children's emergent reading of favorite storybooks: A developmental study. *Reading Research Quarterly, 20*, 458–481.

SULZBY, E. (1985b). *Forms of writing and rereading: Example list.* Unpublished examiner's manual. Evanston, IL: Northwestern University.

SULZBY, E. (1985c). Kindergartners as writers and readers. In M. Farr (Ed.), *Advances in writing research Vol 1: Children's early writing development,* pp. 127–200. Norwood, NJ: Ablex

SULZBY, E. (1987). Children's development of prosodic distinctions in telling and dictating modes. In A. Matsuhashi (Ed.), *Writing in real time: Modelling production processes,* pp. 133–160. Norwood, NJ: Ablex.

SULZBY, E. (1989). *Emergent literacy: Kindergartners write and read, including Sulzby coding system.* Monograph accompanying videotape, a part of Computers in Early Literacy (CIEL) Research Project. Ann Arbor, MI, and Elmhurst, IL: The Regents of the University of Michigan and North Central Regional Educational Laboratory.

SULZBY, E., BARNHART, J., & HIESHIMA, J. (1989). Forms of writing and rereading from writing:

A preliminary report. In J. Mason (Ed.), *Reading and writing connections,* pp. 31–63. Needham Heights, MA: Allyn & Bacon. A more detailed version appears as Technical Report No. 437 (1988) from the Center for the Study of Reading, University of Illinois.

SULZBY, E., & TEALE, W.H. (1985). Writing development in early childhood. *Educational Horizons, 64,* 8–12.

SULZBY, E., & TEALE, W.H. (1987). *Young children's storybook reading: Longitudinal study of parent-child interaction and children's independent functioning.* Final report to the Spencer Foundation. Ann Arbor: University of Michigan.

SULZBY, E., TEALE, W., & KAMBERELIS, G. (1989). Emergent writing in the classroom: Home and school connections. In D. Strickland & L. Morrow (Eds.) *Emerging literacy: Young children learn to read and write.* Newark, DE: International Reading Association.

SULZBY, E., & TEALE, W.H. (in press). Emergent literacy. To appear in P.D. Pearson, R. Barr, M.L. Kamil, & P. Mosenthal (Eds.), *Handbook of reading research,* 2nd ed. New York: Longman.

TAYLOR, D. (1983). *Family literacy: The social context of learning to read and write.* Exeter, NH: Heinemann.

TAYLOR, D., & DORSEY-GAINES, C. (1988). *Growing up literate: Learning from inner-city families.* Portsmouth, NH: Heinemann.

TEALE, W.H. (1984). Reading to young children: Its significance for literacy development. In H. Goelman, A. Oberg, & F. Smith (Eds.), *Awakening to literacy,* pp. 110–121. Exeter, NH: Heinemann.

TEALE, W.H. (1986). Home background and young children's literacy development In W.H. Teale & E. Sulzby (Eds.), *Emergent literacy: Writing and reading.* Norwood, NJ: Ablex.

TEALE, W.H. (1987). Emergent literacy: Reading and writing development in early childhood. *36th NRC Yearbook, 36,* 45–74.

TEALE, W.H. (1988). Developmentally appropriate assessment of reading and writing in the early childhood classroom. *Elementary School Journal, 89,* 173–183.

TEALE, W.H., ANDERSON, A.B., COLE, M., & STOKES, S. (1981, October). *Literacy activities in the homes of low-income preschool children.* Paper presented at the Conference on Home Influences on School Achievement. University of Wisconsin, Madison.

TEALE, W.H., & MARTINEZ, M.G. (1989). Connecting writing: Fostering emergent literacy in kindergarten children. In J.M. Mason (Ed.), *Reading and writing connections,* pp. 177–198. Needham Heights, MA: Allyn & Bacon.

VALENCIA, S.W., PEARSON, P.D., PETERS, C.W., & WIXSON, K. (1989). *Educational Leadership, 46,* 57–63.

VUKELICH, C., & EDWARDS, N. (1988). The role of context and as-written orthography in kindergartners' word recognition. *37th NRC Yearbook, 37,* 85–93.

VYGOTSKY, L.S. (1978). *Mind in society.* Cambridge, MA: Harvard University Press.

WOLFE, D.P. (1989). Portfolio assessment: Sampling student work. *Educational Leadership, 46,* 35–39.

## AUTHOR'S NOTES

This chapter was supported in part by the Spencer Foundation. It was also partially supported by the Center for Research on Learning and Schooling and the program in Curriculum, Teaching, and Psychological Studies of The University of

Michigan. I am particularly grateful to June Barnhart, Joyce Hieshima, George Kamberelis, and Liliana Barro for their assistance in collecting and analyzing data for a number of the studies of writing reported in this chapter. I am also grateful for my long-term colleague William H. Teale of the University of Texas in San Antonio and to the teachers, parents, and children who have made this work possible.

# 7

# ASSESSING CHILDREN'S UNDERSTANDING OF STORY THROUGH THEIR CONSTRUCTION AND RECONSTRUCTION OF NARRATIVE

*Lesley Mandel Morrow*
*Rutgers, The State University of New Jersey*

### Abstract

Lesley Mandel Morrow discusses ways of assessing children's comprehension of text using strategies different from the commonly accepted practice of asking children a series of questions. The first strategy involves the construction of meaning during storybook readings, and the second the reconstruction of meaning after the story has been read, through story retelling. Both contexts involve interactive behavior between adult and child. They encourage integration and personalization of text, helping children see how parts of a story interrelate and how they mesh with one's own experiences. Both contexts provide an approach for assessment and strategies for comprehension instruction as well.

Research in emergent literacy in the last several years has generated new instructional strategies that are starting to be implemented in schools. Publishers of commercial materials are beginning to incorporate them into their programs as well. These new strategies tend to call for different kinds of assessment in early childhood education since most commonly used measures do not reflect many of the elements we now recognize in emergent literacy. We have typically tested children for reading readiness with standardized measures administered once at the end of the kindergarten year.

The tests have measured sets of discrete skills, seen as precursors to reading, but they have not reflected certain crucial elements of emergent literacy nor have they met the need for frequent evaluation. They do not touch, for example, such early attempts in literacy development as a child's scribble writing or attempted reading by focusing on illustrations rather than print. Although there are some predictable stages of development, children's literacy behaviors change frequently and not necessarily in strict, predetermined sequence (Anderson, Hiebert, Scott, & Wilkinson, 1984). Because children change often in their literacy development, assessment should be frequent and include varied procedures within different contexts. We need to collect samples of children's work, both written and oral (Teale, Hiebert, & Chittenden, 1987). We need to observe children's behavior and listen to their responses and comments in various settings, recording them on tape, in continuous written anecdotes, and by prepared checklists. Interviewing children elicits information about their attitudes and insights, developmental levels, and cultural backgrounds. Because instruction and assessment should be closely linked (IRA, 1985), what we assess should match instructional strategies. Teachers should view the instructional setting as one for assessment, as well, for effective assessment involves teachers learning to look systematically at children's learning in various settings. Active and frequent involvement with storybook reading has come to be one of the most valued strategies for developing certain aspects of early literacy (Blank & Sheldon, 1971; Bower, 1976; Pellegrini & Galda, 1982). Yet the most commonly used standardized measures for early literacy do not address children's concepts about books or their comprehension of story. They do not measure a child's sense of story structure; literal, interpretive, and critical levels of comprehension; knowledge of story sequence; or background information concerning topics of stories read. When stories are read to them, children often demonstrate interest in and knowledge of concepts about print. Through their questions and comments, they reveal what they know about stories and what they want to know. Such information not only offers the teacher information about a child's level of achievement but also helps in planning appropriate instruction based on children's interests and needs.

Traditionally, story comprehension has rarely been measured in early childhood, and then only at a literal level. When comprehension is assessed, it is usually done through a series of questions posed after the child has read or listened to a story. The questions typically provide only one avenue for assessing comprehension and thus yield only one perspective on the child's understanding of the story. Because the child usually responds succinctly and is not encouraged to elaborate, comprehension evaluation depends primarily on the questions asked, rather than the child's response.

This chapter describes two storyreading contexts that link assessment of and instruction in children's story comprehension and concepts about print. The first allows assessment of a child's construction of story meaning through discussion with an adult and with other children while a story is being read to them. The second involves assessing a child's reconstruction of meaning through his or her retelling of a story. In either setting, the child has the opportunity to elaborate, relate information to background knowledge and real experiences, and reveal a rich source of information for the teacher. In either setting, the teacher observes and records behavior on prepared checklists or on tape, and then analyzes transcriptions or written anecdotes of the experience.

## RATIONALE FOR STORYBOOK READING

Reading to children has long been recognized as beneficial. Theoretical, correlational, experimental, anecdotal, and case study reports have reinforced the idea and described relationships between reading to children and aspects of their literacy development.

Both Clay (1979) and Smith (1978) articulate the theory that reading to children helps them learn that written language is different from oral, that printed words on a page have sounds, and that print carries meaning. Frequent experiences with story-book reading in early childhood correlate with the development of certain literacy skills. Early readers and children who enter school already knowing how to read have been found to come from homes in which adults read to them often (Clark, 1984; Durkin, 1966; Morrow, 1983; Sutton, 1964; Teale, 1978). Reading to children benefits both their vocabulary development and syntactic complexity (Burroughs, 1972; Chomsky, 1972; Fodor, 1966; Irwin, 1960). Cohen (1968) and Feitelson, Kita, & Goldstein (1986) investigated the effects on children's achievement of frequent storybook reading in the classroom; in both studies, vocabulary, comprehension, and decoding ability improved significantly in experimental groups. Case studies and anecdotal reports indicate that children who have been read to frequently recognized the differences between print and pictures as well as front-to-back and left-to-right directionality in books and reading (Baghban, 1984; Doakes, 1981; Hoffman, 1982; Rhodes, 1979).

## INTERACTIVE BEHAVIOR DURING STORYBOOK READING

Storybook reading is a social activity, with comments from the teacher or parent and comments or questions in children's responses, or vice versa. The event appears to involve cooperative construction or reconstruction of meaning as adult and child negotiate and mediate in their verbal exchanges about the story. As readings continue over time, both children and adults tend to alter their styles of interaction (Heath, 1982; Morrow, 1988 Ninio & Bruner, 1978; Taylor, 1986; Teale & Sulzby, 1987). The dialogue that occurs during interactive story reading thus provides the teacher with a great deal of progressive information about what children know about a story, the complexity of their understanding, how they construct meaning based on their own background information and the information in the story, and what they look for in a story.

Among the interactive behaviors research has identified in read-aloud activities are questioning, scaffolding dialogue and responses, offering praise or positive reinforcement, giving or extending information, clarifying information, restating information, directing discussion, sharing personal reactions, and relating concepts to life experiences. Flood (1977) analyzed parent-child storybook readings to determine characteristics that predict reading success for the child. According to his work with pre-K children, the best predictors of success on readiness test scores were the number of (1) words spoken by the child, (2) questions answered by the child, (3) preparatory questions asked by the parent, (4) post-story evaluative questions asked by the parent, (5) questions asked by the child, and (6) the amount of positive reinforcement offered by the parent.

In an intensive case study of a mother reading to her baby, Ninio and Bruner (1978) identified a four-step parent/child story-reading routine: attention-getting dialogue, questions, labeling and scaffolding, feedback. Scaffolding is a process in which the adult supplies responses that the child is not capable of making, so that the child can discover what is expected and can respond appropriately later on. As the child learns to respond, the adult scaffolds responses less and less (Applebee & Langer, 1983).

Shanahan and Hogan (1983) compared interactive behavior during story reading with children's subsequent achievement on a test of print awareness. They found the best predictors of achievement were the number of (1) answers to the child's questions during readings, (2) minutes of book reading per week, and (3) references to the child's own experiences.

Cochran-Smith (1984) observed storybook readings in school and reported on cooperative negotiation of textual meanings by readers and listeners. The most productive interactions, she learned, involve life-to-text and text-to-life discussions, implying that interpretation of text is based on how it can be related to the child's life and what the child knows about the text. The finding reflects the Piagetian theory that one applies new ideas to existing schemata and thus accommodates new information, and to Ausubel's theory that learning becomes more meaningful as it relates to a child's knowledge (Payton, 1984).

Roser and Martinez (1985) identified three adult roles in story reading. As co-respondents, adults initiate discussion in order to describe information, recount parts of a story, share personal reactions, relate experiences to real life, and invite children to share responses. As informers/monitors, they explain aspects of a story, provide information, and assess a child's understanding of the story. As directors, they introduce the story, announce conclusions, and assume leadership. Roles change, they found, as children participate in more and more story readings: children assume some of the adult behaviors. It has been demonstrated that an adult's reading style affects amount and type of discussion as well as a child's comprehension of story (Dunning, & Mason, 1984; Green & Harker, 1982; Peterman, Dunning & Mason, 1985).

## CHILDREN'S RESPONSES TO LITERATURE

The responses made by children during story readings are important to the interactive process. Literacy must be learned, not just taught (Torrey, 1969). The questions children ask in a read-aloud experience provide a direct channel for information that aids literacy development (Yaden, 1985). Their questions allow immediate feedback and an environment for learning advocated by Holdaway (1979) in his model for literacy instruction. Children are able to regulate their learning by posing questions in literacy situations.

We can learn a great deal about children's understanding of story through their responses during storybook readings. As they participate more frequently in read-aloud events, their responses increase in number and complexity. Initially, their responses relate mainly to illustrations: they label items, restate elements in the story, and, of course, answer questions asked of them (Bloome, 1985; Ninio & Bruner, 1978; Yaden, 1985). Then they begin to narrate a familiar story as the adult reads, and to make interpretive comments, predictions, associations, elaborating on story elements and relating the book to their own life experiences. While children can focus on structural elements within stories, such as character, title, setting, and resolution (Martinez & Roser, 1985; Morrow, 1987; Morrow, 1988), for the most part, they focus on the meaning of a story. With frequent exposure to story readings and as they reach preschool and kindergarten age, they begin to focus on print by asking what a word says, naming a letter, or noticing similar characteristics in words (Yaden, 1985; Morrow, 1988a).

The child learns to understand prose during read-aloud events, then, by interactively engaging in construction of and relationships with textual information. Such active engagement can be described as generative learning (Linden & Wittrock, 1981; Wittrock, 1974, 1981), which in turn is compatible with Vygotsky's (1978) definition of higher mental functions as internalized social relationships. In the story reading event, adult and child interact, initially with mediation by the adult. Together they construct meaning. The interaction has been described as being interpsychological first—that is, negotiated between adult and child—then intrapsychological, when the child has internalized the interactions and can function independently (Teale, 1984).

## CONSTRUCTING MEANING THROUGH INTERACTIVE STORYBOOK READING

Many of the interactions described thus far are discussed in research carried on between parents and children in the home. For the most part, story readings in school take place in whole-group settings where interactive behavior is kept to a minimum. Because of class size, it is difficult to allow interactive discussion throughout the reading of the story. Thus, the teacher typically provides some background information, poses a few questions, then reads the story with few interruptions except at natural pauses. When the story is finished, more questions might be asked with some discussion following (Morrow, 1984). If interactions similar to those in the home are to occur in the classroom, readings must take place with small groups of children or one-to-one with teacher and child.

Generally, those interactive classroom behaviors or the construction of story meaning during reading, fall into three types. Teachers *manage* by introducing each story with a brief discussion that includes the title of the book plus background information to provide some prior knowledge. They also redirect irrelevant discussion back to the text of the story. Teachers *prompt responses* by inviting children to ask questions or share comments throughout a reading. If a child is not at all responsive, the adult scaffolds or models responses and asks questions. Finally, teachers *support* and *inform*, explaining parts of the story when asked and reacting to comments. As much as possible, they relate responses to real-life experiences. After a story has been read, the teacher goes back to the beginning of the book, turns each page, and shares comments or questions about the story (see Table 1). Throughout the entire story reading, teachers provide positive reinforcement and praise for children's responses (Applebee & Langer, 1983; Cochran-Smith, 1984; Flood, 1977; Morrow, 1987; 1988a; Ninio & Bruner, 1978; Roser & Martinez, 1985; Shanahan & Hogan, 1983; Teale, 1984).

Interactive reading or the construction of meaning while reading stories seems to be an important instructional strategy to utilize in an early childhood program at school, especially if children are not being read to at home. Small group and one-to-one readings are time consuming, but asking volunteers, aides, and older children to read to youngsters can alleviate that problem. Or a teacher working alone can read to a small group while other children in the class are independently involved with other activities.

**TABLE 1    Adult Interactive Behavior During Story Reading**

1. Managing
    a. Introduce story.
    b. Provide background information about the book.
    c. Redirect irrelevant discussion back to the story.
2. Prompting
    a. Invite children to ask questions or comment throughout the story.
    b. Scaffold responses for children to model when no responses are forthcoming.
    c. Relate responses to real-life experiences.
3. Supporting and Informing
    a. Answer questions that are asked.
    b. React to comments.
    c. Relate your responses to real-life experiences.
    d. Provide positive reinforcement for children's response

Source: L. M. Morrow (1988a). "Young Children's Responses to One-to-One Story Reading in School Settings," *Reading Research Quarterly, 23,* 89-107 (p. 96).

Two recent research investigations sought to reflect and adapt the interactive behaviors that have elicited positive results in studies of home reading (Morrow, 1987, 1988a). The subjects were preschool and kindergarten children from disadvantaged backgrounds who had not been read to in their homes. The studies involved frequent storybook reading to these children in small groups and one-to-one with a teacher. They demonstrated that the strategies familiar in home reading research can be adapted to school settings and with positive results. Responses of children resembled those of children at home, they increased in complexity and number over time. Although teachers followed guidesheets, drew on a suggested set of specific behaviors, and generally followed procedures prescribed for the study (see Table 1), it became apparent that they shaped their comments to some extent by comments from the children. As children gained confidence in story-reading sessions, they participated more fully and frequently. Teachers needed to manage and prompt them less and less frequently over time, instead offering greater levels of support, positive reinforcement, and information through answers to their questions. Together the teacher and child were involved in the construction of the meaning of the story.

## ASSESSING CHILDREN'S ABILITY TO CONSTRUCT STORY MEANING

Interactive story reading, which involves the construction of meaning about a story, also provides a setting for evaluation. The quality and increased levels of children's participation over time, evident in the controlled studies, gave the teachers rich sources of information about the children as well as a basis for comparing literacy development within each child. Teachers learned what the children knew from the stories, what they wanted to know, and what they did not know, thus identifying specific needs and allowing the design of specific instructional strategies appropriate to individual children.

As designed, the studies were carried out to determine if an interactive story-reading setting, similar to what occurs between parent and child at home, could be adapted for use in school with children from disadvantaged environments. A second goal was to determine if the strategies would contribute to the literacy development of disadvantaged youngsters. To determine if the treatment demonstrated change in children's behavior, a coding system was devised to evaluate story transcriptions. To devise the system, the literature describing children's responses to story reading was first reviewed and gleaned, and my transcriptions of the classroom story readings were used to create categories for children's responses. Taxonomies for traditional comprehension categories and story structure elements were also taken into consideration. Categories, then, were based on the literature studied plus my own data and were directed toward the questions posed for the investigation. There was an effort to limit the categories, thus providing an evaluation system that could be used simultaneously for instruction, assessment and research.

The major categories used were Focus on Story Structure (Bowman, 1981; Gordon & Braun, 1982; Mandler & Johnson, 1977; McConaughy, 1982; Morrow, 1984; Morrow, 1985; Rumelhart, 1975; Stein & Glenn, 1979), Focus on Meaning (Bloom, 1956; Bloome, 1985; Guszak, 1967; Hansen, 1981; Heath, 1980; Lanier & Davis, 1972; Martinez & Roser, 1985; Morrow, 1984; Snow, 1983; Snow & Goldfield, 1983; Sulzby, 1985), Focus on Print, and Focus on Illustrations (Bloome, 1985; Ninio & Bruner, 1978; Sulzby, 1985; Yaden & McGee, 1984). (See Table 2.)

For research purposes, taped transcriptions of storybook readings were analyzed by coding the comments and questions made by the children into the categories spelled out in Table 2. The results of these investigations indicated that children's questions and comments fell mainly into the category of Focus on Meaning. Within that category children tended to label items, narrate portions of the story with the teacher, ask or comment about details, ask for definitions of words, interpret information by frequently drawing from their own life experiences, make predictions, and elaborate on incidents. Few responses indicated concern for Focus on Structure. Children did ask and comment about characters, but referred to most other elements in the category (setting, theme, plot episodes, and story resolution) with no consistent frequency.

**TABLE 2  Categories for Coding Children's Responses**

1. Focus on Story Structure
   a. Setting  _____
   b. Characters  _____
   c. Theme  _____
   d. Plot episodes  _____
   e. Resolution  _____
2. Focus on Meaning
   a. Labeling  _____
   b. Detail  _____
   c. Interpreting (associations, elaborations)  _____
   d. Predicting  _____
   e. Drawing from one's experience  _____
   f. Word definitions  _____
   g. Narrational behavior  _____
3. Focus on Print
   a. Questions or comments about letters  _____
   b. Questions or comments about sounds  _____
   c. Questions or comments about words  _____
   d. Reading words  _____
   e. Reading sentences  _____
   f. Book management  _____
4. Focus on Illustrations
   a. Questions or comments while eyes are focused on
      illustrations or fingers pointing to illustrations  _____
5. Total number of questions  _____
6. Total number of comments  _____

Source: L. M. Morrow (1988a). "Young Children's Responses to One-to-One Story Reading in School Settings," *Reading Research Quarterly, 23,* 89-107 (p. 98).

Children focused a great deal on illustrations during most of the early readings. Illustrations definitely motivated responses and helped the children to construct meaning about the text. Few incidents fell into Focus on Print, especially in the earlier readings. Later, some children began to ask about letters, noticed similarities in words, read a word here and there, wanted to know what certain words said, and asked for information about the purpose of different parts of the book.

With practice through frequent story readings, teachers can, then, assess the types of responses made by children in their classrooms using the coding sheet (Table 2) as a guide without having to tape and transcribe story readings. Selected dialogue samples from story readings between teachers and children demonstrate how one can categorize and thus evaluate the number and types of responses made by children. The teacher can code children's responses or more simply observe children's behavior in this setting and record anecdotes about their comments. Following are segments from transcripts of story readings to illustrate the variety of responses and the general information that both teacher and child can receive from the experience.

In the first segment it is evident that Chris's responses are not very sophisticated. The only type of response he offers is to label as the teacher reads the story *The Little Red Hen* (Galdone, 1973).

TEACHER:   "Not I," said the cat…
CHRIS:   (pointing to the picture)  cat
TEACHER:   That's right, "Not I," said the dog…
CHRIS:   (pointing to the picture)  dog
TEACHER:   Very good, Chris. "Not I," said the duck…
CHRIS:   (pointing to the picture)  duck
TEACHER:   You're right. "Not I." said the goose…
CHRIS:   (pointing to the picture)  goose

His labeling behavior indicates that Chris is listening and attending to the pictures as the teacher reads. We can assume that he understands enough to identify or label the characters as the teacher reads about them. The teacher should try to encourage more sophisticated responses from the child by modeling some for him.

Melony is at a more sophisticated level than Chris. In the reading of *The Little Red Hen,* she began to narrate with the teacher after the third repetitive phrase.

TEACHER:   "Who will help me bake this cake?"
MELONY AND
TEACHER:   "'Not I,' said the cat. 'Not I,' said the dog. 'Not I,' said the duck.
TEACHER:   That was very good, Melony.
MELONY:   Let's do it again.

Narration indicates that a child is listening quite attentively. The child is, in a sense, making a first attempt at reading, although not necessarily attending to the print. The teacher can try to indicate to the child that the words she is saying are printed on the page. She can point to them and suggest that Melony do the same as they read together.

In this next segment, from the story *Madeline* (Bemelmans, 1939), the main character gets sick and is taken off to the hospital. Jill asks a detail question.

> TEACHER: "In a car with a red light they drove out into the night."
> JILL: (pointing) What do you call that kind of car?
> TEACHER: It is called an ambulance. When people are very sick, they use an ambulance to take them to the hospital. Madeline is sick and they had to bring her to the hospital, so they used the special car called an ambulance.

There is no doubt that Jill was not only listening attentively to the story, but also attending to the illustration that motivated her question. Perhaps she had seen an ambulance in real life, which may have stimulated her interest in asking its name.

Jerry's segment concerns *Caps for Sale* (Slobodkina, 1947):

> TEACHER: "One morning the peddler couldn't sell any caps. He walked up the street and he walked down the street calling, 'Caps! Caps for sale. Fifty cents a cap.'"
> JERRY: I don't know why he shouts "Caps for Sale." Why can't he just go to someone's house and knock on their door to sell the caps?
> TEACHER: That's a good idea. I wish you could tell him that.
> JERRY: I can't do that. I ain't in the story.

Jerry's comments are interpretive. In his first response he puts himself in the place of the character to try to solve his problem by offering a logical solution. In his second comment, in response to the teacher's suggestion, Jerry makes it clear that he understands the difference between real life and the story.

In the story *Caps for Sale,* again, monkeys take caps from a peddler when he is asleep. He tries to get the caps back by asking the monkeys for them, but each time they just imitate him and don't return the caps. Katie responds:

> TEACHER: "By this time the peddler was really very angry. He stamped both his feet and shouted, 'You monkeys, you! You must give me back my caps!'
> KATIE: I know what will happen. The monkeys will just stamp their feet like the peddler and say "tsz, tsz, tsz."
> TEACHER: Katie, that's exactly right. I'll read it to you. "But the monkeys only stamped both their feet back at him and said, 'tsz, tsz, tsz.'"

Katie's response is also interpretive. She predicts what will come next, based on her attention to and understanding of what has already happened in the story.

The next segment involves the story *Mr. Rabbit and the Lovely Present* (Zolotow, 1962). In the book a rabbit helps a little girl find a present for her mother's birthday. They decide on a basket of fruit. Notice how Nicky brings additional meaning to the text.

TEACHER: "So she took her basket and filled it with the green pears, the yellow bananas, the red apples and the blue grapes. It made a lovely present."

NICKY: She better give that to her mother right away. If her mother's birthday is a few days away the fruit will get bad. Fruit doesn't stay good for very long.

It is clear that Nicky knows from her own experience that fruit is perishable, and she wants to share that information with the characters in the book.

In this next segment, Jason, too, infers from his own experiences with life to make better sense of the story. At this point in *Mr. Rabbit and the Lovely Present,* the little girl is consulting with the rabbit.

TEACHER: "'I would like to give her something that she likes,' said the little girl. 'Something that she likes is a good present,' said Mr. Rabbit. 'But what?' said the little girl."

JASON: She should give her mother a ring for her birthday.

TEACHER: Why do you think that, Jason?

JASON: Because my Daddy gave my Mommy a ring and she really liked it and I think her Mommy would like a ring, too.

Noting that Jerry, Katie, Nicky, and Jason not only understand the stories they are hearing, but can add interpretive insights as well, their teacher should lead discussions that encourage such interaction.

Children seek information by asking for what various words mean and what things are for. As in the following segment, asking for a definition is a rather sophisticated question:

TEACHER: I'm going to read a story today called *Caps for Sale.*

IAN: What are caps?

TEACHER: A cap is a kind of little hat that you put on your head. Here is a picture of a cap on the cover.

IAN: Oh, I heard of hats before, but I never heard of caps.

Although young children attend mostly to the meaning, they do begin to focus on print as their experience with books increases. Daniel comments about letters after hearing *Mr. Rabbit and the Lovely Present:*

TEACHER: "'Good-bye,' said Mr. Rabbit, 'and a happy birthday and a happy basket of fruit to your mother.'" (The teacher turns to the last page in the book and reads the two words there) "The End."

DANIEL: Let me see that again, "The End." That has a "d" in it, like my name.

TEACHER: You're right, it is a "d," Daniel. Are there any other letters from your name?

DANIEL: Hey, yeh, (pointing to the words "The End") there's an "e" and an "n."

The next segment is from the story *Chicken Soup with Rice* (Sendak, 1962), a book of poems for each month of the year. The teacher has just read about June and July.

CHRIS: Wait, let me see this. (He looks at July and turns back to June.) How come they are the same?

TEACHER: What do you mean, Chris?

CHRIS: They both have a "J" and then a "U," ...ohhh now they're not the same. Just the "J" and "U." But they do look alike.

In the following segment Jerry asks what the words on the front of the book say: *Are You My Mother?* (Eastman, 1960)

JERRY: Hey, what does this say?

TEACHER: It says, "Are You My Mother?"

JERRY: (Pointing, he says slowly) "Are you my mother?" (Pauses again, points with his finger, and says) "Are you my mother?"

TEACHER: Jerry, that is very good. You're reading.

JERRY: Does it say that in the book?

TEACHER: Yes, do you want to look for it?

JERRY: Yeh. (The teacher points it out to him and Jerry reads) "Are you my mother?" (He goes through every page slowly, looking for the words. Each time he finds them, he points and reads slowly) "Are you my mother?"

These last three segments illustrate that the children are interested in print and are capable of learning about its functions and forms, a signal to the teacher to offer children more information along such lines.

Transcription and analysis of story segments give us some insight into what individual children know and want to know about stories. The children quoted in this discussion demonstrated in their questions and comments that they were capable of interpretive responses, including prediction, inference, and relating the text to life experiences (Morrow, 1988a). Teachers need to accommodate such interests, a departure from typical early reading activities, which tend to stress the mechanics of reading more than the meaning, or meaning only at a literal level. With adequate experience with books and ample opportunity to draw meaning from them, children are ready to focus on the more abstract elements of reading, specifically to focus on characteristics of print. Teachers, meanwhile, can note into which categories individual children's responses fall, then focus their instruction so as to increase the complexity and variety of responses children make.

In addition to evaluating the dialogue produced by children, it is important for the teacher to evaluate the quality of his or her own responses, which are crucial to the construction of meaning during interactive story readings. Although the model for interactive behavior described in Table 1 offers a guide that works for most teachers, certain aspects of that model seem to produce richer interactions than others. Transcriptions of story readings were analyzed to determine if certain elements in a teacher's dialogue particularly encouraged responses. It was found that children offered more and richer responses when the teacher used any of the following behaviors:

1. Providing information requested and extending the interaction by requesting a response from the child in reference to what the teacher said.
2. Scaffolding by asking questions and modeling responses.
3. Channeling discussion to direct the focus back to the story when irrelevant comments began to interfere.
4. Providing frequent feedback and positive reinforcement (Stickland, 1988).

The following examples illustrate such teacher behaviors:

1. About to read *Blueberries for Sal* (McCloskey, 1948), the teacher answers the child's question and extends the interaction by incorporating a request for a response.

IAN:     Why does the book have pictures on it?
TEACHER:   The book has pictures to help you know what the book is about. See, look at the picture on the cover and tell me what the book is about.
IAN:     (looks at the book) Ummm, I guess it's about a girl in the country and she looks like she's picking berries.
TEACHER:   That's exactly right, Ian. That's very good. The title of the book is *Blueberries for Sal*. You see how the picture told you what the story is about?

2. In the next illustration, because the child has neither commented nor questioned at all during the story reading, the teacher scaffolds for the child by asking questions and then modeling responses.

TEACHER:  I wonder why the other animals wouldn't help the Little Red Hen?
TIM:  I don't know.
TEACHER:  I think that maybe it is because they didn't want to do the work.
TIM:  Yeh, they didn't want to work. They are lazy.
TEACHER:  Yes, you're right about that. They sure are lazy and that's why the hen didn't let them eat the bread.
TIM:  So the hen didn't let them eat the bread and they got mad.

3. Sometimes discussion strays from a story, especially in small group readings. The teacher needs to channel irrelevant discussion back into productive focus, as in the following example.

TEACHER:  "'What does she like,' said Mr. Rabbit. 'She likes red,' said the little girl. 'But I can't give her red.' 'But you can give her something that is red,' said Mr. Rabbit."
KIM:  I have something red. I have red Play-Dough.
JILL:  I have yellow and blue Play-Dough.
TRACY:  I have Play-Dough, too, and it's mushy.
KIM:  Mine is mushy, too.
TEACHER:  It is nice that you all have colored Play-Dough. You could make red apples and yellow bananas and blue grapes with the Play-Dough, just like the fruit in the story.
JILL:  That's a good idea. We can make fruit for the little girl's mother, just like the story.

4. The use of frequent feedback and positive reinforcement encourages children to continue participating, as in the following interchange about *The Little Red Hen.*

CHRIS:  There's the hen again asking for help.
TEACHER:  You're right.
CHRIS:  But no one will help her.
TEACHER:  Right again, Chris.
CHRIS:  I would help her.
TEACHER:  That's nice of you. I think I would, too.
CHRIS:  The cat and dog want the bread, but they can't because they didn't help.

During interactive storybook reading, assessment by frequent analysis guides the teacher's instructional strategies, while instruction (management, prompting, and supporting) guides the child's responses and their literacy development.

## RECONSTRUCTION OF STORY

Encouraging children to retell stories is a second procedure that allows active participation in literacy development. Retellings are post-reading and post-listening recalls of text or stories in which children tell what they remember from their reading or listening. It is a reconstruction of the text. Research has demonstrated that it aids development of skills in young children. Like story reading, it, too, can be used for instruction, reinforcement, and assessment of early literacy skills.

Verbal rehearsal improves memory and recall (Craik & Watkins, 1973; Ornstein & Naus, 1978). Retelling text helps a reader or listener relate parts of a text to each other and to one's own background experience, and to integrate and personalize information. It engages children in holistic comprehension, in contrast with the more piecemeal approach of traditional teacher-posed questions to which students respond with specific bits of literal information. According to Johnston (1983), "retelling is the most straightforward assessment…of the result of text-reader interaction" (p. 54). Retelling indicates something about the reader's or listener's assimilation and reconstruction of text information and, therefore, reflects comprehension. Retelling, like interactive story reading, reflects Wittrock's generative learning model as children integrate and personalize content, relate parts of a text to the whole, and mesh it with their own background experience. It follows Holdaway's notion that children benefit when their experiences with stories are mediated by interactive adults who provide problem-solving situations. The child is asked to respond (in this case, retell a story), and the adult offers information when necessary (in this case, guides, models, and prompts the retelling). Children and adults interact to integrate, reconstruct, and define relationships with text. (See Chapters 3, 9, and 12).

## RETELLING AS AN INSTRUCTIONAL STRATEGY

Three different research studies with kindergarten children have determined specific instructional benefits of story retelling (Morrow, 1984, 1985, 1986). Once each week for eight weeks, children in experimental groups listened to different stories, then retold them individually to research assistants. Structural elements of stories were emphasized, and retelling was prompted when individual children needed assistance. Experimental groups showed significant improvement in oral language complexity, comprehension of story, sense of story structure during retelling, and inclusion of structural elements.

In another study, elementary grade children who engaged in retelling practice sessions demonstrated superior comprehension performance over children who did not have the opportunity to retell (Gambrell, Pfeiffer, & Wilson, 1985).

## PROCEDURES FOR ELICITING RETELLINGS

Retelling is not an easy procedure for students, no matter what their age and especially if they have had no prior experience, but practice adds to both the quality of retelling and the ease with which children approach the task (Morrow, 1985). Children need guidance and practice before retelling is used for evaluation.

Students should be told before reading or listening to a story that they will be asked to retell it. Further guidance depends on the purpose for retelling. If the immediate intent is to teach or test sequence, the child should be instructed to concentrate on what happened first, second, and so on. If the goal is to teach or assess ability to integrate information and infer from text, the child should be instructed to refer to personal feelings or experiences related to the story.

Props such as felt story characters and a felt board, pictures from the text, or puppets can aid students in their initial retellings. Pre- and postdiscussion of a story often helps improve the skill. Predictable books for initial retelling makes the process easier, as do familiar books with repetitive phrases, conversation, and rhyme. Recording children's retellings lets them playback their own presentations. Retellings can be done alone or with other children. Teachers can engage children in whole class retellings.

Guidelines for eliciting and guiding a child's retelling follow (Morrow, 1985). The format emphasizes elements of story structure: *setting* (introduction of characters, time, and place), *theme* (an initiating event that causes the main character to react and form a goal or face a problem), *plot episodes* (events in which the main character attempts to attain the goal or solve the problem), and *resolution* (attainment of the goal or solution of the problem and the story ending).

1. Ask the child to retell the story by saying, " A little while ago I read the story (name of story). Please retell the story as if you were telling it to a friend who has never heard it before." Young children might be provided with a doll to tell the story to, or they might practice telling the story to other children.
2. Use the following prompts only if and when they are necessary:
    a. If the child has difficulty beginning the story retelling, suggest beginning with "Once upon a time" or "Once there was…".
    b. If the child stops retelling before the end of the story, encourage continuation by asking, "What comes next?" or "Then what happened?"
    c. If the child stops retelling and cannot continue with the prompts offered in step 2b, ask a question about the story that is relevant at the point in the story at which the child has paused. For example, "What was Jenny's problem in the story?"
3. When a child is unable to retell the story, or if the retelling lacks sequence and detail, prompt the retelling step by step. For example,
    a. "Once upon a time" or "Once there was…"
    b. "Who was the story about?"
    c. "When did the story happen?" (for instance, day, night, summer, winter)
    d. "Where did the story happen?"
    e. "What was the main character's problem in the story?"
    f. "How did he or she try to solve the problem? What did he or she do first, second," and so on.
    g. "How was the problem solved?"
    h. "How did the story end?

Source: L.M. Morrow (1989). *Literacy development in the early years: Helping children read and write.* Englewood Cliffs, NJ.: Prentice Hall (p. 115).

The teacher needs to model retellings of whole stories for the children and scaffold or provide responses when children are unable to supply them themselves. The child's ability to retell determines how much guidance and scaffolding are necessary.

## RETELLING AS AN ASSESSMENT TOOL

A child's retellings should be assessed several times during a school year to evaluate change. If retellings are to be evaluated, students should be told before reading or listening to a story that they will be asked to retell it and guided toward the evaluator's specific purpose for the retelling. For example, if a student's sense of story sequence is to be evaluated, the student should be told before the story reading to pay special attention to the order in which things happen.

Retellings for assessment are carried out with no discussion and no prompts, props, or use of the storybook itself. The child should simply be asked to retell the story as if telling it to a friend who has never heard it before. Teachers can, however, keep records of retellings done with props or pictures and compare the results under the different conditions.

Retellings can be scored quantitatively or qualitatively. In quantitative assessment, children should be asked to retell all they can remember from the text. The examiner parses the story into units, for example, idea units or elements of story structure. The child's retelling is parsed into identical units and compared with the text. The match between the child's protocol units and the text units represents the child's comprehension score (Gambrell, Pfeiffer, & Wilson, 1985; Kintsch & Kozimnsky, 1977; Morrow, et al., 1986). Quantitative assessment has both advantages and disadvantages in measuring comprehension. It tends to reflect text recall of facts, details, sequence, and structural elements. It does not, however, always provide for scoring the inferences that can indicate the child's linkage of text and prior experience.

Qualitative assessment focuses on a child's deeper understanding of a story. Sometimes referred to as holistic rating, qualitative analyses take into account a child's generalizations beyond the text (e.g., interpretive remarks, ability to summarize, biases for or against information in the text). In addition to major points and details, qualitative assessments document supplementation, coherence, completeness, and comprehensibility (Irwin & Mitchell, 1983).

The example that follows is an assessment of a child's sense of story structure. The teacher has first parsed the story to be read and then retold into four categories: setting, theme, plot episodes, and resolution. Then the child's retelling has been matched against that parsing to compare or contrast its sequence of events with that in the original story. The child receives credit, by the way, for partial recall or for recounting the "gist" of a story event (Pellegrini & Galda, 1982; Thorndyke, 1977).

*Jenny Learns a Lesson* (Fujikawa, 1980) is the story of a little girl who likes to play "pretend" games and invites her friends to do so. Jenny bosses her friends when they play. They decide to leave her and not to return. Jenny realizes her problem, apologizes to her friends, invites them back to play again, and promises not to boss them. They agree and all "pretend" what they want during their play.

## PARSED STORY: JENNY LEARNS A LESSON

### Setting

a. Once upon a time there was a girl who liked to play pretend.
b. Characters: Jenny (main character), Nicholas, Sam, Mei Su, and Shags (the dog).

### Theme

Every time Jenny played with her friends, she bossed them and insisted that they do what she wanted them to.

### Plot Episodes

*First Episode:*   Jenny decided to pretend to be a queen. She called her friends and they came to play. Jenny told them what to do and was bossy. The friends became angry and left.

*Second Episode:*   Jenny decided to play dancer, with the same results as in the first episode.

*Third Episode:*   Jenny played pirate, with the same results.

*Fourth Episode:*   Jenny decided to play duchess, with the same results.

*Fifth Episode:*   Jenny's friends decided not to play with her again because she was so bossy. Many days passed and Jenny became lonely. She went to her friends and apologized to them for being bossy.

### Resolution

a. Jenny and her friends played together and each person did what he or she wanted to do.
b. They all had a wonderful day and were so tired that they fell asleep.

*Sample Verbatim Transcription—Beth, Age 5*

Once upon a time there's a girl named Jenny and she called her friends over and they played queen and went to the palace. They had to, they had to do what she said and they didn't like it, so then they went home and said that was boring...It's not fun playing queen and doing what she says you have to. So they didn't play with her for seven days and she had...she had a idea that she was being selfish, so she went to find her friends and said, I'm sorry I was so mean. And said, let's play pirate, and they played pirate and they went onto the ropes. Then they played that she was a fancy lady playing house. And they have tea. And they played what they wanted and they were happy...The End.

## STORY RETELLING ANALYSIS*

Child's Name _____ Beth _____ Age ___ 5 ___
Title of Story ___ Jenny Learns a lesson ___ Date _____

General directions: Place a "1" next to each element if the child includes it in his or her presentation. Credit "gist" as well as obvious recall, counting the words *boy, girl*, or *dog*, for instance, under characters named, as well as *Nicholas, Mei Su*, or *Shags*. Credit plurals (*friends*, for instance) as "2".

### SENSE OF STORY STRUCTURE

### Setting

| | |
|---|---|
| a. Begins story with an introduction | 1 |
| b. Names main character | 1 |
| c. Number of other characters named | 2 |
| d. Actual number of other characters | 4 |
| e. Score for "other characters" (c/d) | 0.5 |
| f. Includes statement about time or place | 1 |

### Theme

| | |
|---|---|
| Refers to main character's primary goal or problem to be solved | 1 |

### Plot Episodes

| | |
|---|---|
| a. Number of episodes recalled | 4 |
| b. Number of episodes in story | 5 |
| c. Score for "plot episodes" (a/b) | 0.8 |

### Resolution

| | |
|---|---|
| a. Names problem solution/goal attainment | 1 |
| b. Ends story | 1 |

### Sequence

| | |
|---|---|
| Retells story in structural order: setting, theme, plot episodes, resolution. (Score 2 for proper order, 1 for partial, 0 for no sequence | 1 |

| | | | |
|---|---|---|---|
| Highest score possible: | 10 | Child's score | 8.3 |

*L.M. Morrow (1988b) Retelling as a diagnostic tool. In S. Glazer, L. Searfoss & L. Gentile (Eds.) *Re-examining reading diagnosis: New trends and procedures in classrooms and clinics.* Newark, DE: International Reading Association pp. 128-149 (pp. 142-144).

From this measurement of her retelling we learn that Beth is quite competent at the task. Her weaker areas in this sample include remembering characters and plot episodes and being able to sequence the story properly. But she is able to remember the most important elements in the story, the basic theme and the resolution. Samples of Beth's retelling of other stories would be helpful to indicate if she omits the same elements in those. If so, it would suggest that the teacher help Beth in her ability to understand and remember characters, episodes, and story sequence.

Beth can obviously listen to a story and then tell its main idea. She inserts her own interpretation when she uses *mean* and *selfish,* words not in the original text. In the story, Jenny is said to be bossy, perhaps a word unfamiliar to Beth. Yet Beth is able to understand the "gist" of its meaning from the context of the story. From her own background, she substitutes words with similar meanings ("selfish" and "mean" for "bossy"), which illustrates her basic understanding.

Retelling is valuable for both assessment and instruction. Analysis of a retelling can help a teacher identify problems not obvious when a student is asked simply to answer questions.

Different retelling assessment strategies can be used to measure different skills. Teachers should be aware, however, that there are strengths and weaknesses in different measures and contexts. One form of analysis and its resulting intepretations may be very different from another. Variables such as memory, linguistic frequency, and task awareness can confound the results of retelling assessment. Other variables can make differences in the results such as (1) the nature of the instructions given to the subject before retellings, (2) the type and length of text that is asked to be retold, and (3) the tenor relationships in the retelling. This refers to whether the child is retelling to someone they believe knows the story being retold or is unfamiliar with the narrative.

## CONCLUDING REMARKS

The strategies discussed in this chapter for story reading and retelling link assessment and instruction. They make it possible for assessment and instruction to take place concurrently. They provide alternative measures for evaluation that can be carried out frequently throughout a school year. As assessment tools they can be used formally with careful item analyses or informally simply by listening and recording anecdotes about the literacy behaviors of different students. They identify the teacher as a careful observer, recorder, and analyst of children's performance.

Interactive story reading makes the child an active participant in the construction of meaning related to story. Retelling allows the child to reconstruct meaning and personalize information. Both settings utilize new concepts of emergent literacy that stress active involvement in story events and social interaction with adults and peers.

# REFERENCES

ANDERSON, R. C., HIEBERT, E. H., SCOTT, J. A., & WILKINSON, I. A. G. (1985). *Becoming a nation of readers.* Washington, DC: National Institute of Education.

APPLEBEE, A. N., & LANGER, J. A. (1983). Instructional scaffolding. Reading and writing as natural language activities. *Language Arts, 60,* 168-175.

BAGHBAN, M. J. M. (1984). *Our daughter learns to read and write: A case study from birth to three.* Newark, DE: International Reading Association.

BEMELMANS, B. (1939). *Madeline.* New York: Viking.

BLANK, M., & SHELDON, F. (1971). Story recall in kindergarten children: Effects of method of presentation on psycholinguistic performance. *Child Development, 42,* 299-313.

BLOOM, B. S. (1956). *Taxonomy of education objectives. Handbook I: Cognitive domain.* New York: David McKay.

BLOOME, D. (1985). Bedtime story reading as a social process. In J. A. & R. V. Lalik (Eds.), *Issues in literacy: A research respective.* Thirty-fourth yearbook of the National Reading Conference, pp. 287-294. Rochester, NY: National Reading Conference.

BOWER, G. (1976). Experiments on story understanding and recall. *The Quarterly Journal of Experimental Psychology, 28,* 511-534.

BOWMAN, M. (1981). *The effects of story structure questioning upon reading comprehension.* Paper presented at the annual meeting of the American Educational Research Association, Los Angeles, April 1981.

BURROUGHS, M. (1972). The stimulations of verbal behavior in culturally disadvantaged three-year-olds. Unpublished doctoral dissertation, Michigan State University, East Lansing.

CHOMSKY, C. (1972). Stages in language development and reading exposure. *Harvard Educational Review, 42,* 1-33.

CLARK, M. M. (1984). Literacy at home and at school: Insights from a study of young fluent readers. In J. Goelman, A. A. Oberg, & F. Smith (Eds.), *Awakening to literacy,* pp. 122-130. London: Heinemann.

CLAY, M. M. (1979). *Reading: The patterning of complex behavior.* Auckland, NZ: Heineman.

COCHRAN-SMITH, M. (1984). *The making of a reader.* Norwood, NJ: Ablex.

COHEN, D. (1968). The effects of literature on vocabulary and reading achievement. *Elementary English, 45,* 209-213, 217.

CRAIK, F. I., & WATKINS, M. J. (1973). The role of verbal rehearsal on short memory. *Journal of Verbal Learning and Verbal Behavior, 12,* 599-607.

DOAKES, D. (1981). Book experiences and emergent reading behavior in preschool children. Unpublished doctoral dissertation, University of Alberta.

DUNNING, D., & MASON, J. (1984, November). An investigation of kindergarten children's expressions of story characters' intentions. Paper presented at the annual meeting of the National Reading Conference, St. Petersburg, FL.

DURKIN, D. (1966). *Children who read early.* New York: Random House.

EASTMAN, P. D. (1960). *Are you my mother?* New York: Random House.

FEITELSON, D., KITA, B., & GOLDSTEIN, Z. (1986). Effects of listening to series stories on first graders' comprehension and use of language. *Research in the Teaching of English, 20,* 339-867.

FLOOD, J. (1977). Parental styles in reading episodes with young children. *The Reading Teacher, 30,* 846-867.

FODOR, M. (1966). The effects of systematic reading of stories on the language development of culturally deprived children. Unpublished doctoral dissertation, Cornell University, Ithaca, NY.

FUIKAWA, G. (1980). *Jenny learns a lesson.* New York: Grosset & Dunlap.

GALDONE, P. (1973). *The little red hen.* Boston: Houghton Mifflin.

GAMBRELL, L., PFEIFFER, W., & WILSON, R. (1985). The effects of retelling upon reading comprehension and recall of text information. *Journal of Educational Research, 78,* 216-220.

GORDON, C., & BRAUN, C. (1982). Metatextual aid to reading and writing. In J. Miles & L. Harris (Eds.), *New inquiries in reading and research and instruction,* pp. 262-268. Thirty-first yearbook of the National Reading Conference. Rochester, NY: National Reading Conference.

GREEN, J. L., & HARTER, J. O. (1982). Reading to children: A communicative process. In J. A. Langer & M. T. Smith-Burke (Eds.), *Reader meets author/Bridging the gap: A psycholinguistic and sociolinguistic perspective,* pp. 196-221. Newark, DE: International Reading Association.

GUSZAK, F. (1967). Teacher questioning and reading. *The Reading Teacher, 21,* 227-234

HANSEN, J. (1981). An inferential comprehension strategy to use with primary-grade children. *The Reading Teacher, 34,* 665-669.

HEATH, S. B. (1980). The functions and uses of literacy. *Journal of Communication, 30,* 123-133.

HEATH, S. B. (1982). What no bedtime story means: Narrative skills at home and school. *Language in Society, 11,* 49-76.

HOFFMAN, S. J. (1982). Preschool reading-related behaviors: A parent diary. Unpublished doctoral disseration, University of Pennsylvania, Philadelphia.

HOLDAWAY, D. (1979). *The foundations of literacy.* Sydney, Aus: Ashton Scholastic.

International Reading Association. (1985). *Literacy development and pre-first grade.* Newark, DE: International Reading Association.

IRWIN, O. (1960). Infant speech: Effects of systematic reading of stories. *Journal of Speech and Hearing Research, 3,* 187-190.

IRWIN, P. A., & MITCHELL, J. N. (1983). A procedure for assessing the richness of retellings. *Journal of Reading, 26,* 391-396.

JOHNSON, D. M. (1983). *Reading comprehension assessment: A cognitive basis,* pp. 54-56. Newark, DE: International Reading Association.

KINTSCH, W., & KOZIMNSKY, E. (1977). Summarizing stories after reading and listening. *Journal of Educational Psychology, 69,* 491-499.

LANIER, R., & DAVIS, A. (1972). Developing comprehension through teacher made questions. *The Reading Teacher, 26,* 153-157.

LINDEN, M., & WITTROCK, M. C. (1981). The teaching of reading comprehension according to the model of generative learning. *Reading Research Quarterly, 17,* 44-57.

MANDLER, J., & JOHNSON, M. (1977). Remembrance of things passed: Story structure and recall. *Cognitive Psychology, 9,* 111-151.

MARTINEZ, M., & ROSER, N. (1985). Read it again: The value of repeated readings during storytime. *The Reading Teacher, 38,* 782-786.

MCCLOSKY, (1948). *Blueberries for Sal.* New York: Penguin.

MCCONAUGHY, S. H. (1982). Using story structure in the classroom. *Language Arts, 57,* 157-164.

MORROW, L. M. (1983). Home and school correlates of early interest in literature. *Journal of Educational Research, 76,* 221-230.

MORROW, L. M. (1984a). Reading stories to young children: Effects of story structure and traditional questioning strategies on comprehension. *Journal of Reading Behavior 16,* 272-288.

MORROW, L. M. (1984b). Effects of story retelling on young children's comprehension and sense of story structure. In J. Niles (Ed.), *Changing perspectives on research in reading/language processing and instruction.* Thirty-third yearbook of the National Reading Conference. Rochester, NY: National Reading Conference.

MORROW, L. M. (1985). Retelling stories: Strategies for improving children's comprehension, concept of story structure, and oral language complexity. *Elementary School Journal, 85,* 647-661.

MORROW, L. M. (1986). Effects of structural guidance in story retelling. *Journal of Reading Behavior, 18,* 135-152.

MORROW, L. M. (1987). The effects of one-to-one story reading on children's questions and responses. In J. Readence & S. Baldwin (Eds.), *Research in literacy: Merging perspectives.* Thirty-sixth yearbook of the National Reading Conference. Rochester, NY: National Reading Conference.

MORROW, L. M. (1988a). Young children's responses to one-to-one story readings in school settings. *Reading Research Quarterly, 23,* 89-107.

MORROW, L. M. (1988b). Retelling as a diagnostic tool. In S. Glazer, L. Searfoss, & L. Gentile (eds.) *Re-examining reading diagnosis: New trends and procedures in classrooms and clinics.* Newark, DE: International Reading Association, pp. 128-149.

MORROW, L. M. (1989). *Literacy development in the early years: Helping children read and write.* Englewood Cliffs, N.J.: Prentice Hall.

MORROW, L. M., GAMBRELL, L., KAPINUS, B., KOSKINEN, P., MARSHALL, N., & MITCHELL, J. (1986). Retelling: A strategy for reading instruction and assessment. In Jerome A. Niles & Rosary V. Lalik (Eds.), *Solving problems in literacy: Learners, teachers, and researchers.* Thirty-fifth yearbook of the National Reading Conference. Rochester, NY: National Reading Conference.

NINIO, A., & BRUNNER, J. S. (1978). The achievement and antecedents of labeling. *Journal of Child Language, 5,* 1-15.

ORNSTEIN, P. A., & NAUS, M. J. (1978). Rehearsal processes in children's memory. In P. A. Ornstein (Ed.), *Memory development in children,* pp. 69-99. Hillsdale, NJ: Erlbaum.

PAYTON, S. (1984). Developing awareness of print: A young child's first steps toward literacy. Unpublished master's thesis, University of Birmingham, England.

PELLEGRINI, A., & GALDA, L. (1982). The effects of thematic-fantasy play training on the development of children's story comprehension. *American Educational Research Journal, 19,* 443-452.

PETERMAN, C. L., DUNING, D., & MASON, J. (1985, December). A storybook reading event: How a teacher's presentation affects kindergarten children's subsequent attempts to read from the text. Paper presented at the annual meeting of the National Reading Conference, San Diego, CA.

RHODES, L. K. (1979, May). Visible language acquisition: A case study. Paper presented at the annual meeting of the International Reading Association, Atlanta, GA.

ROSER, N., & MARTINEZ, M. (1985). Roles adults play in preschooler's response to literature. *Language Arts, 62,* 485-490.

RUMELHART, D. (1975). Notes on a schema for stories. In D. Bobrow & A. Collins (Eds.), *Representation and understanding: Studies in cognitive science,* pp. 211-236. New York: Academic Press.

SENDAK, M. (1962). *Chicken soup with rice.* New York: Harper & Row.

SHANAHAN, T., & HOGAN, V. (1983). Parent reading style and children's print awareness. In J. Niles (Ed.), *Searches for meaning in reading/language processing and instruction,* pp. 212-217. Thirty-second yearbook of the National Reading Conference. Rochester, NY: National Reading Conference.

SLOBODKINA, E. (1947). *Caps for sale.* New York: Scholastic.

SMITH, F. (1978). *Understanding reading* (2nd ed.). New York: Holt, Rinehart and Winston.

SNOW, C. E. (1983). Literacy and language: Relationships during the preschool years. *Harvard Educational Review, 53,* 165-189.

SNOW, C. E., & GOLDFIELD, B. A. (1983). Turn the page, please: Situation-specific language acquisition. *Journal of Child Language, 10,* 535-549.

STEIN, N., & GLENN, C. (1979). An analysis of story comprehension in elementary school children. In R. Freedle (Ed.), *New directions in discourse processing,* Vol. 2, pp. 53-120. Norwood, NJ: Ablex.

STICKLAND, L. (1988). An investigation of teacher-child interactions during story readings. Unpublished masters thesis. Rutgers, The State University of New Jersey, New Brunswick.

SULZBY, E. (1985). Children's emergent reading of favorite books: A developmental study. *Reading Research Quarterly, 20,* 458-481.

SUTTON, M. M. (1964). Readiness for reading at the kindergarten level. *The Reading Teacher, 17,* 234-240.

TAYLOR, D. (1986). Creating family story: "Matthew we're going to have a ride!" In W. H. Teale & E. Sulzby (Eds.), *Emergent literacy: Writing and reading,* pp. 139-155. Norwood, NJ: Ablex.

TEALE, W. M. (1978). Positive environments for learning to read: What studies of early readers tell us. *Language Arts, 55,* 922-932.

TEALE, W. H. (1984). Reading to young children: Its significance for literacy development. In H. Goelman, A. A. Oberg, & F. Smith (Eds.), *Awakening to literacy,* pp. 110-130. London: Heinemann.

TEALE, W. H., HEIBERT, E., & CHITTENDEN, E. (1987). Assessing young children's literacy development. *Reading Teacher, 40,* 772-778.

TEALE, W. H., & SULZBY, E. (1987). Literacy acquisition in early childhood: The roles of access and mediation in storybook reading. In D. A. Wagner (Ed.), *The future of literacy in a changing world,* pp. 111-130. New York: Pergamon.

THORNDYKE, R. (1977). Cognitive structures in comprehension and memory of narrative discourse. *Cognitive Psychology, 9,* 77-100.

TORREY, J. (1969). Learning to read without a teacher. *Elementary English, 11,* 550-556, 658.

VYGOTSKY, L. S. (1978). *Mind in society: The development of psychological processes.* Cambridge, MA: Harvard University Press.

WITTROCK, M. C. (1974). Learning as a generative process. *Educational Psychologist, 11,* 87-95.

WITTROCK, M. C. (1981). Reading comprehension. In F. J. Pirozzolo & M. C. Wittrock (Eds.), *Neuropsychological and cognitive processes in reading,* pp. 229-259. New York: Academic Press.

YADEN, D. B., Jr. (1985). Preschooler's spontaneous inquiries about print and books. Paper presented at the annual meeting of the National Reading Conference, San Diego, CA.

YADEN, D. B., Jr., & McGEE, L. M. (1984). Reading as meaning-seeking activity: What children's questions reveal. In J. Niles (Ed.), *Changing perspectives on research in reading/language processes and instruction,* pp. 101-109. Thirty-third yearbook of the National Reading Conference. Rochester, NY: National Reading Conference.

ZOLOTOW, C. (1962). *Mr. Rabbit and the lovely present.* New York: Harper & Row.

# 8

# THE ROLE OF DECODING IN EARLY LITERACY INSTRUCTION AND ASSESSMENT

*Connie Juel*
*University of Texas at Austin*

### Abstract

Connie Juel outlines the home, preschool, and kindergarten experiences that prepare children for learning to decode. She provides an outline of the stages through which children seem to pass in learning to decode and encode words, and how teachers can assess a child to facilitate growth. She discusses the role that decoding plays in early reading and writing, as well as in later school experience.

In January of their first grade year two children are asked to read aloud a passage.[1]

Sherry reads:

> ~~Mary was on her way to school.~~ (She omits the first line)
>
>    want out to play
> She ~~came to the corner.~~
>
> A fun puppy said, "Will
> ~~She saw a red light.~~
>
> you play with me? But I
> ~~Then she saw the green light.~~

can't show you how to play.
~~Then she went on to school~~.

Mike reads:

Mare
~~Mary~~ was on her way to school.

              curmal
She came to the ~~corner~~.

   sa
She ~~saw~~ a red light.

         sa
Then she ~~saw~~ the green light.

Then she went on to school.

In May of first grade the two children once again read the passage.

Sherry reads:

My      we      here guess    last
~~Mary was~~ on ~~her way~~ to ~~school~~.

           my             cars
She ~~came~~ to the ~~corner~~.

       so      line
She ~~saw~~ a red ~~light~~.

       had          line
Then she ~~saw~~ the green ~~light~~.

       will   so   the   house
Then she ~~went on to school~~.

Mike reads:

Mary was on her way to school

           cur (1)   cor (2)   corner (3)
She came to the corner.

She saw a red light.

Then she saw the green light.

Then she went on to school.

In January and May of first grade, the children are shown a colorful picture of animals (e.g., mice, a rabbit, rats, a squirrel, a porcupine) who are seated in a classroom. In this classroom there are pictures that look as if they were drawn by the animals and hung on a wall. Also pictured are books and a blackboard. The children talk about the animal classroom picture and are asked to imagine what might be going on. They are then asked to write a *story* about what might be happening.

In January, Sherry writes:

lauveinsill.                  (Sherry copies as much  as she can from
ßaigavrabes.                  the board or someone else's paper.)
hiitisasK.landput.
tryctsareihn.iershiecKcl.
The wateriesthe.

In January, Mike writes:

| rabbits | moses | drees |
|---------|-------|-------|
| class   | book  |       |
| door    | chair |       |
| desk    | pitcher |     |

In May, Sherry writes:

Nrics trneyneriohncsqfntri.
dicknrcnserirh:tnsrappnickri.
ciADcniL.smerabbitand
flancKraBAtrnickp.

In May, Mike writes:

A door closed
A mouse talking to the techer.
glasses A class some books
Some pitchers A classroom
A rabbit  A window.
A chalk-boad  A pitcher
8 deskes.  A pitcher of leafs
A pensole  2 mouse.
8 childrin  A porcopine
wals  A pitcher  flowers
A dress  A pitcher of a tree

These children are real children and the preceding are their actual readings and writings, collected as part of a research study. Both children were in the same classroom in a low-socioeconomic-status (SES) neighborhood school. Both are competent speakers of English. They received the same phonics program that the teacher delivered to the whole class for the first 20-30 minutes of the reading period. Then both Sherry and Mike went to their reading group assignments. They were both reading from the same basal reading series. Mike was in the high reading group and was soon ahead of Sherry in the series. Sherry was in the low reading group and would later be retained at the end of first grade. At the end of first grade, she scored a 30 on the reading comprehension subtest of the *Iowa Tests of Basic Skills* (ITBS) (1980 Hieronymous, A.N., Lindquist, E.F., & Hoover, H.D., Form 7, Level 7), which translated into a 1.4 grade equivalent; Mike got every question right on this subtest (66 questions), and this score translated into a 4.7 grade equivalent.

We don't need the standardized test to tell us that Mike read better than Sherry. It is doubtful that Mike is really reading on a fourth grade level. It is also doubtful that Sherry is reading as well as a 1.4 grade equivalent suggests. Standardized tests are worst at differentiating between children who score at the extremes (i.e., either very high or very low), as they have fewer questions aimed at these ends of the continuum. One less question correct, for example, and Mike's score would have produced a 4.2 grade equivalent. Would a child who scored one point less really be five months behind in reading ability? The question of the actual meaning of a 4.2 or 4.7 grade equivalent is also debatable.

The reading comprehension subtest had a total of 66 questions of which 32 involved choosing either yes or no, 11 involved choosing among one of four alternatives as answers, and 23 involved choosing among one of three alternatives. A chance score on the subtest would be about 27, which would have given a child a grade equivalent score of 1.2. Sherry's score of 30 is hardly above what she might have gotten by random guessing. It's most unlikely she's reading any better than a child who received a 1.2 (or below) grade equivalent on the ITBS. She certainly did not read from the 1.4 grade equivalent Spache (1981) at a "passing" level.

In addition to questionable discrimination between either the set of very poor or the set of very good readers, standardized scores tell us little about what children specifically need to do to improve. Since these tests are usually administered late in the school year, they provide little assistance to the current classroom teacher.

Teachers must often rely on other, informal, assessments. These assessments involve either commercial reading inventories (as in the foregoing examples) or less formal assessments made by the teacher, as when the child reads from his or her own classroom books. Informal assessments are also more likely to include writing samples than standardized tests, as such samples of writing are not easily machine scorable.

How should the preceding samples of reading and writing be interpreted? How are Sherry and Mike really doing? Clearly Mike is reading and writing better than Sherry, but is he doing as well as he can? What could a teacher do to help Sherry and Mike be better readers and writers? This chapter will attempt to answer these questions.

## THE ROLE OF THE "CODE" IN EARLY READING AND WRITING

The role of the code[2] can be seen in the earlier samples of reading and writing. No matter how bright, creative, and knowledgeable about oral language and the world a child may be, he or she cannot read and write well unless the code of written English is known. Mike reads and writes better than Sherry because he has more knowledge about the code that he can use to translate spoken words into printed words (and vice versa).

How can it be said with such conviction that the fundamental difference in the reading ability between Mike and Sherry lies in knowledge of the code? To answer this question, let's look at often mentioned alternatives to using the code: (1) "holistic" recognition and (2) use of context.

The child could try to memorize the "holistic" visual sequence of letters in a word. The existence of ideographic writing systems (like Chinese) shows that this type of "visual" learning can indeed occur. But it is very difficult. A child in Japan is only expected to learn 76 Kanji (based on Chinese characters) in first grade and only 996 by the end of sixth grade. In contrast many Japanese children are already reading Kana, which is based on phonetic segments, prior to entering formal schooling (Kuhara-Kojima (1988), personal communication). Most ideographic writing systems have been (or are in the process of being) replaced by alphabetic writing systems (Perfetti, 1985).

In the United States, the child is often exposed to between 300 and 1,100 *different* words in first grade readers (Juel & Roper/Schneider, 1985; Willows, Borwick, & Hayvren, 1981). These words occur in running text of well over 7,000 words (to over 20,000 words in some series). The beginning reader in the United States is constantly encountering words that have not been seen before, and words that may not be repeated for some time. To *learn* such words by recalling the "visual" sequence of letters would appear to be a formidable task. Through years of reading an adult may be able to recognize many words as "visual" sequences of letters, without reference to spelling-sound information, but it is doubtful that the adult *began* that way.

What about context? Adult readers can accurately use context to predict one out of four words (Gough, Alford, & Holley-Wilcox, 1981). This suggests an upper bound to how much growth could be expected in use of context by the child. Those words that can be predicted on the basis of context are frequently function words (which are so high frequency that context is rarely needed to recognize them) (Alford, 1980). It is the content words—those words that carry the meaning in text—that can be least accurately predicted and that require the most decoding skill.

In extensive literature reviews, Stanovich (1980, 1986) has shown that it is the *poor* reader who most frequently uses context for word recognition. These reviews of the literature indicate that the poor reader uses context because he or she cannot use the code. The primary advantage of an alphabetic language is that there is some correspondence between graphemes and phonemes—and it is these correspondences that form the most reliable and important cues for word identification. The primary difference between the good and poor reader lies in the ability to use these correspondences to identify words.

### Prerequisites to Learning the Code

The question needs to be examined as to how the child learns the code. Downing (1979) views the process of becoming literate as consisting in "the rediscovery of (a) the functions and (b) the coding rules of the writing system..." (p. 37). Learning the communicative function of print frequently occurs in the preschool years and frequently occurs through exposure to environmental print and being read to at home. It is not necessarily an easy discovery, however. The compelling colors and shapes in which environmental print is embedded (e.g., the shape and red color of "STOP" signs) and the enticing and telling nature of pictures in storybooks can obscure the role of the print itself. The individualized, underlying meaning of the objects attached to print tends to predominate over the specific, generalized message of the *actual* print. The child thus labels the printed word "Crest" as "toothpaste" or "brush your teeth" (Harste, 1980). It would appear that one basic prerequisite to learning to read and write is for the child to understand that print also has a *specific* communicative function.

Assuming that the child knows that printed words contain a specific message, the child needs to know how to decode the print to get that message. Children's first attempts at using the print itself to "read" a word frequently involves recalling some arbitrary feature of the word's printed form. Such arbitrary features may include distinctive visual cues such as the double "oo's" in "moon" or the dot in the middle of "pig" or the length of "elephant" (Gates & Boeker, 1923). Distinctive visual cues may include aspects of the environment in which the word occurs, for example, recalling the long word at the end of the page is "elephant" or recognizing "Budweiser" due to its distinctive font (Gough & Hillinger, 1980). First and last letters frequently serve as recall cues in this early reading period (Samuels & Jeffrey, 1966). This type of arbitrary association will become progressively more difficult as more words need to be recalled (i.e., "d" for "dog" will no longer work when "duck" is introduced). With each new word, decoding by random or positional cues alone can become an increasingly difficult and frustrating activity. A new, less arbitrary system for word identification must be found if reading progress is to develop smoothly into a skilled performance.

The realization that the system is not random and that there are some systematic relationships between the printed symbols and spoken sounds is a necessary precursor for learning spelling-sound correspondences. For some children, "formal" instruction may be necessary to facilitate this understanding (Mason, 1980). Ehri and Wilce (1985), referring to a study by Masonheimer, Drum, and Ehri (1984), write: "movement into effective printed word learning requires a qualitatively different way of processing printed words, one that prereaders do not naturally hit upon as they encounter print in their environment. The problem is that they habitually process context and configurational cues, and this precludes their attending to phonetic cues that must be done to begin reading words reliably" (pp. 174-175).

The foregoing realization has been termed "cryptanalytic intent" by Gough and Hillinger (1980). Cryptanalytic intent is the understanding that *print is encoded speech* and that there is some systematic relationship between the printed symbols and spoken words which must be uncovered. Cryptanalytic intent is one of four conditions that Gough and Hillinger (1980) believe are necessary prerequisites for learning the spelling-sound correspondences (or cipher) which is written English.

A second condition Gough and Hillinger (1980) view as necessary for learning the cipher is that the child has alphabetic understanding. *The child must understand that words are composed of letters.* Third, *the child must have phonemic awareness;* that is, the child must be aware that words are composed of phonemes. Fourth, *the child must have data;* that is, the child must have pairings of the spoken and written words.

A common question of preschoolers who "teach themselves to read" is: "What's this word?" (Clark, 1976; Durkin, 1966). We know that the child who asks this question knows (1) what a word is, (2) that text consists of words printed between spaces, and (3) that printed words carry the meaning of a text. Presumably the child could learn to read, given enough answers (i.e., data) to the question, if the child also has (1) alphabetic understanding (i.e, knows that words are composed of letters), (2) phonemic awareness (i.e., the awareness that a word is composed of a sequence of meaningless and somewhat distinct spoken sounds), and (3) cryptanalytic intent (i.e, the realization that there is some systematic relationship between the printed letters and spoken sounds). Thus, when the answers to "What's this word?" include "goat," "float," "oatmeal," and "toad," the child will, over time, induce the sound of "oa" and the sounds of other consonants, and so on. This knowledge can then be applied to decode a novel word in a story, such as "load."

Phonemic awareness is probably the most "unnatural" prerequisite skill. The realization that words are composed of sequences of meaningless sounds (i.e., phonemes) that can be independently manipulated (as in Pig Latin) is not necessary for understanding or producing *speech.* In speech production, there is no clear distinction between phonemes, as one phoneme overlaps another (in the word "goat," the pronunciation of the /o/ begins before the /g/ ends).

Phonemic awareness is not a unitary, indivisible insight or ability. Rather there are various "phonemic" insights (e.g., being able to judge which is a longer word in spoken duration, rhyming words, syllable sense, knowing that "goat" is composed of three distinctive-albeit overlapping and abstract—sounds). Some phonemic abilities (such as phoneme blending) appear prerequisite to learning to read, while other abilities (such as identifying the number of phonemes in a word) are not, and may in fact be learned *from* reading (Perfetti, Beck, Bell, & Hughes, 1987). There is considerable evidence from both experimental and longitudinal studies conducted in several countries that some form of phonemic awareness is necessary for successfully learning to read and write alphabetic languages (Blachman & James, 1985; Bradley & Bryant, 1983; Elkonin, 1963, 1973; Fox & Routh, 1975; Juel, Griffith, & Gough, 1986; Lundberg, Oloffson, & Wall, 1980; Share, Jorm, Maclean, & Matthews, 1984; Tornéus, 1984; Tunmer & Nesdale, 1985; Williams, 1984).

### Stages in Learning the Code

There appear to be qualitative shifts in the dominant strategies that children employ at various stages in their literacy development to read and write words. (For a review of the literature that supports these stages, see Juel, in press.) Children's movement through these stages depends, in part, upon how quickly they develop the prerequisite insights discussed in the prior section and, in part, upon their interaction with others (e.g., parents and teachers).

In the first stage, the "selective-cue" stage, the child identifies words by selection of some *random* feature of either the environment in which the print occurs (i.e., place on a page) and/or some distinctive feature of the print (i.e., first letter). If a child fails to identify a specific word correctly, he or she is likely to substitute a *real* word that looks like the target word (e.g., perhaps it shares the same first letter). This substituted word is often a "good guess," as it is a word that the child knows is likely to be in the text (e.g., it has been a word previously encountered in the book or just introduced by the teacher as a word that will appear in a story) and/or a word that fits to some degree the meaning of the surrounding text which the child could read.

Children who are in the "selective-cue" stage appear to read by reaching into the bag of words stored in their heads that they know are likely candidates for a printed word and pulling out one that contains some of the letters of the unrecognizable word. This strategy is very evident when children read words in isolation. Juel et al. (1985) found that in response to the word "rain," the reading errors of first grade children with no spelling-sound knowledge were "ring," "in," "runs," "with," "ride," "art," "are," "on," "reds," "running," "why," and three "ran"s. Even more revealing about word processing in this stage are the spelling errors of these children. Their lack of spelling-sound knowledge leaves them to spell by locating a complete image of the word, substituting another real word for the target, or recalling an incomplete image and filling it in with random letters. In response to "rain" used in a sentence, their spelling errors were "weir," "rach," "yes," "uan," "ramt," "fen," "rur," "Rambl," "wetn," "wnishire," "rup," five "ran"s, and one drawing of raindrops.

Clearly there is a range in orthographic understanding among the writers of the preceding words. The child who spelled "rain" as "wetn" may well have recalled the last letter in "rain" (and no other letters) but thought something like, "Well, I know how to spell 'wet.'" The children who spelled "rain" as "rach" and "ramt" probably recalled the first two letters in "rain" and its length, but their choice of what to add to the initial "ra" indicates little knowledge of letter sounds. The five children who spelled "rain" as "ran" may have recalled an incomplete "image," *or* they may have been using their knowledge of the sounds contained in letter names to spell. In this respect they may have engaged in a common form of "invented" spelling. Indeed, invented spelling may signal the beginning of the second stage, the "spelling-sound" stage. The child who uses invented spelling certainly has the prerequisite alphabetic understanding, cryptanalytic intent, and phonemic awareness with which to enter this stage.

Read (1971, 1975, 1986) has made extensive studies of "invented spellings," showing that there is a phonetic reason for certain nonstandard spellings frequently produced by young children. Schreiber and Read (1980) state that:

> children's spelling is phonetic, not merely in the expected sense that it represents each
> phoneme of English more or less consistently, but also in the sense that it represents

details of pronunciation that adults are unaware of. A spelling such as "SIK" for "sink" is phonetically accurate in that for many, if not most pronunciations, "sink" does have only three phonetically distinct segments: [sIk]. Any trace of a velar nasal that does occur is typically so short that it is by no means obvious that is it the "same sound" (same phoneme) as the one that occurs at the end of "sing" [sIn]. (p. 212)

The child who is on the threshold of the spelling-sound stage may first try to recall words by using the same type of letter-name knowledge that is used frequently in "invented" spelling. Ehri and Wilce (1985, 1987) have shown that children who know the names of the letters of the alphabet (e.g., through "Sesame Street," preschool, or the home) sometimes use the sounds captured in letter names to identify words. A child may identify the printed word "jail," for example, by associating the names of the letters "j" and "l" with the sounds in the spoken word. Such children are using the phonetic cues contained in the letter names as mnemonics for recall. To advance they will need to develop more accurate and extensive spelling-sound knowledge so that they can truly "sound and blend" the letter-sound patterns in a word.

As children learn more specific spelling-sound knowledge, the form of their spelling and reading "errors" change. Juel et al. (1985) found that when first grade children with good spelling-sound knowledge made a spelling error, the error was often homophonous with the target word (e.g., "raine" and "rane" for "rain"). When these children made word recognition errors on words in isolation, they frequently substituted a nonsense word reflecting unsuccessful attempts to "sound out" the target (e.g., "rannin" for "rain").

At some point in the spelling-sound stage there appears a "gluing" to print phase, a laborious "sounding-it-out" phase. During this phase attention is consciously focussed on getting the words (i.e., on breaking the code). When a child is not able to identify a word, the child may give a nonsense word (reflecting an unsuccessful attempt to "sound out" the word) or may refuse to pronounce the word (Biemiller, 1970; Söderberg, 1977; Sulby, 1985). This represents a change from earlier substitutions of real words (and often more contextually appropriate words) for unknown words. As Chall (1979) describes,

> To advance, to build up the skill for making choices, beginners have to let go of their pseudomaturity. They have to engage, at least temporarily, in what appears to be less mature reading behavior—becoming glued to the print—in order to reach the real maturity later. They have to know enough about the print in order to leave the print. (pp. 40-41)

This "glued-to-print" phase has sometimes been blamed on too much attention to letter sounds in school. But such a phase has also been found in children who learned to read prior to school, without formal letter-sound instruction (see Bissex, 1980; Söderberg, 1977; Sulzby, 1985). The phase does not appear to be a very long one in either the home or school environment. Biemiller (1970) found that by the end of first grade, children were fairly consistent in combining the products of spelling-sound knowledge with contextual checks for appropriateness. Gough, Juel, &

Roper/Schneider (1983) found that first grade "spelling-sound" stage readers were not insensitive to semantic appropriateness, making as many self-corrections based on context as "selective-cue" readers. Lesgold and Curtis (1981) found that even the oral reading errors of children in "code-emphasis" programs were almost always contextually appropriate—even by the middle of first grade.

In the third stage, the "automatic" stage, the child can identify many words without conscious "sounding out." Words the child frequently saw and "sounded out" in the second stage now elicit either automatic phonological recodings or become recognizable purely on the basis of orthographic features. By second or third grade, children can "automatically" recognize a large number of high-frequency words (Doehring, 1976; Golinkoff & Rosinski, 1976; Guttentag & Haith, 1978, 1979, 1980; Rosinski, 1977; Rosinski, Golinkoff, & Kukish, 1975; West & Stanovich, 1979).

The relatively effortless word recognition in the "automatic" stage leads to wider reading. With wide reading the child learns even more spelling-sound information which can be applied to new words until the novel words also become "automatically" recognized. Venezky (1976) indicates that spelling-sound knowledge continues to grow at least through eighth grade. Only when it becomes necessary will the child (or adult) consciously apply the spelling-sound knowledge that has accumulated over the years. The adult, for example, may be conscious of applying such knowledge when a novel or foreign word pops up in their reading (e.g., when reading a gardening book and finding sweet peas referred to as "lathyrus odoratus").

While some words can be correctly spelled purely from their spoken sounds (e.g., "jump"), many words cannot (e.g., "green" could just as well be spelled "grean" or "grene"). The more exposure a child has had to a printed word, the more likely the child is to have formed a "mental" image of the word. In the "automatic" stage we are likely to find more correct spellings of words with ambiguous sound-spelling patterns (e.g., "green," "pencil") than was found in the spelling-sound stage.

## ASSESSMENT IN THE EARLY GRADES

To determine what a child needs to learn to decode, and what instruction or experiences need to be provided in school to prepare children for mastery of the code, a teacher needs to assess the child's phase in literacy development. There are various ways (informal and formal) to determine what a child knows about the function of print and the way print is utilized (e.g., that it is composed of words, read left to right). Chapters 3 (Teale), 6 (Sulzby), and 9 (Mason and Stewart) give suggestions for such evaluation. The focus of this chapter is on evaluating decoding processes, and as such the assumption is made that the person doing the assessment already has determined that the child has basic knowledge about the function and basic conventions of print. (If the child does not have such basic knowledge, then worrying about decoding seems premature.)

The goal of decoding assessment is to determine how the child processes words. The evaluator is interested in answering two basic questions: (1) At what stage of literacy development (i.e., selective-cue, spelling-sound, or automatic stage) is the child? and (2) Does the child have the necessary prerequisites to advance to the next stage?

To illustrate how to make such determinations, let's return to the reading and writing samples of Sherry and Mike. In what stage is Sherry in January of first grade? She recognizes only one word, "she" and makes a story up for the rest. Her writing gives little indication that she knows text is composed of words with spaces in between them. She seems to know something about punctuation, but her knowledge is rudimentary; she puts periods anywhere. Her writing is composed mainly of random letter strings, with the exceptions of one nonletter and some words that were likely copied from the board or someone else's paper.

Sherry is clearly in the first stage. Does she have the prerequisites to advance to the next stage? To answer this question definitively, we would need to do some additional assessment. She appears to lack clear alphabetic understanding that print is composed of words and words are composed of letters; she seems to lack any cryptanalytic understanding in that she does not have any systematic approach to word identification. To judge if Sherry has any phonemic awareness we would need to ask her some questions. We could see if she can judge spoken duration of words (e.g., Which is a longer word when we speak it, "Timothy" or "Tim"?). We could see if she can rhyme words (e.g., "If I say, 'cat,' 'hat,' 'rat,' 'mat,' can you think of a word that sounds the same?). We can discover if she can blend sounds (e.g., What word does /n/, /i/, /s/ make?). We can determine if she can delete sounds (e.g., "Stop" without the /s/ is what word?). We can ask if she can add sounds (e.g., "If I put a /s/ sound at the start of "at," what word is made?). We can hear if she can segment a word into its sounds (e.g., What is the *first* sound in "up"?). (We did, in fact, ask Sherry questions like these, and her responses indicated she lacked phonemic awareness.)

How about Sherry's reading and writing in May? She now recognizes a few more words (e.g., "to," "the," "then," "a," "red," and "green"). Notice that she tends to be correct on high-frequency words, particularly function words. These are the same words that context best enables the reader to predict. It is the content words (like "corner" and "light") that can be least accurately predicted based on context. These words require the most decoding skill, which Sherry lacks. If she does not recognize a word, she substitutes a real word, often one that starts with the same letter as the target word (e.g., "cars" for "corner" and "line" for "light"). Some of her substitutions share several letters with the target word (e.g., "my" for "Mary" and "here" for "her"). Although a little more advanced than in January, she is still in the first, selective-cue, stage. Her writing shows little significant improvement. Indeed, a check on her phonemic awareness showed it had not improved. Without some improvement in that skill, she will remain in the selective-cue stage in both reading and spelling.

What about Mike's reading in January? For each word he missed, he gave a "nonsense" word (e.g, "curmal" for "corner"). Clearly he is in the spelling-sound stage. In fact, since he is not correcting his mistakes based on context, one would suspect he is in the throes of the "glued to print" phase of this stage. What does he need to advance? More practice. If Mike reads more he should be able to respond to more words "automatically," which will increase his ability to "unglue from the print" and be more cognizant of contextual appropriateness of his choices, and so on.

Analysis of Mike's writing in January supports the idea that he is focused at the word level, as he wrote nothing but a list of words. One could investigate whether he knows what a story is, by asking him to tell an oral story (see Chapter 7). We did ask Mike to tell a story about the picture, and he told a simple one. His writing reflects his level of concern: the word. We see misspellings that retain much of the sound sequence of words (e.g., "moses" for "mouses" and "pitcher" for "picture"). These fairly homophonous misspellings are typical of a "spelling-sound" stage child.

In May, Mike's only reading mistake suggests he can now combine spelling-sound cues with contextual ones. He also read the text considerably faster than he did in January. His increased reading rate suggests that some of the high-frequency words (e.g., "she," "came," "then") are now recognized automatically. Mike's writing in May still does not tell a story, but the content words are now in short phrases. He has "unglued" a bit. His misspellings are *clearly phonetically based* (e.g., "childrin" for "children" or "pensole" for "pencil"). Practice will improve both his reading and his spelling (the only way to learn the standard spelling for "pencil" is to see it several times in print). Mike would seem to be well on his way to the third, automatic, stage of reading. His spelling-sound knowledge will be consciously applied only when he does not instantly recognize a word, or needs to spell a word for which he does not possess a complete mental "image."

## INSTRUCTION IN THE EARLY YEARS

Literacy development in preschool and kindergarten may help to prevent the failure in first grade of a child like Sherry. Sherry clearly entered first grade without many of the understandings about print, about spoken words, and about their connection that are necessary for reading and writing. Sherry's writing at the end of first grade is similar to the first grade children in the Juel et al. (1985) study who spelled "rain" as "yes" or "wnishire." It is not even at the "invented" spelling level that has been found in much younger children.

Sherry, and the children in the Juel et al. (1985) study came from a low-SES neighborhood and may represent a different group from those children whose early writing development has often been studied and found to contain "invented" spellings. It is unlikely that children who are nonphonetic spellers in first grade engage in "invented" spelling (or much writing) at home. The child who spells "rain" as "wnishire" in first grade will need very different instruction to learn the code than will the child (Paul) who at home at age 5 writes above his workbench, "DO NAT DSTRB GNYS AT WRK." (Bissex, 1980 p. 23).

What should the instructor/teacher do to foster decoding skill in the early grades? Clearly, the first step is to assess what the child already knows about print. Determine the child's current stage of development. Find out if the child has the necessary knowledge, experiences, or materials to progress to the next stage. Then instruction and experiences conducive to further growth can be created.

It is clear that a child like Paul is much less dependent on school instruction for literacy development than is a child like Sherry. He no doubt learned about the communicative function of print and developed many of the preliminary understandings about the relationship between spoken and written words at home.

The first critical insight that the child must gain is understanding the communicative function of print. Parents who read stories to children at home, who talk to children about print on signs, cereal boxes, and so on, have already laid the foundation for this understanding. In school, practices which may foster such understanding include: (1) pointing out environmental print and creating it by labeling objects in the classroom; (2) reading to children and showing them you are reading the "print"; (3) "language experience" activities where students "dictate" words, sentences, or stories to the teacher to write; (4) the use of "Big Books" where children can clearly see the print as their teachers read it (see Holdaway, 1979); and (5) the use of patterned predictable text in chart stories, "Big Books," and so on, which can facilitate the "feel" for and enjoyment of reading as well as induce some "selective-cue" recognitions of words (Bridge, 1986). The foregoing activities also foster alphabetic understanding (especially if, while reading, the teacher provides some commentary, such as pointing out how words are composed of letters). These activities are probably sufficient to induce most children to enter the "selective-cue" stage of word recognition.

To prepare children to enter a spelling-sound stage, we need to foster phonemic awareness, alphabetic knowledge, and cryptanalytic intent and to provide lots of printed words paired with their spoken equivalents (e.g., as in reading a story). There are various ways that this can be done—through writing activities, reading activities, and direct instruction.

Lundberg, Frost, and Petersen (1988) showed that preschool children can be successfully taught to discover and manipulate the phonological elements in words. Their eight-month training program involved a variety of games, nursery rhymes, and rhymed stories. (A typical game designed to foster syllable synthesis included a "troll," who had a peculiar way of speaking. The troll would try to tell children what they would receive as presents by giving them hints. The troll produced the words syllable by syllable, until the child could correctly identify the present.) Danish children in the program showed dramatic gains in certain phonemic awareness skills, such as phoneme segmentation skill, compared to children who did not go through the program. The preschool program had a facilitating effect on reading and spelling acquisition through the second grade.

The use of patterned, rhymed text (such as found in nursery rhymes and many Dr. Seuss books) in oral story reading as well as in chart stories or "Big Books," probably would foster phonemic awareness. In a 15-month longitudinal study of British children from the age of 3 years, 4 months, Maclean, Bryant, and Bradley (1987) found (1) that there was a strong relationship between children's early knowledge of nursery rhymes and the later development of phonemic awareness; and (2) that phonemic awareness predicted early reading ability. Both relationships were found after controlling for the effects of IQ and SES.

Clay (1979) found that many 6-year-old children who were not making adequate progress learning to read could not hear the sound sequences in words. She adapted a phonemic awareness training program developed by the Russian psychologist Elkonin to train these children (Elkonin, 1973). Teachers may find some of the procedures in this program, which are outlined in Clay (1987), useful for children who are having real difficulty hearing the sound sequences in words. Clay (1987) describes her thinking on phonemic awareness, and one of the initial recovery procedures, as follows:

> For many decades and in many different programmes teachers have tried to teach children a sound to go with a letter they can see. The children who succeeded in those programmes were able to do just that, and those who failed were probably unable to hear the sound sequences in words anyway.
>
> For children who cannot hear the order of sounds in words, the teacher can act as analyzer of the words. She articulates the word slowly, but naturally, and gradually develops the same skill in her pupils. It is an essential feature of the theory behind this tutoring to hear sounds in words in sequence. The child's first lessons take place *in the absence of letters or printed words.* The child must *hear* the word spoken, or speak it himself and try to break it into sounds by slowly articulating it. He is asked to show what he can hear with *counters* not *letters.* (pp. 64-65)

As an example, the teacher would have cards on which squares were drawn for each phoneme (not letter) in words with up to four sounds. As the teacher slowly articulates the word, the child puts counters into the squares when a new sound is heard. The child then articulates the word and fills in the counters. Later, when the child can do this and knows the alphabet, the counters can be replaced with letters. Through dialogue with the teacher over what letters can be used for certain sounds in words the child want to write, the learning of spelling-sound relationships occurs.

Bissex (1980), in a detailed case study of her son's (Paul) literacy acquisition, shows how a child can learn the code through interaction while writing. Two examples of 5-year-old Paul's questions to his mother, while attempting to write words, illustrate how he learned the code:

PAUL:    What makes the "ch" (in TECH)?
MOTHER:  c-h.
PAUL:    What makes "oo"?
MOTHER:  o-o

| PAUL: | In "to"? |
| MOTHER: | Only one o.   (p. 12) |
| PAUL: | What makes the "uh" sound? |
| MOTHER: | In what word? |
| PAUL: | "Mumps." |
| MOTHER: | u          (p. 13) |

To ask such questions, it is clear that Paul has phonemic awareness (e.g., or else he could not have segmented the "uh" sound in "mumps"). He also has cryptanalytic intent, alphabetic understanding, and "data" provided by a very special one-to-one partner.

Bissex and her son, Paul, provide a good example of the type of interaction during writing that can teach spelling-sound knowledge. Most children, regrettably, do not have such individualized help at home. Teachers of young children may be able to foster similar interaction as they encourage their students' attempts to write and respond to their questions about how to write the sounds in certain words.

Children who have some phonemic awareness, alphabetic understanding, and cryptanalytic intent may also begin to induce spelling-sound correspondences from seeing printed words paired with their spoken counterparts. Children who have been read to frequently at home will have had considerable opportunities to make such connections; children who have not will be more dependent on teachers to provide such pairings.

Sometimes teachers can encourage the induction of spelling-sound correspondences by informing children that the print to sound system is not random and that their job is to be a detective and "break the code" (i.e., we can foster cryptananalytic intent). We can even point out that there are "trick" words (i.e., irregular words) which contain some unexpected sounds, and are designed to throw them off the track. We can let children know that the best adults can do is give them some clues (i.e., approximations of the sounds that some letters make). This is where explicit spelling-sound instruction, such as that found in explicit phonics, can be helpful. While the letter-sounds presented in phonics are only approximations to the spelling-sound system of written English, they may point the child in the right direction to discovering the code. The child may get the idea of what to look for in matching letters to sound through only a few examples of such correspondences. Juel and Roper/Schneider (1985) found that first grade children who were taught some letter sounds (initial and final consonants and short vowels) were able to induce untaught sounds (e.g., double vowels) when they read text that contained a number of words with these sounds.

Obviously some children (like Paul) may need little or no instruction in spelling-sound correspondences. Other children (particularly those who have had little exposure to print prior to school) will need more. This "instruction" can be informal (as occurs in interaction over how to write sounds in particular words) or "formal" (as in explicit phonics). It should be remembered that children like Sherry (who have little or no phonemic awareness) will have a difficult time benefiting from either activity and may even become quite frustrated by them until they can "hear" the sound sequences in words (Clay, 1987; Juel, Griffith, & Gough, 1986).

## IMPORTANCE OF INSTRUCTION TO PREPARE CHILDREN TO DECODE

It is certain that teachers of young children are not helping their students very much if they do not prepare them for "breaking the code." Early decoding skill very accurately predicts later reading comprehension. Lesgold and Resnick (1982) found that a child's speed of word recognition in first grade was an excellent predictor of that child's *reading comprehension* in second grade. Juel (1988) found there was a .88 probability that a child at the bottom quartile on the Iowa Reading Comprehension subtest at the end of first grade would still be a poor reader at the end of fourth grade. Of 24 children who remained poor readers through four grades, only 2 had average decoding skills. Most of these poor readers entered first grade with little phonemic awareness.

Lundberg (1984), in a longitudinal study of children learning to read in Sweden (where school does not begin until the child is age 7), found that linguistic awareness of words and phonemes in first grade correlated .70 with reading achievement in sixth grade. Of the 46 Swedish children in this study with low linguistic awareness and low reading achievement in first grade, 40 were still poor readers in sixth grade.

Clay (1979) discusses results of a study of children learning to read in New Zealand, where reading instruction begins at age 5: "correlations from a follow-up study of 100 children two and three years after school entry lead me to state rather dogmatically that where a child stood in relation to his age-mates at the end of his first year at school was roughly where one would expect to find him at 7:0 or 8:0." (p. 13)

The problem with a year of reading failure is that it tends to be self-perpetuating. Those children who learn to decode early read more, both in and out of school (Juel, 1988). They thus have the opportunity through reading to gain the vocabulary, complex syntax, knowledge of text structures, concepts, and general knowledge that provides a strong foundation for reading comprehension. Children who do not learn to decode do not have this avenue for growth. This phenomenon of the "rich get richer and the poor get poorer" (i.e., the children who learn early to decode continue to make improvement in their reading, and those who do not lag farther and farther behind) has been termed the "Matthew effect" (Stanovich, 1986).

Preschool and kindergarten teachers can be instrumental in preventing this vicious cycle of failure. The gap in reading achievement between the Sherry's and Paul's or Mike's of our country can be decreased by recognizing and acting upon the fact that there are *early* differences in exposure to print and knowledge about print. Sherry desperately needed early help in school; Paul did not, since he got it at home. We need to help those who can least help themselves by doing more in the preschool and kindergarten years to develop the prerequisites of decoding (i.e., alphabetic understanding, phonemic awareness, and cryptanalytic intent). We foster these prerequisites when we discuss a child's attempts to write words, when we discuss the printed words in stories, when we rhyme, when we play word games, and when we simply read to children. In this way, we can ease the transition from an oral to a literate world, a transition that for too many children like Sherry has been far too painful.

## END NOTES

[1]This passage is from the *Diagnostic Reading Scales,* G.D. Spache (1981). It is labelled grade level 1.4.

[2]I use the word "code" here as it is most commonly used in the literature. The more appropriate term would be "cipher" as discussed by Gough & Hillinger (1980).

## REFERENCES

ALFORD, J. A., Jr. (1980). *Lexical and contextual effects on reading time.* Unpublished doctoral dissertation, University of Texas at Austin.

BIEMILLER, A. (1970). The development of the use of graphic and contextual information as children learn to read. *Reading Research Quarterly, 6,* 75–96.

BISSEX, G. L. (1980). *Gnys at Wrk.* Cambridge, MA: Harvard University Press.

BLACHMAN, B. A., & JAMES, S. L. (1985). Metalinguistic abilities and reading achievement in first-grade children. In J. Niles & R. Lalik (Eds.), *Issues in literacy: A research perspective,* pp. 280–286. Rochester, NY: National Reading Conference.

BRADLEY, L., & BRYANT, P. E. (1983). Categorizing sounds and learning to read—a causal connection. *Nature, 301,* 419–421.

BRIDGE, C. A. (1986). Predictable books for beginning readers and writers. In M. R. Sampson (Ed.), *The pursuit of literacy.* Dubuque, IA: Kendall/Hunt.

CHALL, J. S. (1979). The great debate: Ten years later, with a modest proposal for reading stages. In L. B. Resnick & P. A. Weaver (Eds.), *Theory and practice of early reading,* Vol. 1, pp. 29–55. Hillsdale, NJ: Erlbaum.

CLARK, M. (1976). *Young fluent readers.* London: Heinemann.

CLAY, M. M. (1979). *Reading: The patterning of complex behaviour.* Auckland, NZ: Heinemann.

CLAY, M. M. (1987). *The early detection of reading difficulties* (3rd ed.). Hong Kong: Heinemann.

DOCTOR, E., & COLTHEART, M. (1980). Children's use of phonological encoding when reading for meaning. *Memory and Cognition, 8,* 195–209.

DOEHRING, D. G. (1976). Acquisition of rapid responses. *Monographs of the Society for Research in Child Development, 41,* (2, Serial No. 165).

DOWNING, J. (1979). *Reading and reasoning.* New York: Springer-Verlag.

DURKIN, D. (1966). *Children who read early.* New York: Teachers College Press.

EHRI, L. C., & WILCE, L. S. (1985). Movement into reading: Is the first stage of printed word learning visual or phonetic? *Reading Research Quarterly, 20,* 163–179.

EHRI, L. C., & WILCE, L. S. (1987). Cipher versus cue reading: An experiment in decoding acquisition. *Journal of Educational Psychology, 79,* 3–13.

ELKONIN, D. B. (1963). The psychology of mastering the elements of reading. In B. Simon & J. Simon (Eds.), *Educational psychology in the U.S.S.R,* pp. 165–179. London: Routledge & Kegan Paul.

ELKONIN, D. B. (1973). U.S.S.R. In J. Downing (Ed.), *Comparative reading,* pp. 551–579. New York: Macmillan.

FOX, B., & ROUTH, D. K. (1975). Analyzing spoken language into words, syllables, and phonemes: A developmental study. *Journal of Psycholinguistic Research, 4,* 331–342.

GATES, A. I., & BOEKER, E. (1923). A study of initial stages in reading by preschool children. *Teachers College Record, 24,* 469–488.

GOLINKOFF, R. M., & ROSINSKI, R. R. (1976). Decoding, semantic processing, and reading comprehension skill. *Child Development, 47,* 252–258.

GOUGH, P. B., ALFORD, J. A., Jr., & HOLLEY-WILCOX, P. (1981). Words and contexts. In O. J. L. Tzeng & H. Singer (Eds.), *Perception of Print,* pp. 85–102. Hillsdale, NJ: Erlbaum.

GOUGH, P. B., & HILLINGER, M. L. (1980). Learning to read: An unnatural act. *Bulletin of the Orton Society, 30,* 179–196.

GOUGH, P. B., JUEL, C., & ROPER-SCHNEIDER, D. (1983). A two stage model of initial reading acquisition. In J. A. Niles & L. A. Harris (Eds.), *Searches for meaning in reading/language processing and instruction,* pp. 207–211. Rochester, NY: National Reading Conference.

GUTTENTAG, R. E., & HAITH, M. M. (1978). Automatic processing as a function of age and reading disability. *Child Development, 49,* 707–716.

GUTTENTAG, R. E., & HAITH, M. M. (1979). A developmental study of automatic word processing in a picture classification task. *Child Development, 50,* 894–896.

GUTTENTAG, R. E., & HAITH, M. M. (1980). A longitudinal study of word processing by first-grade children. *Journal of Educational Psychology, 72,* 701–705.

HARSTE, J. (1980, April). Written language learning as a social event. Paper presented at the meeting of the American Educational Research Association, Boston.

HIERONYMOUS, A. N., LINDQUIST, E. F., & HOOVER, H. D. (1980). *IOWA test of basic skills, primary battery, form 7, level 7.* New York: Houghton Mifflin.

HOLDAWAY, D. (1979). *The foundations of literacy.* New York: Ashton Scholastic.

JUEL, C. (1988). Learning to read and write: A longitudinal study of fifty-four children from first through fourth grade. *Journal of Educational Psychology, 80,* 437–447.

JUEL, C. (in press). Beginning reading. In P. D. Pearson, R. Barr, M. L. Kamil, & P. Mosenthal (Eds.), *Handbook of reading research,* Vol. 2. New York: Longman.

JUEL, C., GRIFFITH, P. L., & GOUGH, P. B. (1985). Reading and spelling strategies of first grade children. In J. A. Niles & R. Lalik (Eds.), *Issues in literacy: A research perspective,* pp. 306–309. Rochester, NY: National Reading Conference.

JUEL, C., GRIFFITH, P. L., & GOUGH, P. B. (1986). Acquisition of literacy: A longitudinal study of children in first and second grade. *Journal of Educational Psychology, 78,* 243–255.

JUEL, C., & ROPER-SCHNEIDER, D. (1985). The influence of basal readers on first grade reading. *Reading Research Quarterly, 20,* 134–152.

KUHARA-KOJIMA, K. Personal Communication March 31, 1988.

LESGOLD, A. M., & CURTIS, M. E. (1981). Learning to read words efficiently. In A. M. Lesgold & C. A. Perfetti (Eds.), *Interactive processes in reading,* pp. 329–360. Hillsdale, NJ: Erlbaum.

LESGOLD, A. M., & RESNICK, L. B. (1982). How reading disabilities develop: Perspectives from a longitudinal study. In J. P. Das, R. Mulcahy, & A. E. Wall (Eds.), *Theory and research in learning disability*, pp. 155–187. New York: Plenum.

LUNDBERG, I. (1984). Learning to read. *School Research Newsletter* (August). (National Board of Education in Sweden.)

LUNDBERG, I., FROST, J., & PETERSON, O. (1988). Effects of an extensive program for stimulating phonological awareness in preschool children. *Reading Research Quarterly, 23*, 263–284.

LUNDBERG, I., OLOFFSON, A., & WALL, S. (1980). Reading and spelling skills in the first school years predicted from phonemic awareness skills in kindergarten. *Scandinavian Journal of Psychology, 21*, 628–636.

MACLEAN, M., BRYANT, P., & BRADLEY, L. (1987). Rhymes, nursery rhymes, and reading in early childhood. *Merrill-Palmer Quarterly, 33*, 255–281.

MASON, J. M. (1980). When do children begin to read: An exploration of four year old children's letter and word reading competencies. *Reading Research Quarterly, 15*, 203–227.

MASONHEIMER, P. E., DRUM, P. A., EHRI, L. C. (1984). Does environmental print identification lead children into word reading? *Journal of Reading Behavior, 26*, 257–271.

PERFETTI, C. A. (1985). Reading Ability, NY: Oxford University Press.

PERFETTI, C. A., BECK, I., BELL, L. C., & HUGHES, C. (1987). Phonemic knowledge and learning to read are reciprocal: A longitudinal study of first grade children. *Merrill-Palmer Quarterly, 33*, 283–319.

READ, C. (1971). Pre-school children's knowledge of English phonology. *Harvard Educational Review, 41*, 1–34.

READ, C. (1975). *Children's categorization of speech sounds in English*. Urbana, IL: National Council of Teachers of English.

READ, C. (1986). *Children's creative spelling*. London: Routledge & Kegan Paul.

ROSINSKI, R. R. (1977). Picture-word inference is semantically based. *Child Development, 48*, 643–647.

ROSINSKI, R. R., GOLINKOFF, R. M., & KUKISH, R. S. (1975). Automatic semantic processing in a picture-word interference task. *Child Development, 46*, 247–263.

SAMUELS, S. J., & JEFFREY, W. E. (1966). Discriminability of words and letter cues used in learning to read. *Journal of Educational Psychology, 57*, 337–340.

SCHREIBER, P., & READ, C. (1980). Children's use of phonetic cues in spelling, parsing, and —maybe—reading. *Bulletin of the Orton Society, 30*, 209–224.

SHARE, D. L., JORM, A. F., MACLEAN, R., & MATTHEWS, R. (1984). Sources of individual differences in reading achievement. *Journal of Educational Psychology, 76*, 1309–1324.

SÖDERBERG, R. (1977). *Reading in early childhood: A linguistic study of a preschool child's gradual acquisition of reading ability*. Washington, DC: Georgetown University Press.

SPACHE, G. D. (1981). *Diagnostic reading scales*. Monterey, CA: CTB/McGraw-Hill.

STANOVICH, K. E. (1980). Toward an interactive-compensatory model of individual differences in the development of reading fluency. *Reading Research Quarterly, 16*, 32–71.

STANOVICH, K. E. (1986). Matthew effects in reading: Some consequences of individual differences in the acquisition of literacy. *Reading Research Quarterly, 21*, 360–406.

SULZBY, E. (1985). Children's emergent reading of favorite storybooks: A developmental study. *Reading Research Quarterly, 20*, 458–481

TORNÉUS, M. (1984). Phonological awareness and reading: A chicken and egg problem? *Journal of Educational Psychology, 76*, 1346–1358.

TUNMER, W. E., & NESDALE, A. R. (1985). Phonemic segmentation skill and beginning reading. *Journal of Educational Psychology, 77,* 417–427.

VENEZKY, R. L. (1976). *Theoretical and experimental base for teaching reading.* The Hague: Mouton.

WEST, R. F., & STANOVICH, K. E. (1979). The development of automatic word recognition skills. *Journal of Reading Behavior, 11,* 211–219.

WILLIAMS, J. P. (1984). Phonemic analysis and how it relates to reading. *Journal of Learning Disabilities, 17,* 240–245.

WILLOWS, D. M., BORWICK, D., & HAYVREN, M. (1981). The content of school readers. In G. E. MacKinnon & T. G. Waller (Eds.), *Reading research: Advances in theory and practice,* Vol. 2, pp. 97–175. New York: Academic Press.

# 9

# EMERGENT LITERACY ASSESSMENT FOR INSTRUCTIONAL USE IN KINDERGARTEN

*Jana M. Mason*
*University of Illinois*

*Janice P. Stewart*
*Rutgers, The State University of New Jersey*

### Abstract

Jana M. Mason and Janice P. Stewart demonstrate how emergent literacy concepts are part of instruction and can be connected to correspond with assessment. Mason and Stewart propose a framework for instructionally based assessment: (1) concepts and functions of literacy, (2) knowledge of letters and words, (3) listening comprehension and word understanding, and (4) writing and composing. These aspects of emergent literacy are presented with examples from a project in which teachers were learning to link assessment of children's literacy concepts to their instruction.

Assessment instruments that are intended to evaluate students' performance hold a prominent position in American schools, having become "the engine for implementing educational policy" (Petrie, 1987, p. 175). Their widespread use in schools today, however, does not compel all of them to be based on the same model. In this chapter we examine how instruments intended to evaluate kindergarten children's emergent reading and writing might be constructed so as to provide instructional information for teachers.

Reading assessment instruments are not without criticism. For example, there are newspaper accounts by the Friends of Education that all states have reported above-average performance of their students. While we would like to believe that "all the children are above average" (a Garrison Keillor pronouncement), such results are likely instead to be caused by score distributions that have out-of-date norms. Another criticism is whether assessment instruments are valid, that is, whether they actually measure the concepts intended and are instructionally important. Furthermore, tests need to be authentic, containing items that assess the concepts the test makers say they are measuring, and tests need procedures for administration and scoring that yield unbiased, realistic responses. Finally, tests can be criticized for not being sufficiently functional (see Chapter 4). Linn (1988) suggests that the use of test results should go beyond ranking groups, perhaps by providing evaluative information of instructional programs and curricula or by suggesting instructional implications to teachers.

Assuming a test has addressed these criticisms, it could still be of no value unless it served an important goal. According to Farr and Carey (1986), assessment instruments can be used to hold teachers, schools, and school systems accountable through evaluation of regular and new programs. Another goal is to provide guidance to teachers for improving their instruction in the classroom and to administrators and teachers concerning individual student placement into special programs and classes.

The first goal is a global reporting score that allows comparisons among schools and districts; the second one is to describe students' proficiencies for purposes of reforming or improving curriculum and instruction. Unfortunately, most instruments serve the first goal, yielding global comparisons of classrooms or schools. This information cannot easily be interpreted by school personnel to figure out how to change instruction. For example, although reading readiness tests typically contain four or more subtests (see Chapter 2), high intercorrelations among the subtests encourage gross judgments about children's ability. Moreover, because the assessment procedures are unlike classroom instruction tasks, it is difficult for teachers to make direct comparisons between test responses and instruction.

Global comparison instruments feature decisions about test form, administration, reliability, and validity. For example, decisions about form and administration have emphasized efficiency. Through administration to large groups and reliance on machine-scored, multiple-choice student responses, test time and scoring costs have been minimized. These procedures, however, reduce the possibility of understanding why children choose particular responses. This process information is better obtained with open response test formats and individual test administrations. Test items are made reliable by the use of construction techniques that differentiate students by overall ranking, a process which obscures differences in ethnicity, region, and background experience. Items are made valid by being grouped into macro concepts, such as word attack, vocabulary, and comprehension, rather than into narrowly defined concepts that might uncover the process of thinking or reasoning or lend diagnostic information or allow evaluation of particular instructional objectives. Thus, most of our reading tests are designed to serve the first objective, evaluation of schools and systems, rather than the second, curricular decision making.

A more realistic view about reading assessment may be to admit that the tests should not simultaneously serve both global assessment and instructional application goals.  In fact, Calfee (1987) argues that the way tests are constructed leads to divergent assessment instruments and goals.  Group-administered instruments contain multiple-choice tasks and are mandated and supervised by administrators or other authorities for evaluating teachers and schools.  Individually administered and informal instruments measure progress in particular skills and knowledge about subject matter being taught.  They are usually administered by teachers to monitor student progress task processing and to aid in curricular decision making.  Unfortunately, many instructional process tests, according to Calfee, have been modeled after group assessment instruments, making even these tests difficult to use for instructional evaluation.  An emphasis on global scores and school evaluation has apparently led to a neglect of effective testing techniques that can help teachers improve instruction.

Instruments that evaluate curricular decision making are important, particularly for evaluating young children's early reading and writing.  To create more appropriate mechanisms to fulfill this need, Calfee (1987) recommends the following: (1) analysis of the basic concepts surrounding literacy acquisition into a coherent set, (2) movement away from an emphasis on the content of lesson detail toward an analysis of the processes students need to use for extracting underlying concepts, and (3) a change in school policy to support informed teacher judgment of student performance and effective instruction.  In this chapter we discuss the second mechanism, followed by the notion of a coherent set of reading concepts concluding with ways that teachers might use the information.  Our goal is to suggest how curricular-based assessment instruments could be constructed so that teachers of young children could apply assessment information for their reading instruction.

## TASKS THAT FOCUS ON ANALYSIS OF THE READING PROCESS

How might teachers move toward an analysis of young children's processes of thinking and reasoning as they attempt to read and write?  Such a move requires more than a simple change of attitude; judgments about students' progress must be made with a new view about how and when to evaluate students' knowledge and progress.

Group tests have been standardized based on the assumption that the directions for their administration are followed exactly, assuming that students will be sufficiently familiar with the procedures and concepts making up the tasks to be evaluated fairly.  Such a position is usually an unsatisfactory role for teachers to take.  Can they be advocates rather than adversaries as they test children?  According to Holdaway (1979) and Johnston (1987), teachers can be advocates if they judge and interpret students' knowledge processing through a dynamic assessment approach, an approach that involves varying the amount of support before and during the test.  Teachers might, for example, demonstrate a test procedure by describing how they might think about the question and answers. Then they could provide additional examples if children seem confused, a technique that cannot be followed when administering standardized tests because sample examples are predetermined. Teachers might also systematically vary the amount of help during the testing itself to differentiate when children can accomplish the task with and without assistance (Campione & Brown, 1987).

Teachers can also become experts at informally evaluating and interpreting children's literacy development, according to Johnston (1987), by recognizing important patterns in their responses. Errors, for example, signal weak processing approaches or misinterpretations, while changes in errors can indicate new insights and a developmental progression. Teachers can become aware of response patterns in children's errors, and then learn to differentiate between errors based on new insights and errors that are affected by task procedures. Teachers can figure out how to stage a range of responses, evaluate children with different materials, and write down, tabulate, and interpret children's responses while interacting with them. Reading in context and recalling information that children read or listen to also provides valuable information if teachers learn how to record and interpret errors that children make while reading in context (Clay, 1985).

Finally, because valuable information oftentimes comes not from staged test situations but from unplanned incidents, teachers should learn to be good listeners and observers. If they react to children's comments and questions with other questions, they will be able to probe for more information about what children understand and will be able to infer what processes children are using to carry out the tasks. In these diverse ways teachers will gain invaluable insights into what children know and how they carry out reading tasks.

When teachers use the information they receive from students during instruction and try to enhance their teaching by understanding and reacting to students' responses, we see a situation where dynamic instruction is taking place. When coordinated with dynamic assessment, teachers have a powerful set of instructional techniques. Dynamic assessment can be used to initiate instruction, can occur informally throughout the school year, and can become a part of the instruction because it is grounded in the ongoing social interaction between teacher and student and in the concepts and skills being studied.

By contrast, teachers who rely only on static assessment are limited in several ways: to questions that are to be asked, to particular responses from children, and to a few tasks. The profile emitted by this testing situation does not permit adult assistance, partially correct answers, or unusual but acceptable answers. In essence, static assessment does not take into account children's potential to respond nor does it permit flexibility from adult-mediated assistance.

When dynamic assessment is used in the context of instruction, children's responses provide cues that help teachers structure the next step of the assessment as well as to plan the next phase of instruction. Now, when a teacher is simultaneously providing instruction and testing a child, it becomes apparent that there is no longer a strong distinction between tester and teacher. As Johnston (1987) states, "The roles of teacher and evaluator allow teaching and evaluation to occur at the same time, while encouraging and modeling independence" (p. 747). It is this interactive effect that we advocate when measuring young children's reading and writing development and interpreting their responses.

## A COHERENT SET OF READING CONCEPTS

To make instructional use of assessment instruments, Calfee (1987) advocates that teachers be informed about the basic concepts surrounding literacy acquisition. Discussion of these basic concepts has been suggested for decades. As early as 1939, Gates, Bond, and Russell provided an illuminating base for studying reading readiness (see Chapter 2). More recent work by Clay (1979, 1985), Dickinson and Snow (1987), Lomax and McGee, (1987), and Teale, Hiebert, and Chittenden (1987) describes current emergent literacy perspectives. In Table 1 we list the basic assessment concepts that span this era. We suggest that there are four aspects of emergent literacy: concepts and functions of literacy, knowledge of letters and words, listening comprehension and word understanding, and writing and composing. A discussion of each shows how they can be interpreted for a dynamic assessment approach that has instructional improvement as the goal.

### Concepts and Functions of Literacy

Literacy concepts that children have upon entry into school are influenced by the support children receive at home as well as in kindergarten or preschool (Gates, Bond, & Russell, 1939; Dickinson & Snow, 1987). Although these concepts cannot be defined in terms of discrete stages of development (Hiebert, 1981), there are early and later developing characteristics that can be distinguished (Lomax & McGee, 1987; Mason, 1980), so that children's progress in understanding how reading occurs can be measured with dynamic and informal assessment instruments. In one instrument developed by Clay (1985), for example, children are handed a book and are asked to show where the front of it is and where to begin and continue reading. They are asked to identify upper- and lowercase letters and punctuation marks; to distinguish between letters and words, first and last words, top and bottom of the text; and to point to the words as the examiner reads them.

Children are also asked to write as many words as they know, and to write out the words in a sentence or two that is dictated by the examiner. This test is scored in terms of the number and quality of concepts children describe (Stewart, 1986). Children who are aware of how they are learning to read understand how to analyze and talk about their own actions. From work by Vygotsky (1962) we know that young children are able to analyze and talk about their own actions, verbalize the steps they are carrying out in learning tasks, and express the difficulties or problems they confront. When children are asked, "How are you learning to read (or write)," many

**TABLE 1    Four Proposed Aspects of Emergent Literacy Sketched Across 50 Years**

**Concepts and functions of literacy**

Knowledge of terms used to talk about reading (e.g., terms for describing print and reading tasks, location of top and bottom of the page, book cover, knowledge of punctuation marks) (Clay, 1985; Hardy, Stennet, & Smythe, 1974; Lomax & McGee, 1987)

Understanding functions of print (able to provide uses for print materials such as newspapers, ads, lists, greeting cards) (Lomax & McGee, 1987; Schickedanz, 1986)

Knowing how the act of reading is carried out (including where to begin and continue reading; knowing how to separate speech into words, syllables, and letters; and being able to track or follow along as a printed text is read) (Clay, 1979, 1985; Mason & McCormick, 1979; Morris, 1983)

Emergent reading of storybooks (Clay 1985; Mason & Kerr, 1988; Sulzby, 1983, 1985)

Self-perception of learning to read (Johns, 1984; Stewart, 1986)

Context-sensitive strategies for word reading (Ferreiro & Teberosky, 1982; Peterman & Mason, 1984)

Knowledge of environmental print words in context (Harste, Woodward, & Burke, 1984; Mason, 1980; Hiebert, 1981; Lomax & McGee, 1987)

**Knowledge of letters and words**

Letter knowledge (Clay, 1985; Ehri, 1983; Gates, Bond, & Russell, 1939; Lomax & McGee, 1987; Mason & McCormick, 1979)

Phonological awareness of beginning and ending sounds of words (Gates, Bond, & Russell, 1939; Lomax & McGee, 1987)

Grapheme-phoneme correspondence knowledge (Gates, Bond, & Russell, 1939; Lomax & McGee, 1987; Mason & McCormick, 1979)

Word recognition (common words and words containing generalizable patterns) (Clay, 1985; Gates, Bond, & Russell, 1939; Lomax & McGee, 1987; Mason & McCormick 1979)

**Listening comprehension and word understanding**

Recall, retell, or complete a partially told story (Gates, Bond, & Russell, 1939; Genishi & Dyson, 1984; Jensen, 1984; Mason & Dunning, 1986; Chapter 7, Morrow, this volume; Sulzby, 1989)

Define, classify, and draw analogies to words (Dickinson & Snow, 1987; Mason & Dunning; 1986; Watson & Olson, 1987)

Multiple cue strategies for reading texts (Clay, 1985)

**Writing and composing**

Writing words (Clay, 1985; Ehri, 1989; Harste, Woodward, & Burke 1984; Read, 1971)

Sentence dictation (Clay, 1985)

Story composition (Applebee, 1980; King, 1989)

---

will talk about what happens at home or school and what literacy materials are used. More advanced and older children will also describe help they obtain from others (Pramling, 1983; Stewart, 1986).

Knowledge of print functions can be evaluated by showing children a range of printed materials and asking children to explain their use. An ability to identify words in the context of their pictures can be addressed at the same time. Children can be asked to read logo words in context (e.g., "stop," "Coke," "milk") and then in standard print out of context (Mason & McCormick, 1979). Another approach is to insert less appropriate words in place of the expected words, for example, by placing the word "wheel," instead of the word car, under a picture of a car (Peterman & Mason, 1984).

### Knowledge of Letters and Words

Letter and word identification tasks have been the mainstay of early reading tests for years (e.g., Gates, Bond, & Russell, 1939). Today, tasks that measure this important construct are more extensive, with recognition of lower- as well as upper-case letter forms, finer distinctions made in phonological awareness (Stanovich, Cunningham, & Cramer, 1984, or Yopp, 1988); word recognition which differentiates sight recognition of familiar words from ability to figure out unfamiliar words; and word analysis. Again, such instruments, if they contain flexible procedures and take into consideration variations in difficulty of items, can be organized with a dynamic assessment approach. Children can be asked to recognize, name, or construct letters, sounds, or words. They can manipulate letters in words. They can try to read old, newly learned, or wholly new words or asked to analyze parts of words, such as initial or final consonant sounds, medial vowel, consonant blends, digraphs, and letter cluster patterns. Finally, they can be given the same words in and out of context to determine whether and how they use syntactic and semantic information.

Recognition of letters, names, and sounds can be organized as a dynamic assessment task. First, children would be asked to name uppercase letters, and those who do not know the first few can be given easier tasks of reciting the alphabet and matching named letters. Those who know uppercase letters can be given harder tasks such as naming lowercase letters, copying a sample of letters, printing letters without seeing the model, and telling which letters begin the names of pictured objects. None of these tasks requires testing knowledge of all 26 letters; 10 to 15 of the more common letters is usually sufficient to test children's development of the underlying concepts, unless a teacher also wants to know exactly which letters children know and do not know.

Phonological awareness is the ability to hear sounds in words that are labeled phonemes or letters sounds. It can be tested with a number of tasks, including recognizing or producing a word that rhymes or begins the same as another word, moving sounds around in words (e.g., replace the $p$ sound in "pie" with $t$ to get "tie"), and tapping for each sound heard in words. The important concept here is to evaluate whether children have begun to analyze words into their phonemes to uncover and understand the fundamental letter-to-sound patterns of English.

Recognition of common words out of context includes words important to children and common two- to four-letter words in reading primers. A dynamic assessment instrument can be scaled, beginning with the easiest items which are words important to children such as their own names and frequently seen environmental print words. Harder words include common, concrete nouns found in books and other common book words. Less familiar words are harder still. Word recognition tasks have often been constructed from basal reading lists, the A & P sight words, selected words from the Dolch list, or high-frequency words from the Carroll, Davies, and Richman *Word Frequency Book* (1971). These words can be administered as recognition tasks (e.g., find the word the examiner says) or in varying ways as production tasks (e.g., read the list of words, where the easiest words are placed first so the test can be stopped when the words become too difficult; or read a set of words and select the one that describes a picture).

Recognition of uncommon words, which requires word-to-sound analysis, is the subject of a large body of literature regarding an understanding of the regularity of letter-to-sound correspondences. These tasks build from an understanding of phonological awareness by having children move letters around in words to create other words, match words on the basis of their letter-sound patterns, break words into syllables, and recognize new words by analogy to known patterns or generalization of regular patterns. One effective approach is to ask children to read a set of pseudowords, beginning with the easiest patterns (e.g., fet), and then harder patterns (e.g., splink, vate, joit). Recognizing patterns of this nature indicates an ability to draw on or generalize from the regular patterns of English spelling.

### Listening Comprehension and Word Understanding

Before and during the early stages of reading stories, children make use of written language concepts and reading strategies. This is an area of research that can be viewed from a dynamic assessment perspective (Clay, 1985; Genishi & Dyson, 1984; Lundberg, 1988; Mason, in press; Sulzby, 1989; Chapter 7, this volume). Several important dimensions of oral and written language understanding are conjoined, particularly listening comprehension, text structure knowledge; ability to define, classify, and draw analogies to words; and use of multiple text cues when reading.

Listening comprehension is based on the notion that as children listen to and discuss stories that are read to them and listen to and tell stories to family members, they develop approaches for identifying and making sense of the ideas, and strategies for remembering them. They are likely, for example, to build connections between the text information they hear and their own experiences. We know that at first parents and teachers make these connections for children (e.g., Snow & Ninio, 1986; Mason & Kerr, 1988) and it is likely that these text-connecting experiences foster listening comprehension abilities. Listening comprehension questions which tap the important aspects of a story are used in beginning reading and language tasks. Recalling a story that was read to children is frequently used in comprehension research studies. Repetition of sentences, in which sentences are increasingly longer, evaluates the amount of syntactic information children can absorb and report.

Sulzby (1983, 1985), drawing on children's rereading of favorite stories, recommends that children be asked to give story retellings. She scores responses as a scale that begins with a recounting of events as though they were isolated incidents and moves toward an integrated accounting using a written language style. Morrow (Chapter 7) indicates that children's retellings can be analyzed for sense of story structure such as setting, theme, plot episodes, and resolution.

The importance of definition, classification, and organization of information is evident from research by Watson and Olson (1987) and a treatise by Egan (1987) about the orality/literacy shift and its conceptual role in attaining literacy. Mason and Dunning (1986) found that a word definition task correlated with listening comprehension measures and can be used to help predict later reading. Word definition can be tested by asking children to define words, with a higher score assigned to classificatory and functional responses.

When children begin to read, they also begin to use strategies of competent readers: letter and letter-sound cues, syntactic information, and semantic information (Clay, 1985). When they do not know or remember a word, they ask appropriate questions or challenge its meaning and as they read, they keep track of meaning by predicting and summarizing (Mason, McCormick, & Bhavnagri, 1986). A working knowledge of these strategies can be assessed in individual sessions with children by asking them to read parts of storybooks that vary in difficulty. They can be asked what they think the story will be about, a running record can be kept of their reading errors and corrections, their comments and questions can be noted, and their responses to questions about how they figured out certain parts of the text can be collected. Children who are learning to make appropriate use of text strategies will rely on picture, letter, and text information to predict, figure out words, and interpret the story information and will adjust their strategies with the difficulty of the text.

### Writing and Composing

Although writing and composing must be closely related to listening comprehension and word understanding, we distinguish abilities to read or recount from abilities to write. There are varying levels, according to Dobson (1989), and Sulzby (1989). We distinguish three aspects of writing and composing. One involves the ability to print and spell words. A second is with regard to dictating stories, and a third follows an activity in which children watch a teacher write a story or report and then discuss its contents.

Notions about printing and spelling development emanates from work by Read (1971) who showed that young children mirror the regularity of the language in their writing and spelling attempts. Ehri (in press) and Morris (1983) developed this concept more fully, showing connections between spelling and reading and providing a model of developmental change. Printing and spelling words can be tested by asking children to write all the words they know (Clay, 1985) and then, when they have finished, reading all the words to the examiner. Drawings, scribbles, as well as letter and word understanding can be analyzed using a scale suggested by Sulzby (1989). Or, if children are more literate, fidelity to conventional spellings can be the basis for analysis (Clay, 1985).

Dictating a known story or a new one can capture children's understanding of what a story is. Genishi and Dyson (1984) and King (1989) assess the language of the retelling in terms of fluency, complexity, and vocabulary. The story itself is analyzed according to major events and the linking of events. Applebee (1980) suggests that written productions can be classified and ranked into heaps, sequences, primitive narratives, unfocused chains, focused chains, and narratives.

Watching a teacher construct and then answer questions about a brief message has been a favorite approach for years; only a change of names, "Chart Writing" or "Language Experience" or "Morning Message," seems to suggest different tasks. When teachers write messages for instructional purposes, either the teacher or students compose the message, children usually watch as the teacher writes it out, and either the teacher or the children say the words while it is being written. Even though messages may be produced by children, rephrased from the children's ideas, or produced by the teacher, they all have in common an opportunity for children to see a text being constructed and then to work with it, whether by discussion of the ideas or analysis of its form or structure. Informal tasks can be constructed about a text after it has been written out and discussed regarding meaning, words, or prominent letter sounds in the text. Tests can be constructed from the written productions, with either reading or rewriting as the goal, and with the task geared to children's level of competency.

## A WORKING EXAMPLE OF EMERGENT LITERACY ASSESSMENT

In the foregoing presentation, two points were emphasized. One is that assessment tasks can be instructionally relevant, that is, useful to teachers for purposes of diagnosis, remediation, and group instruction. The other is that assessment instruments can be constructed based on a construct of dynamic assessment. When both these constructs are present, assessment can be used by teachers as part of their instruction and for informal and formal evaluation of their students' progress.

In this section we show in examples from ongoing work how teachers can profit from an assessment instrument that meets these assumptions. We do not intend to imply that our assessment instrument is unique; rather, we intend the examples to demonstrate how an instrument of this nature can be used in classrooms.

Three kindergarten teachers the first year and four the second year were trained to use information from our assessment instrument for their instruction. Their children's progress was later compared with that of other classes in which teachers had not been trained. Preliminary results show that instructional use of dynamic assessment leads to greater progress among kindergarten children.

In the study, all the kindergarten classrooms were from low-income schools in the Virgin Islands. Assignation of low income is based on the fact that about 79 percent of the children were eligible for free lunches. Stewart worked closely with the four teachers. In the first year, she explained what the test scores meant and how teachers could interpret errors. She continued with demonstrations about how they could use the tasks and testing procedures in their curriculum to teach reading. Eventually, they learned also how to modify some parts of the assessment battery for informal testing in order to monitor their students' progress.  She found not only that teachers learned ways of integrating the testing techniques with their curriculum that led to improvements in their instruction but that they developed more positive attitudes toward their students' ability to learn to read.

### Concepts About Print

Knowledge of print concepts was evaluated in kindergarten, before children could read independently, by using picture-phrase books and books that repeat the same phrases on each page and contain words on each page that are easily predicted through picture information.  In the Mason and Stewart *Early Childhood Screening and Diagnostic Instrument* (1989), children are handed the book upside down and are asked to find the front of the book and identify the print ("Show me where there is something to read").  They are told the name of the book and then are asked to read it.  If they say they can't read, they are told they can "pretend read."  As mentioned earlier, an alternative approach was developed by Clay (1985).

Most kindergarten children find the front of the book and point to print rather than to picture information.  They are evaluated principally on their reading attempts.  Some simply repeat the title for each page, and some do better by labeling each picture or by elaborating on the pictures to construct a plausible story.  A few who are further along attempt to read the printed words or try to use print and picture information.  Thus the measure gives information about how children handle books and what information they can use from it to try to read.

Teachers working with Stewart were shown how to extend this task by making predictable book reading a daily classroom activity.  For many children in these classrooms, it was their first exposure to handling books, and so the teachers made sure they felt successful and comfortable about reciting the stories and pretend-reading the texts.  Because many of the children were not able to orient the books properly for reading and exhibited minimal language responses for text reading, teachers introduced seven to ten books during the school year in an order that fit the rest of their curriculum.  Each book was no more than six pages in length and usually had three to five words on a page (McCormick & Mason, in press).

The teachers read the books to small groups of children, with children sitting around the teacher and able to see the teacher and the book.  The teachers reread each book several times and led discussions concerning aspects of the print and picture.  Drawing on information gained from children's responses, teachers were able to adjust their questions and help, gradually withdrawing support until children were able to read the books to one another and independently.

Children became aware of the text pattern when listening and rereading, and teachers used other books, pictures, objects, or shared experiences to activate and extend children's knowledge about the story topic.  Teachers modeled the correct way to hold books, turn pages, and read.  After children heard the story, they were given copies of the book for participation and individual reading. Then the teacher was able to note which children could orient the books correctly and attend to pictures and print, hear sounds in words, and reread. The children were often asked questions about the print that engaged them in phonetic analysis. After the lessons the teachers placed the books in the class library or on tables for children to pick up and read and borrow for home use. Then the teachers listened to some children reading from memory, to others who were focusing on word recognition, and still others who were using the pictures.

Teachers also encouraged the children to take the books home so that parents could listen to the child read or reread with their aid. To help parents, videotapes were shown at parent-teacher meetings that demonstrated effective book reading approaches.

To learn how children perceive learning, or awareness about how to read and how to learn to read, Stewart tested children with three interview questions:

> Tell me, how are you learning to read at home? (Prompt: What are you doing that will help you?)
>
> Pretend this teddy bear wants to learn to read. How might you teach him? (In scoring, note the bear's position and the materials the child uses as well as what the child says.)
>
> How are you learning to read in school? (Prompt: Who helps you? What does that person say?)

Similar questions were asked about writing. Evaluations of all responses are based on the appropriateness of response (e.g., use of book materials, noting importance of knowing words, admission that others can help). Children who are more advanced describe interactions with adults assisting them or describe their self-monitoring behavior while reading or decoding; children who are not as aware of how they are learning often describe household chores or playing outside.

Responses to the awareness task helped teachers to determine how their children perceived the school reading program. Children in a curriculum that was highly dependent on workbooks and drill gave more limited responses to learning, for example, "We circle the right answer in our book" or "We sit in groups and read." Children in a literature and language-enriched program often talked about learning words, reading books, trying to figure out words, and listening to the teacher read to them. Teachers noted whether children attributed any of the learning to significant others, whether they said they used phonetic cues, and whether they confused reading with unrelated activities. It was not uncommon for a teacher to see some children unable to respond at all while others were able to discuss how they sounded out words. Differences were usually dependent on the extent of salient communications between children and their family members and children's perceptions of the school reading program. If children expressed confusion about learning to read or write in school, teachers often adjusted their instructional strategies.

Responses for learning to read home in September were in some cases richer and reflected more help than responses given later in the kindergarten year. Mc-Cormick and Mason (1986) obtained a similar finding from a questionnaire given to parents at the beginning and end of the school year. Apparently some parents reduce their support for literacy at home when children begin school, perhaps believing, erroneously, that they could conflict with the teacher's instruction or that the teachers will take over the job of literacy instruction now. Thus, responses to these questions can signal a need to work more closely with parents.

### Knowledge of Letters and Words

In this section we describe four tasks: letter naming, phonetic knowledge with a spelling task, common word recognition, and pseudoword recognition.

A letter-naming score discriminates children who know some or all of their letter names from those who confuse letters with numbers or confuse visually similar letters or know few or no letters. However, if teachers can also see errors when the task requires children to name upper- and lowercase letters, they will be able to judge the nature of letter recognition problems and confusions.

At the beginning of kindergarten, the teachers found children's letter knowledge to vary from none to all correct. At the lower end, some children could volunteer a little information, for example, "I know it's for Calvin's name" or "I see that in my name." Some called every letter by two or three letter names they knew or with number names. At the end of the kindergarten year, the majority of children knew all their letters, though some confused *b* and *d* visually or *C* and *S* (because of the name-sound confusion).

Teachers found that letter-name errors enabled them to distinguish the kind of instruction children needed, such as those who could recognize letters from their name from children who were still confusing letters with numbers. Later, they worked more closely with children whom they found were confused by phonics instruction because they still misidentified letter names.

Phonetic knowledge can be assessed by asking children to write words from dictated sentences and by writing words that they know (Clay, 1985). While appropriate in first grade, an easier task to use with kindergarten children is to dictate words for them to construct from magnetic letters (Mason & McCormick, 1979; Mason & Stewart, in preparation). Children can be asked to spell unfamiliar words, beginning with three-letter words containing short vowels (e.g., "pat"). If they are partially successful, they can be given four-letter words containing short vowels (e.g., "sick") and long vowels (e.g., "kite"). Their attempts, or errors, are most instructive for teachers.

As documented by Read (1971), there are regular changes in children's spelling responses. Children at the first phonetic stage usually represent the beginning consonant sound or beginning and ending consonants. Then they analyze middle sounds; later still they recognize varying long vowel patterns.

Teachers working with Stewart used the spelling task as a teaching tool and observed carefully their responses. They allowed children to experiment with spellings through play with magnetic letters and encouraged them to make words on their pictures. The teachers found that they could obtain useful information even at the beginning of the school year when most children did not use phonetic information. Some children might play with the magnetic letters, standing them on their side or in a pile; some might create "lines of text" by exhausting all the letters with a long string of letters; and those who understood a little more might create wordlike units bounded by spaces. By the middle of the year teachers differentiated children who could identify initial and final consonants (e.g., spelling "pat" as "pt") from those who knew that more letters were needed (e.g., spelling "pat" as "pet") or who used one vowel for all middle letters. By the end of the year, they could see that some children could hear some of the middle letters in four-letter words (e.g., spelling "sick" as "sik" or "tape" as "taep").

The teachers found the spelling task information valuable. In the beginning of kindergarten teachers were able to determine in a matter of minutes the phonetic orientation of their students. They provided magnetic boards and letters for the children to use to construct and sound out words. They worked individually with them and encouraged children to work in pairs or small groups. During writing sessions, children often experimented with magnetic letters before deciding how to spell something. Often teachers used these writing attempts and word play to make an instructional point. One teacher, for example, noticed a child spelling "hat" as "ht" and so she sat beside him and together they played with words that had the letter a in the middle. Other teachers had children use blanks where they knew letters belonged, writing, for example, "The g__t ate the f__d" for "The goat ate the food." Teachers also noticed that children's writing attempts mirrored their willingness to take risks at guessing or figuring out how to read or spell words. Some children, for example, liked to practice correct spelling by using the magnetic board to reconstruct words that the teacher had written on the blackboard.

Teachers were able to translate the spelling responses into valuable phonetic instruction during the daily Morning Message, an activity in which teachers wrote relevant messages in natural language on the chalkboard. Children could then be led through various activities to encourage reading: a use of multiple cues, structural analysis, semantic analysis, and phonetic analysis. Often the children were so excited about reading the message that they would predict words from the first few letters and use context cues. Teachers asked questions based on particular children's phonetic development. For example, a child just beginning to identify and differentiate letters and sounds was asked to find two words beginning with a particular letter or sound. Other children were asked to decode words, find words that rhymed, or use structural and context cues to figure out a word.

Teachers found that asking children to spell words was an easy and reliable method of diagnosing their phonetic knowledge and could be used flexibly. The words for children to spell were made more complex and less familiar as children moved developmentally from an understanding of single letter-sound patterns toward understanding some of the letter-cluster patterns and from memorizing words into sounding out words.

An ability to recognize common words is tested in most, if not all, beginning reading tests. Commonness is based on frequency of usage in written English. Words from among the 100 or 200 highest ranked (most frequent) are usually used. Because the words are also among those taught in preprimers and featured in practice sheets, children may have learned some by sight, that is, memorized them, rather than by applying a decoding strategy. To obtain a clearer measure of decoding ability, Mason and McCormick (1979) devised two sets of words, one of high-frequency words, some of which had been taught to the children, and the other of three-letter pseudowords (though other versions of this test have used very unfamiliar words instead). Common words on the subtest included go, bed, ten, little, at; examples of pseudowords were fam, pag, lac, jav. Thus, the common words were comprised of several types of letter patterns, while the pseudowords were restricted to the pattern consonant, short *a*, consonant which children could only read by sounding out the letters.

The common words gave teachers an idea of which children knew sight words and words that they had been taught. In the beginning of kindergarten, few children could even attempt the word reading task. Some tried by saying letters or numbers for words, using words they knew (e.g., out for ran), or using initial or final sounds of the word and saying a word they had learned (e.g., girl for go, sat for at). By the end of kindergarten, most children were at least matching the initial consonant (e.g., like for lunch, ham for had) and more advanced children were attempting to decode them (e.g., hone for honey).

The responses children made on the task helped teachers to understand what strategies children were using to recognize words. In their instruction, for example, they differentiated children who called at "h" from those more advanced children who said "hat" for at. They realized that some children called every *b* word "bed" because the word "bed" was their key word. These children were learning letter and word sounds by rote and had not yet realized that there were many words beginning with *b*! They also understood why a child who looked at "go" and said "gorilla" then gave animal names for each word thereafter. This child apparently thought that word lists were like stories and contained related words.

As children became more conscious of letter sounds and how to use them to decode words, teachers encouraged children to look for text meaning clues as well. For example, a child who mispronounced laugh as la-ef was helped when the teacher constructed a sentence about a funny joke.

Pseudoword reading tests children's willingness to rely singularly on letter-sound information. Although many children in kindergarten are not willing to try this task, or will only say real words, children's errors often indicate whether they are beginning to assign sounds to letters in words. If so, their errors will indicate that they are attending to initial or final consonant sounds (e.g., fish for fam, cup for kap, red for ras). Hence, this task (as well as the spelling task) is scored in two ways—number of words correctly read or spelled and number of letters correctly matched to appropriate sounds. Those children who know some common words and can use magnetic letters to form words will usually attempt this task and correctly match a third or more of the letters and form some of the words as well. By the end of kindergarten, children who have learned to hear initial and final consonants in words will perform at a higher level.

Teachers preferred the pseudoword and spelling tasks to the common word task for understanding how children were progressing in word analysis. They noticed some children were able to sound out initial and final consonants, others were able to work with initial sounds, and a few were able to include vowels in the blending. Teachers also commented that becoming aware of children's spelling response patterns helped them interpret and make use of the pseudoword task, particularly when helping children in the writing sessions.

### Listening Comprehension

Individual story recall following group storybook reading was used to illuminate problems children had in reconstructing important story information, a task which was studied by Mason, Peterman, and Kerr (1988). Children were also occasionally asked to repeat sentences the teacher has said, which suggested how familiar children were with varying types of sentence structures and phrases. This task as well as asking children to define words was used by Mason and Dunning (1986) to indicate the extent to which children were organizing meaningful information effectively.

The teachers working with Stewart were encouraged to read storybooks several times and then have children retell or pretend-read the storybooks. Some also used the Peabody language activities, read-along book cassettes, and peer and group storybook reading.

### Writing and Composing

Stewart used two forms of writing tasks to determine children's understanding of writing and their attempts at writing. Children were asked what they write at home and to write something for the examiner and tell what it said. They were then asked to tell how they were learning to write and/or how they knew what to write. Responses to these questions provided evidence of levels of development of children's writing. Children at a low level drew without labeling their picture or write isolated letters with no explanation. At the next level, they drew and labeled one or more letters or words. At the third level, they wrote a connected statement or idea. Those at a high level wrote sentences and connected their ideas.

The teachers were helped to utilize the discussion of the Morning Message and children's writing assessment responses for their instructional writing program. Stewart helped them to distinguish children's writing based on what they wrote in connection with its meaningfulness. Teachers used a four-phase writing activity: prewriting (discussion of a topic and sharing of ideas among children with the teacher's help), writing (drawing, scribbling, or letter and word construction, with the form chosen by the children), teacher conferencing (teacher helps and discusses the writing with each child), and sharing (children share what they have written with the class).

Teachers relied on their assessments of children's writing to tailor instruction for children. One teacher, for example, provided children with a clue of a letter sound in the word they wrote. The conferencing allowed the teacher to nudge the child toward a higher level of phonetic awareness. Sharing time allowed children to reveal their story to peers and lead a discussion about what they wrote. The teacher usually guided the discussion and, when necessary, assisted the child in reading the message. Teachers noted that it was important not to pressure children. Often a child who could write would simply decide to draw on one day and write sentences on another. This means that multiple measures of writing are required to achieve a reliable measure.

Because the teachers did not add writing to their program until the second year, they were very excited about the effects that writing had on their children's progress. With only four months of writing experience (writing was begun in January of the kindergarten year), many children were able to write with only a little help. Never before had these teachers expected children to write in kindergarten: copying letters, words, and sentences as a penmanship exercise had been the norm. By the end of the school year, however, most of the children could write in sentences or label pictures they had drawn and could even accurately describe what they had written. Children not in the writing program, by contrast, could at most write down names of some of the characters from their reading book. Teachers also commented that the writing program was favorably received by parents. One remarked, "Clive had started hating reading. Probably because we drilled him so much on phonics before he went to kindergarten. But now that he is writing, he likes reading. We are so pleased."

## CONCLUSION

It is our position that assessment instruments can foster curricular decision making, and when they do, they can play a valuable role in the classroom. In our exploration of its use in the classroom, however, we believe that the key is dynamic assessment. Coordinated with a wider range of measures, including informally administered tasks and more flexible scoring techniques, teachers can improve their teaching. Currently, many assessment instruments convey important information for teachers, but some involve quite complex approaches for administration, and others require fine distinctions for judging children's responses, either of which could lead to unreliable judgment decisions in scoring. Thus, more work is needed to make the instruments more accessible to teachers.

We believe that emergent literacy can be assessed with the four clusters of concepts we explained, namely, concepts and functions of literacy, knowledge of letters and words, listening comprehension and word understanding, and writing and composing. These provide a range of information that can be adapted for curricular decision making. Our use of an assessment instrument in a hard-to-teach setting provides a tough way to evaluate this framework, though which measures are most useful, and which are interesting but not necessary for effective curricular decision-making, ought to be considered in future research.

Among the other questions that must be addressed are the following: When developing assessment instruments that meet teachers' instructional needs, what information should test makers provide so that teachers might reliably interpret children's responses? Does the notion of clusters of concepts for assessment meet this need? To what extent will a task measure the same ability under a dynamic assessment procedure and under a more formal testing situation? Will the former always provide more useful information to the teacher? If not, why?

In this chapter we have described tasks that can be used to measure emergent literacy and have explained how teachers can use the underlying concepts to initiate and adjust their instruction. These tasks can provide valid information for teachers so that they might analyze young children's processes of thinking and reasoning as they begin to read and write. But will teachers use them appropriately? Perhaps the key is in the dynamic nature of instruction. One cannot test a child and use the response as something static, unchanging, impervious to the social context of instruction. Teachers will find the information obtained from assessment instruments only as valuable as their interactions with the children. Thus, with changes toward dynamic assessment and instruction, it will be the child and teacher together who ultimately coordinate improvements in the learning environment.

## REFERENCES

APPLEBEE, A. N. (1980). Children's narratives: New directions. *The Reading Teacher, 34,* 137–42.

CALFEE, R. C. (1987). The school as a context for assessment of literacy. *Reading Teacher, 40,* 738–743.

CAMPIONE, J. C., & BROWN, A. L. (1987). Linking dynamic assessment with school achievement. In C. S. Lidz (Ed.), *Dynamic assessment,* pp. 82–115. New York: Guilford.

CARROLL, J. B., DAVIES, P., & RICHMAN, B. (1971). *The American Heritage word frequency book.* Boston: Houghton Mifflin.

CLAY, M. (1979). *Reading: The patterning of complex behavior.* Portsmouth, NH: Heinemann.

CLAY, M. (1985). *Early detection of reading difficulties* (3rd ed.). Portsmouth, NH: Heinemann.

DICKINSON, D. K., & SNOW, C. S. (1987). Interrelationships among prereading and oral language skills in kindergartners from two social classes. *Early Childhood Research Quarterly, 2,* 1–25.

DOBSON, L. (1989). Connections in learning to write and read: A study of children's development through kindergarten and grade one. In J. M. Mason (Ed.), *Reading and writing connections.* Needham Heights, MA: Allyn & Bacon.

EGAN, K. (1987). Literacy and the oral foundations of education. *Harvard Educational Review, 57,* 445–472.

EHRI, L. (1983). Beginning reading: Summaries and critique. In L. Gentile, M. Kamil, & J. Blanchard (Eds.), *Reading research revisited.* Columbus, OH: Charles E. Merrill.

EHRI, L. (1989). Movement into word reading and spelling. In J. M. Mason (Ed.), *Reading and writing connections.* Needham Heights, MA: Allyn & Bacon.

FARR, R., & CAREY, R. F. (1986). *Reading: What can be measured?* Newark, DE: International Reading Association.

FERREIRO, E., & TEBEROSKY, A. (1982). *Literacy before schooling.* Portsmouth, NH: Heinemann.

GATES, A., BONE, G., & RUSSELL, D. (1939). *Methods of determining reading readiness.* New York: Columbia Teachers College.

GENISHI, C., & DYSON, A. H. (1984). *Language assessment in the early years.* Norwood, NJ: Ablex.

HARDY, M., STENNETT, R., & SMYTHE, P. (1974). Development of auditory and visual language concepts and relationship to instructional strategies in kindergarten. *Elementary English, 51,* 525–532.

HARSTE, J. C., WOODWARD, V. A., & BURKE, C. L. (1984). *Language stories and literacy lessons.* Portsmouth, NH: Heinemann.

HIEBERT, E. (1981). Developmental patterns and interrelationships of preschool children's print awareness. *Reading Research Quarterly, 16,* 236–260.

HOLDAWAY, D. (1979). *The Foundations of Literacy.* Gosford, AUS: Ashton-Scholastic.

JENSEN, J. M. (1984). *Composing and comprehending.* Urbana, IL: NCTE/ERIC.

JOHNS, J. (1984). Students' perceptions of reading: Insights from research and pedagogical implications. In J. Downing & R. Valtin (Eds.), *Language awareness and learning to read.* New York: Springer-Verlag.

JOHNSTON, P. (1987). Teachers as evaluation experts. *Reading Teacher, 40,* 744–748.

KING, M. (1989). Speech to writing: Children's growth in writing potential. In J. M. Mason (Ed.), *Reading and writing connections.* Needham Heights, MA: Allyn & Bacon.

LINN, R. L. (1988). State-by-state comparisons of achievement: Suggestions for enhancing validity. *Educational Researcher, 17,* 6–9.

LOMAX, R. G., & MCGEE, L. M. (1987). Young children's concepts about print and reading: Toward a model of word reading acquisition. *Reading Research Quarterly, 22,* 237–256.

LUNDBERG, I., FROST, J., & PETERSEN, O. (1988). Effects of an extensive program for stimulating phonological awareness in preschool children. *Reading Research Quarterly, 23,* 263–284.

MASON, J. (1980). When do children begin to read? *Reading Research Quarterly, 15,* 203–227.

MASON, J. (in press). Reading stories to preliterate children: A proposed connection to reading. In P. B. Gough (Ed.) *Reading acquisition.* Hillsdale, NJ: Erlbaum.

MASON, J., & DUNNING, D. (1986). *Proposing a model to relate pre-school home literacy with beginning reading achievement.* American Educational Research Association Convention, San Francisco.

MASON, J., & KERR, B. (1988). Transmission of literacy to young children. Paper presentation at the annual CORR preconvention of the International Reading Association, Toronto.

MASON, J., & MCCORMICK, C. (1979). *Testing the development of reading and linguistic awareness* (Tech. Rep. No. 26). Champaign: University of Illinois, Center for the Study of Reading.

MASON, J., MCCORMICK, C., & BHAVNAGRI, N. (1986). How are you going to help me learn? Lesson negotiations between a teacher and preschool children. In D. Yaden & S. Templeton (Eds.), *Metalinguistic awareness and beginning literacy*. Portsmouth, NH: Heinemann.

MASON, J., PETERMAN, C., & KERR, B. *Fostering comprehension by reading books to kindergarten children* (Technical Report). Urbana, IL: University of Illinois, Center for the Study of Reading.

MASON, J., & STEWART, J. (1989). *Early Childhood Screening and Diagnostic Instrument*. Chicago, IL.: American Testronics.

MCCORMICK, C., & MASON, J. (1986). *Use of little books at home: A minimal intervention strategy for fostering early reading* (Technical Report No. 388). Urbana, IL: University of Illinois, Center for the Study of Reading.

MCCORMICK, C., & MASON, J. (in press). *Little books*. Glenview, IL: Goodyear.

MORRIS, D. (1983). Concepts of word and phoneme awareness in the beginning reader. *Research in the Teaching of English, 17*, 359–373.

PETERMAN, C., & MASON, J. (1984). *Kindergarten children's perceptions of the forms of print in labeled pictures and stories*. Paper presented at National Reading Conference, St. Petersburg, FL.

PETRIE, H. G. (1987). Introduction to "evaluation and testing." *Educational Policy, 1*, 175–180.

PRAMLING, E. (1983). The child's conception of learning. *Göteborg Studies in Educational Sciences, 46*. Göteborg, Sweden: University of Göteborg.

READ, C. (1971). Preschool children's knowledge of English phonology. *Harvard Educational Review, 41*, 1–34.

SCHICKEDANZ, J. A. (1986). *More than the ABCs: The early stages of reading and writing*. Washington DC: National Association for the Education of Young Children.

SNOW, C. E., & NINIO, A. (1986). The contracts of literacy: What children learn from reading books. In W. H. Teale & E. Sulzby (Eds.), *Emergent literacy: Writing and reading*, pp. 116–138. Norwood, NJ: Ablex.

STANOVICH, K., CUNNINGHAM, A., & CRAMER, B. (1984). Assessing phonological awareness in kindergarten children: Issues of task comparability. *Journal of Experimental Child Psychology, 38*, 175–190.

STEWART, J. (1986). *A study of kindergarten children's awareness of how they are learning to read: Home and school perspectives*. Doctoral dissertation, University of Illinois, Champaign, Urbana (ERIC Document Reproduction Service, No. ED285 120).

SULZBY, E. (1983). *Children's emergent abilities to read favorite storybooks* (Final report to the Spencer Foundation). Evanston, IL: Northwestern University.

SULZBY, E. (1985). Children's emergent reading of favorite storybooks: A developmental study. *Reading Research Quarterly, 20*, 458–481.

SULZBY, E. (1989). Forms of writing and rereading from writing. In J. M. Mason (Ed.), *Reading and writing connections*. Needham Heights, MA: Allyn & Bacon.

TEALE, W., HIEBERT, E., & CHITTENDEN, E. (1987). Assessing young children's literacy development. *Reading Teacher, 40*, 772–777.

TEALE, W. H., & SULZBY, E. (1986). Emergent literacy as a perspective for examining how young children become writers and readers. In W. H. Teale and E. Sulzby (Eds.), *Emergent literacy: Writing and reading*. Norwood, NJ: Ablex.

VYGOTSKY, L. (1962). Thought and language. Cambridge, MA: MIT Press.

WATSON, R., & OLSON, D. R. (1987). From meaning to definition: A literate bias on the structure of word meaning. In R. Horowitz & S. J. Samuels (Eds.), *Comprehending oral and written language*, pp. 329–353. San Diego, CA: Academic Press.

YOPP, H. K. (1988). The validity and reliability of phonemic awareness tests. *Reading Research Quarterly, 23*, 159–177.

## AUTHOR NOTES

This chapter was based on work that was supported in part by OERI under cooperative agreement #OEG 0087-C1001 (University of Illinois) and (Rutgers University) Program #2-02315.

We would like to acknowledge the assistance of Dr. Linda White Benjamin of the University of the Virgin Islands. We are deeply grateful for the participation and enthusiasm shown by the administrators and teachers from the St. Thomas, V.I. School District. Special thanks to the following principals: Mr. Carver Farrow, Mrs. Carmen Lake, and Mrs. Valaria Wheatley and teachers: Mrs. Marysharon Marin, Ms. Regina Sapp, Mrs. Claire Simmonds, and Mrs. Delia Simmonds.

# 10

# THE CONSTRUCT OF EMERGENT LITERACY: PUTTING IT ALL TOGETHER

*Irene Athey*

Rutgers, The State University of New Jersey

### Abstract

Irene Athey's chapter summarizes the second part of this text, "Ways of Assessing Early Literacy in the Classroom." The author begins by placing the chapters in an historical perspective and reflecting upon them in light of current research and practice. Professor Athey then expands upon the ideas and examines their consequences for teachers and teaching.

This chapter will review the four papers that comprise the part on "Ways of Assessing Early Literacy in the Classroom" with additional comments by the author. Each of the papers is thought provoking in its own right and complementary to the other three. Together, they make a substantial contribution to the concept of emergent literacy.

## THE NEW CONTEXT FOR READING RESEARCH

Although reading research has a long and venerable tradition spanning almost 200 years, its progress has been marked by periods of rapid growth alternating with periods of relative stagnation (Venezky, 1984). While the middle decades of this century were characterized by a voluminous amount of research of a somewhat repetitious and inconclusive nature, the 1970s and 1980s have witnessed a resurgence of interest in the cognitive interactions between reader and text.    As a result, a corresponding acceleration in research productivity has ensued, adding considerably to our understanding of the reading process.

Two areas of inquiry have contributed to the burgeoning research literature of the past twenty years.  The first is the movement away from the earlier preoccupation with the mechanisms of decoding and a refocussing of attention on the complex cognitive processes involved in the comprehension of text (picking up on the earlier work of Huey, 1908; and Thorndike, 1917).  Schema theory, from which hypotheses concerning the related concepts of background knowledge and inferential thinking could be derived, was possibly the primary stimulus for this line of research, which has had far-reaching theoretical and practical implications.

A second, and more recent area of inquiry is the growth of the emergent literacy movement.  This relatively new field of study represents a long-overdue rapprochement among several hitherto independent disciplines; early childhood education, language development, and the psychology of reading, among others.  But this new area does more than integrate these formerly disparate disciplines.  From an educational standpoint, it creates, at least to some extent, a more appropriate balance among the language arts.  Writing, for example, has come into its own in the past two decades. As noted earlier, reading research has a long and impressive history; research into the writing process, by contrast, is of a more recent vintage, while research regarding listening and speaking is still quite sparse.  This neglect is all the more surprising when we consider that (1) students spend a large portion of their school hours listening and responding to teachers and other students, and (2) a prerequisite of learning to read is the realization that print is encoded speech (see Chapter 8).

In brief, then, early childhood education extending from birth to 7 or 8 years of age has been infused by a most salutary, if belated, recognition stemming from the cognitive movement in instruction that learning consists of the construction of meaning through assimilation of new information to the existing mental structures of the learner.  From this basic premise we can proceed one step further to allow that not only the receptive modes of language (listening and reading) but also the productive modes (speaking and writing) involve the construction of meaning.  This train of thought may lead the reader to infer that the language arts curriculum as a whole, and possibly each lesson in the curriculum, should contain a balance of listening, speaking, reading, and writing, all permeated by thinking in pursuit of the construction of meaning.  If this educational outcome becomes a reality, then research in emergent literacy will have made a substantial contribution indeed, both in bringing education under the aegis of the cognitive science movement, and also in laying the foundation for the cultural literacy reputedly so lacking in today's high school students (Ravitch & Finn, 1986; Kirsch & Jungeblut, 1986).

## THE ASSESSMENT OF EMERGENT LITERACY

Such a thoroughgoing revision of the preschool and elementary language arts curriculum must, of necessity, confront the issue of assessment.  As several of our authors point out, the ubiquity of the testing movement owes much to the demand for school reform and teacher accountability. Standardized tests are well suited to this goal, but, as Mason and Stewart (Chapter 9) note, the advantages of validity, reliability, and efficiency built into the construction of these tests make them inappropriate for other purposes such as continuous recording of individual students' progress and modification of instructional content or methods in response to insights gleaned from the test data. Morrow notes that the rapid growth of language skills in young children calls for much more frequent assessment than the typical annual evaluation by means of standardized reading tests. In answer to the question of how frequently assessment should occur, the current thinking as represented in these chapters appears to be leaning to the view that assessment should be *continuous, multifaceted,* and *radically different in kind* from that accorded by standardized tests. Continuity speaks to the need for frequent evaluation. The multifaceted nature of testing comes about by reason of the broader view of literacy described earlier. From the simple concept of reading as a composite of a few decoding skills plus literal comprehension, we have come (some would say "light years") to the more inclusive construct of literacy. Standardized reading tests were not developed with this construct in mind and hence are inadequate to the task of assessing the new construct. We need new, and radically different, tests for this construct.

It could be argued, of course, that the skills management systems were developed to answer these very criticisms. In the first place, they offer opportunities for frequent testing as the teacher sees the need for it. Second, by use of criterion-referenced tests, they permit the teacher to record individual student progress toward a predetermined goal. Third, by the inclusion of specific objectives and related outcome measures, they permit the construct (literacy) to be as broad as the test maker wishes. Fourth, if properly constructed, they incorporate those virtues of reliability, validity, and efficiency typically associated with standardized tests. Finally, they avoid the problem noted by Juel (Chapter 8) of misrepresenting the ability of individuals falling at the two extremes of the distribution.

## INTEGRATING ASSESSMENT AND INSTRUCTION

Why then will criterion-referenced tests systematically geared to instructional objectives not meet the assessment needs of the field of emergent literacy? Partly because, as Morrow (Chapter 7) points out, in measuring discrete skills, test makers frequently ignore crucial elements of literacy. Another possible reason is that, in the process of dissecting literacy into a finite number of discrete skills, its essential nature, which consists of the dynamic interplay of such skills, is lost.

It appears that the type of assessment that is being proposed by the present authors, while avoiding the problems associated with the formal global assessment afforded by standardized tests on the one hand and the semiformal discrete subskill measurement by criterion-referenced tests on the other, combines some of the advantages of each of these forms of assessment. It has the overwhelming advantages of the latter in being closely tied to instructional objectives and of providing data on individual student progress (telling us what a child needs to do to improve), but it is also efficient (being part and parcel of the instruction itself) and, given the amount of data it yields, can be easily made valid and reliable. But there are two other important advantages to the informal assessment techniques described in these pages. First, they are as easy to modify as the instruction itself. A perennial criticism of both norm- and criterion-referenced tests is that their construction is so costly as to preclude frequent revision, so that both the tests and the instructional content to which they are geared become "frozen" for long periods. By contrast, the informal tests constructed, administered, and interpreted by teachers are changeable at will. Moreover, they may sample a much broader range of behaviors than is provided by written responses alone. A second advantage is the consistency of contexts and roles between instruction and assessment. As Mason and Stewart (Chapter 9) note, by abstracting the tasks from the instructional contexts in which they were learned, formal testing situations change the nature of the task as well as alter the teacher's role from supportive to adversarial. Morrow (Chapter 7) suggests that whether or not a teacher provides prompts or elicits information by means of questions depends upon whether the purpose is instruction or assessment. Mason and Stewart, on the other hand, seem to be saying that each condition embodies its own means of both instruction and assessment. For example, it is not inappropriate, they aver, even during the administration of an instructional process test, for the teacher "to model the approach to the task and provide additional examples if children seem confused" (p. 6). This view, which appears eminently reasonable in light of the previous discussion, is clearly a departure from the traditional constraints on test administration.

All four chapters are, I think, extremely helpful in describing ways in which teachers can integrate instruction and assessment for the mutual improvement of both areas. It is fortunate, in light of our earlier comments, that they include all four modes of oral/written and receptive/productive language: listening and speaking (Morrow, Chapter 7), reading (Juel, Chapter 9), and writing (Sulzby, Chapter 6).

Assessment experts have long recognized that the type of question appearing on a test changes not only the difficulty of the item but also the processes involved in arriving at an answer. We know, for example, that students go about answering a true-false question differently than a multiple-choice item, both of which involve recognition and are different in kind from, say, open-ended questions that require reconstruction. Few, if any, standardized tests call for the kind of memory and reasoning process involved in reconstructing a complete narrative. Morrow's (Chapter 7) work is highly interesting in this regard. It recognizes that the ability to use the various modes of language follows no strict sequence in its development, since the four modes depend on and reinforce one another, so that even young children are capable of such complex tasks as recapturing the central theme, reconstructing sequences of events, and inferring characters' motivations and actions in a story. She notes that, through the medium of dialogue, teachers can detect improvement over time in a number of skills such as children's ability to bring their own background knowledge to bear in attempting to understand particular aspects of a story or in their ability to assume various roles while trying to understand the motivations, assumptions, and so on of different protagonists. I think there are many other insights an astute teacher can gain from observing and drawing out children's comments in the context of story dialogue. It is clear that children make judgments about the motives and actions of the characters and compare them with their own. For example, Chris's comments reveal that he takes a poor view of the animals' behavior and maintains that his own responses would be different (Chapter 7, p. 123). In making this value judgment, the teacher's prompts and questions can help him to explore the reasons for such decisions and ultimately to formulate some general principles of behavior that can be applied in other circumstances.

It is also noteworthy that, in asking questions, scaffolding, keeping the discussion on track, and so on, the teacher is modeling the appropriate techniques and conventions that characterize an intelligent and mutually informative conversational style. Through their cooperative dialogue, the children are learning such important techniques as (1) carrying the discussion forward or to a higher level (Cazden, 1985), (2) formulating questions in ways most calculated to obtain an answer (Wilkinson & Spinelli, 1983), (3) evaluating and, where necessary, deferring to others' opinions, (4) passing the "conversational ball" at appropriate points in the discussion, (5) digressing only for clarification and returning thereafter to the main theme, and (6) probably many others. As previously noted, none of these abilities can be assessed by traditional assessment methods.

The pioneer work in this area of retelling stories was done by Bartlett (1932), primarily as a means of studying the effects of prior knowledge on memory as manifested through the retelling of stories from an alien culture. Bartlett identified the by now familiar processes of nonassimilation, distortion, or inappropriate elaboration of information that failed to fit the listener's existing mental structures. Similarly, teachers can use the retelling of stories to reveal and correct students' misconceptions, their failure to recognize the importance of certain information, or their passive acceptance of information even though it violates their own experience. These kinds of initiatives by teachers would seem to be especially useful in classrooms that house great numbers of students from cultures unlike the white middle-class culture represented in many children's stories.

The wealth of data provided by continuous assessment of student behaviors such as those described earlier can be overwhelming, even if systematically recorded. Morrow's checklist (Chapter 7) is useful in providing teachers with a readily available and easy-to-use schedule. It is also suggestive of ways teachers might construct their own checklists and other recording instruments for other literary skills. Only through the use of informal measures like these can the vast amount of information on each child be reduced to manageable proportions.

The more teachers know about the development of literacy in young children, the better equipped they will be to observe, record, and interpret children's literary productions. The Juel and Sulzby chapters (6 and 8) are very informative in providing research data showing the types of behaviors that precede and contribute to the attainment of conventional reading and writing. Juel's (Chapter 8) articulation of the various prerequisites to learning the code—itself a necessary precursor of reading—is particularly helpful for parents who, though well intentioned, are at a loss to know the best ways of preparing their children for the kind of literacy tasks they will encounter in school. While many parents probably realize intuitively that children must recognize the communicative function of print, it is probably less obvious to them that children need not only to abstract the print from the total stimulus situations (the word "McDonald's" from the golden arches, etc.) but to acquire alphabetical understanding, that is, that the word is comprised of letters and can also be segmented phonemically. Parents, no doubt, are delighted when their child points from the car window and utters the magic word "McDonald's," but they probably do not realize that alphabetic understanding will come about only as a result of many "data pairings," to use Juel's terminology. Nor can we expect children to pay attention to the phonetic cues provided in print unless they have first understood that print is encoded speech.

Similarly, Juel's (Chapter 8) identification and elaboration of the stages of reading provide a useful guideline for teachers, for whom assessment, she points out, must consist of the two basic questions: the stage the child has reached and the prerequisites for moving on to the next stage. Both instruction and further assessment can then be tailored to helping each student gain the necessary insights to proceed to the next stage.

There are certain parallels between Juel's (Chapter 8) paper and that of Sulzby (Chapter 6). Although the latter also enumerates various "stages" of writing, they are not stages in the generally accepted sense of the word, but rather different *forms* of writing that are dominant at different times. If all these forms are not preserved and carried into the child's later writing, the subsequent repertoire of expressive forms is unnecessarily limited. It follows, as Mason and Stewart (Chapter 9) assert, that a reliable and valid measure of writing must include multiple measures of writing. Given the close relationship between instruction and assessment advocated in these pages, it follows that teachers will then begin to teach a broader repertoire of writing abilities.

It has already been noted that "informal testing permits observation and interpretation of behaviors that would not be tapped in a standardized test, but are nonetheless relevant to assessment of the child's understanding." Most evident among these behaviors are errors in speaking, reading, writing, and spelling. Some of these errors are based on children's incorrect hypotheses (e.g., Mason and Stewart's (Chapter 9) example of a child's belief that word lists were based on meaning rather than sound or spelling) that teachers can readily correct if they are aware of them. As Mason and Stewart point out, the nature of these errors can be more revealing than the number or type of items answered correctly in elucidating ways children use to arrive at answers. Task responses are also indicative of personality dispositions, such as the willingness to take risks. (The Wechsler intelligence scales, as their author once pointed out, are also to some extent personality measures.) Again, the teacher can help students in appropriate ways on the basis of such information. Sulzby includes among such important, but rarely assessed, behaviors the metalinguistic speech accompanying the composing process (or, indeed, any other literary activities) and the rereading attendant on writing connected discourse. As these authors point out, even the information patterns children use during reading and writing can provide information about the process of constructing meaning as this process occurs.

While the papers reviewed so far in this chapter concentrate on defining and elaborating specific aspects of literacy, Mason and Stewart's chapter adopts a more inclusive approach of the type that has served well in previous attempts to define a hitherto unmeasured construct, e.g., Binet's (1905) initial attempts to define intelligence through enumeration of various kinds of intelligent behavior. An initial survey of this type must err on the side of including abilities that may later be discarded rather than risk the danger of excluding important aspects prematurely. Mason and Stewart have been quite comprehensive in developing their construct of emergent literacy to include a wide range of abilities which they then reduce to four major categories: concepts and (understanding the) functions of literacy, knowledge of letters and words, language comprehension, and writing and composing. A variety of suggestions for ways to test these abilities informally is provided. It may be noted in passing that the four modes enumerated earlier—listening, speaking, reading, and writing—are all represented in the construct as evolved by Mason and Stewart. While recognizing the possibility that reliability and validity may be sacrificed in the interest of continuous, informal assessment, these authors conclude that the way out of this dilemma is to pay close attention to test directions and to train teachers more thoroughly in techniques of observation, recording, and interpretation. It will be interesting to see how well future informal tests will achieve acceptable standards of reliability and validity while preserving such features as teacher modeling and support seen as advantages of this form of testing.

Whatever helps the teacher to improve instruction and assessment also helps those persons involved in the training and evaluation of student teachers. Just as teachers can learn to observe and interpret children's learning from their behavior, so supervisors can become more sensitive to such interpretive behavior on the part of student teachers and can guide them toward improved performance.

Increasing teachers' awareness and sensitivity to the nuances and possibilities of instructional situations thus becomes the major task of teacher education at both preservice and in-service levels. As teachers become more proficient, they can provide new insights into children's cognitive processing and can suggest additional ways of demonstrating their competencies. For example, Mason and Stewart observe that, in exploring children's concepts of literacy, teachers learn a great deal about literacy events in the home and that greater parental cooperation and greater freedom for the children to engage in such events tends to follow as a result.

Informal assessment may well reduce the traditional gulf between school and college. As teachers become more proficient, they can further researchers' understanding of children's cognitive processing and can suggest additional ways of demonstrating their competencies.

As a final comment, we may note that the integration of instruction and assessment that is occurring in the emergent literacy movement restores to teachers the evaluation component that should be an inherent part of the instructional process, thereby enhancing the sense of professionalism that is the right of every teacher.

## REFERENCES

BARTLETT, F. C. (1932). *Remembering*. Cambridge: Cambridge University Press.

BINET, A. (1905). A propos de la mesure de l'intelligence. *Année Psychologique, 11,* 69–82.

CAZDEN, C. (1985). Adult assistance to language development: Scaffolds, models and direct instruction. In R. P. Parker & F. Davies (Eds.), *Young children's use of language.* Newark, DE: International Reading Association.

HUEY, E. B. (1908). *The psychology and pedagogy of reading*. Cambridge, MA: MIT Press.

KIRSCH, I. S. & JUNGEBLUT, A. (1986). *Literacy: Profiles of America's young adults*. Princeton, NJ: National Assessment of Educational Progress.

RAVITCH, D. & FINN, C. E. (1986). *What 17-year-olds know*. Washington, DC: Department of Education.

THORNDIKE, E. L. (1917). Reading as reasoning: A study of mistakes in paragraph reading. *Journal of Educational Psychology, 24,* 220–234.

VENEZKY, R. L. (1984). The history of reading research. In P. D. Pearson (Ed.), *Handbook of reading research*, pp. 3–38. New York: Longman.

WILKINSON, L. C., & SPINELLI, F. (1983). Using requests effectively in peer-directed instructional groups. *American Educational Research Journal, 20,* 4479–4501.

# 11

# SOCIOLINGUISTIC STUDIES OF CLASSROOM COMMUNICATION: IMPLICATIONS FOR INFORMAL ASSESSMENT

*Louise Cherry Wilkinson*
*Rutgers, The State University of New Jersey*

**Abstract**

Louise Cherry Wilkinson considers the contribution that sociolinguistic research on classroom communication already has made, and potentially can make, to the assessment of literacy abilities of school children. A review of theoretical and empirical work is presented, as well as a discussion of the implications of this work for informal assessment. The chapter includes a discussion of descriptive tools that can be used systematically to study student's language usage.

Adequate assessment of children's literacy abilities should include an analysis of their use of language in typical situations. The approach taken here, nonformal assessment, refers to methods based on direct observation and/or documentation both by the school personnel that children typically encounter and by the nonschool personnel who examine children in school, their language, and their environments. The use of formal assessment instruments (e.g., tests) needs to be supplemented by noticing, hearing and seeing, what children do with and by means of language in school. Assessment is a way of obtaining information about a child and relating that information to the instructional practices in which the child participates, the teaching and learning environments that constitute the child's school experience, and individual differences among children. It can include a variety of methods and can be continuous over the course of the school year. It involves periodic collection of information, as for example tape recordings of children's oral language to note changes in the use of language and/or grammar. Using these methods leads us to a more complete picture of each child's strengths, weaknesses, capacities, and abilities for language.

The purpose of the present chapter is to consider the contribution that sociolinguistic research on classroom communication already has made, and potentially can make, to the assessment of literacy abilities of school children. A review of theoretical and empirical work will be presented, as well as a discussion of the implications of this work for nonformal assessment. Specifically, the concluding section of the chapter will include a discussion of descriptive tools that can be used to study students' language usage systematically. The chapter begins with an overview and definition of the sociolinguistic approach to communicating and teaching in classrooms. A review of the authors' research on one language function central to classroom communication, the request function, will be presented to illustrate the potential application of sociolinguistic research to assessment.

## THE LEGACY OF SOCIOLINGUISTIC STUDIES

In the early 1970s, a tradition of educational research arose that focused on language used by teachers and students in classrooms. This tradition has been referred to as a sociolinguistic approach (Wilkinson, 1982a, b). Essentially, this approach is defined as description of students' and teachers' use of language in the classroom as it spontaneously occurs. Initially, the hope was that these descriptions, by themselves, would provide understanding of life in classrooms, revealing the diversity of students and the complexity of communication. Some believed that these descriptions could serve as reference points for the improvement and/or evaluation of specific educational programs. In addition, some believed that these descriptions could serve as a source of new ideas for investigating the processes of teaching and learning.

Until the appearance of sociolinguistic studies, classroom research was dominated by the process-product tradition, which focused on relationships between teachers' and students' behavior (e.g., teacher praise, higher-order questions) and academic outcomes for students (mainly achievement as measured by students' performance on standardized tests (e.g., Dunkin & Biddle, 1974)). One of the most important consequences for educational research of the early sociolinguistic studies was to challenge the ways by which classroom processes were studied by the process-product researchers. Many systems for coding teachers' and students' behavior in classrooms were developed by process-product researchers, with the Flanders (1970) being one of the first and most widely used. These systems were not specifically focused on language or linguistic categories per se. All used a priori categories, and many were highly inferential, which required the researcher to make complex decisions about the meaning of behavior on the spot. As a result, attempts were made to encapsulate classroom processes into tables of frequency counts of teachers' and students' behaviors. Gender, cultural, ethnic, and social class diversity was not a specific feature typically built into the design of studies. The focus of these studies was on the basic principles of teaching and learning without concern for diversity among students.

Almost two decades have elapsed since the publication of the first volume that brought together sociolinguistic research on classroom communication (*Functions of Language in the Classroom,* edited by Cazden, John, & Hymes, 1972). Since then, a great deal of activity has been stimulated by this approach in a relatively short period of time. Numerous studies have been conducted, some of which have been published in widely circulated, peer-reviewed journals in education, psychology, linguistics, anthropology, and sociology. Several reviews of selected research in this area have already appeared (e.g., Cazden, 1988; Green & Smith, 1983), including volumes that have synthesized work across disciplines (e.g., Wilkinson, 1982a).

## SOCIOLINGUISTIC STUDIES OF CLASSROOM COMMUNICATION: THE FOCUS

Sociolinguistic studies focus on communication of school-age children and their teachers in a variety of classroom situations, including some that may attempt to mimic those "real" situations in more restricted, experimental ones (e.g., Cohen 1984; Cooper, Marquis, & Ayers-Lopez, 1982). Because research considered to be under this rubric has been generated within a variety of disciplinary perspectives (education, linguistics, psychology, sociology, anthropology) and across disciplines, generalizations about guiding theoretical assumptions and consequent methodological practices are somewhat problematical. For example, psychologists have investigated individual differences in language use and communication (e.g., Wilkinson & Calculator, 1982; Wilkinson & Spinelli, 1983; Cooper, Marquis, & Ayers-Lopez, 1982), linguists have studied the development of some communicative functions of some primary school children (e.g., Griffin & Shuy, 1978); sociologists have studied the regulation of social order through communicative processes such as turn taking and attentional norms (e.g., Eder, 1982; Merritt, 1982); educators have studied the organization of formal activities such as the lesson (e.g., Green & Wallat, 1981; Mehan, 1979), and anthropologists have investigated verbal and nonverbal aspects of communicating within and between cultural groups (e.g., Erickson & Shultz, 1982; Florio & Shultz, 1979).

Despite the apparent diversity of even these few studies that are cited here, there are some commonalities throughout the corpus of sociolinguistic research. Virtually all researchers studied processes and patterns of language and communication as they occur spontaneously. Differences in communication which are associated with selected social variables, such as gender, ethnicity, and social class, are examined. Developmental differences also are examined, but the emphasis is upon age as a social role, not chronological age per se.

## ASSUMPTIONS UNDERLYING SOCIOLINGUISTIC APPROACHES

Several assumptions underlie sociolinguistic approaches to the study of language and communication in classrooms: (1) that communicative competence in school involves knowing about both the structure of language and the functions of language in classrooms; (2) that the classroom is a unique communicative context that makes unique demands on the use of language; and (3) that students differ in competence and in how they use language appropriately and effectively in classrooms (Wilkinson, 1982b). Each of these assumptions will be examined in turn.

### Assumption: Competence Includes Both the Structure and Function of Language

Knowledge of language structure, grammar, is largely developed by the time children enter school, yet knowledge of language functions, pragmatics, continues to develop all throughout the school years. Indeed, some have argued that development continues well into adulthood. To be able to participate in all classroom activities, students must develop a special competence; this involves both the production and the interpretation of language and nonverbal communicative behaviors. According to Mehan (1979), students

> must know with whom, when and where they can speak and act, and they must provide the speech and behavior that are appropriate for given classroom situation. Students must also be able to relate behavior, both academic and social, to varying classroom situations by interpreting implicit classroom rules. (p. 133)

The competence referred to here must be viewed as an end in itself, that is a set of rules that must be learned by students so that they can understand and participate in what is going on in classrooms. In addition, the competence must also be viewed as a means of attaining other educational objectives. Failing to understand or participate in classroom communication can preclude students learning the academic content of those communications.

One example of the consequences of not participating effectively in school activities can be seen in the work of Heath (1982). From her description of the language used by black children and their teachers in a southern, rural community, we have a sense of the educational and language problems presented by the children. In the following excerpt, one teacher articulates the communicative inadequacy of students in her class:

> They don't seem to be able to answer even the simplest questions. I would almost think some of them have a hearing problem; it is as though they don't hear me ask a question. I get blank stares to my questions. Yet when I am making statements or telling stories which interest them, they always seem to hear me. The simplest questions are the ones they can't answer in the classroom; yet on the playground, they can explain a rule for a ballgame or describe a particular kind of bait with no problem. Therefore, I know they can't be as dumb as they seem in my class. I sometimes feel that when I look at them and ask a question, I'm staring at a wall I can't break through. There's something there;

yet in spite of all the questions I ask, I'm never sure I've gotten through to what's inside the wall. (Heath, 1982, pp. 107-108)

## Assumption: The Communicative Demands of Classrooms

A second assumption underlying sociolinguistic approaches is that the classroom is a unique context, with specific demands regarding the way language is used to communicate effectively. There is undoubtedly a significant degree of overlap between the way language is used in preschool and elementary classrooms, and the home. For example, the purpose of a large majority of teacher-student talk in school is to facilitate the acquisition of academic information by students. In addition, research has shown that parent-child communication is focused on information exchange during the early years (e.g., Ervin-Tripp, 1977; Cherry, 1979). One difference between home and school contexts, however, is that in school, exchanges between teachers and students typically take place during lessons and students' responses are evaluated more frequently and a more formal way in school (Cherry, 1978).

Examples of the formality of lessons can be found in the work of several researchers (e.g., Cherry, 1978; Sinclair and Coulthard, 1975; Griffin and Shuy, 1978; and Mehan, 1979). These analyses show that classroom lessons have a distinct organization, characterized by communicative units of increasing size. The most central unit, from an instructional viewpoint, consists of communicative sequences between teachers and students, which in turn, consist of an initiation by the teacher (I), a response by the student (R), and a follow-up by the teacher (F) (Cherry, 1978). In the work of Griffin and Shuy (1978) and Cherry (1978), the next organizational level identified is the topical sequence, followed by phases of the lesson, and the entire lesson as the overarching structure. The following example is taken from a kindergarten lesson on trees; the first excerpt describes the lesson as whole, which lasted only 4 minutes. The basic sequence of the lesson includes determining various attributes of trees, including types of trees. Two verbatim excerpts follow, one example of the IRF sequence follows the other.

The class is gathered in a circle in front of the teacher. The teacher writes the word 'tree' on the board and asks if someone can read it. The teacher then asks the students to provide the names of things they think of when they think of "tree." The teacher writes appropriate responses on the board. The lesson ends when the teacher reads a story about trees. (Cherry, 1978, p. 19)

> TEACHER: Alright, Mary had her hand up. (I)
> MARY: Tree. (R)
> TEACHER: Tree we have. (F)
>
> TEACHER: Arthur. (I)
> ARTHUR: Cherrytree. (R)
> TEACHER: Cherrytree, alright. (F) (Cherry, 1978, p. 48)

Students must learn to read classroom events to participate effectively in school. Children have to learn the subtle cues that teachers give to signal changes in the lesson or his or her attention, such as just saying "Arthur" in the immediate example to call on that student, or in the previous sequence, referring to the fact that Mary had her hand up, presuming that Mary is indicating a desire to respond to the teacher's overall initiation.

The consequences of not learning how to read lessons can be far reaching for students. Not only will they be unable to take turns at talk and be unsuccessful in interacting with other students and teachers, they may be deprived of the opportunity to participate in classroom lessons. Thus, the discontinuities between the classroom context and other contexts may present special problems for some students, interfering with their development of communicative competence, and their overall adjustment to school. The effects of students' not knowing the "rules of the game," the standard ways of communicating in the classroom, are not limited to the obvious problems that these students face in their unsuccessful communications with students and teachers. In addition to such immediate problems, if some children do not understand the classroom and its unique communicative demands, then they may learn little from the classroom experiences in which they participate. Furthermore, accurate assessment of their achievement is unlikely, since access to their knowledge is predicted upon optimal communicative performance.

### Assumption: Students Differ in Communicative Competence

A third assumption is that students differ in communicative competence, particularly in aspects that are central to classroom activities such as responding appropriately to teachers' questions. These uses of language are not necessarily taught by teachers or learned by all students. Certainly, children come to elementary school already knowing something about using language, and they have certain expectations about classrooms because of preschool experiences. However, not all students may have learned all the "rules of the game." These students may experience a discontinuity between home and school.

One of the implications of this fact is that some children may have differential access to the school activities that catalyze learning. Learning is not the transfer of knowledge from teacher to student, from our point of view. Learning and development emerge from the highly complex interaction among teacher and students in a variety of school activities, all of which involve communication. The extent to which children participate in school activities that involve communication, such as reading aloud, question and answer exchanges with teachers, and receiving evaluation of their narratives from teachers, will determine their access to learning to a significant degree. From this point of view, then, the educational failure of some students may be caused in part by differences in the communicative patterns between students and teachers who come from different cultural backgrounds.

One example of cultural differences between students and their teachers can be seen in the work of Michaels (1986), who investigated black and white elementary children's production of narratives during "sharing time," a classroom activity during which teachers call on students to share stories with the class. Michaels found that black and white children differed in the style of topical development of their stories, and their narratives were differentially evaluated by teachers. White children produced *topic-centered* narratives, which focus on a single object or event, while black children tended to produce *episodic* narratives, which focus on multiple objects and events. The stories of the black students were more likely to be negatively evaluated by their teachers, and one of the implications of this work is that stylistic differences can be misconstrued and not understood by teachers. Cazden (1988) comments that many factors may influence teachers' decisions about evaluation of ongoing communicative performance of students, such as the amount of time available for activities such as sharing time and teachers' goals for such activities. She notes that *episodic* narratives tend to be longer than *topic-centered* narratives, and the connections among multiple topics and other students' knowledge may be limited, thus rendering *episodic* narratives more difficult to assimilate into the ongoing lesson goals of teachers in class. Nevertheless, the role of teachers in facilitating the development of communicative competence and in resolving miscommunication is critical. Their decisions affect the opportunities that students have to develop academic achievement and communicative competence.

## SOCIOLINGUISTIC STUDIES: DESCRIPTIVE METHODOLOGY

All sociolinguistic studies employ descriptive tools, which are used by observers to obtain a verbatim account of the actual language used, along with a detailed description of the context within which the language use occurs. Observers are typically concerned with identifying a developing process and/or a pattern of behavior, such as the IRF (initiation-response-follow up) sequence described by Cherry (1978). The hallmark of descriptive tools as they are applied to language is that stream of talk and accompanying action are recorded in everyday language, which is sometimes supplemented by additional symbol systems, such as dance notation or graphic symbols that capture what is going on in addition to the language (e.g., Erickson, 1982). Although there are many kinds of descriptive tools, the key aspect of descriptive tools is the use of transcriptions of audio and video recordings of the actual talk. Thus, descriptive tools, by necessity, involve the written records of audio and visual recordings, and analysis of these transcriptions occurs retrospectively, not on-line.

Descriptive tools are characterized by key elements. First, they depend on the use of some technology, such as audio or video taping as the basis for transcription. The initial step in using descriptive tools is to make a good-quality recording for transcription. The second step is the transcription of the audio and video records into everyday language, which may be supplemented by other notation, as needed. Third, some descriptive tools specify predetermined categories, such as the kinds of requests for help, into which language is coded, while other descriptive tools allow the categories to emerge from the data. Descriptive tools are used for retrospective analysis, which is derived from audio and visual recording. This kind of analysis allows the observer to note patterns and sequences of talk that may occur very fast in real time and may elude even the most perceptive clinician. Recordings and transcriptions allow for the infinite retrievability of the actual speech as it occurs in real time. In addition, multiple analyses are possible; the observer can analyze the syntax, the speech function, the lexicon, the paralinguistic cues, among other dimensions, when using transcription and recordings. Finally, descriptive tools incorporate a knowledge of the context within which the recordings are made, so that interpretation can be as accurate and complete as possible. There are many systems used to describe the context within which language is used and recorded.

The following excerpt ("What's that word?") from a transcription of the author's work illustrates the use of a descriptive tool to capture the ways that children use language to request help. This example is a central communication among three first grade students who have been instructed to "help each other" in their reading groups while the teacher is working with another group. In this example, we see how one student, Amy, demonstrates through the use of langauge, a strategy to enlist the help of a reluctant, if knowledgeable, student, Dave. Amy has been successful in obtaining help from Dave in doing her assignment in the previous 15 exchanges between the two of them. Amy shifts her attention to another student, Joe, in an attempt to enlist his help. Joe does not provide assistance, and Amy shifts her attention back to Dave, by requesting his help in providing the answer to a particular question. At first, Dave hesitates and resists Amy's initial request, which is interrupted by Joe also requesting the answer. However, Amy persists, and Dave eventually gives in to the pressure and provides the answer. Both Dave and Amy continue to work together on the assignment, which consists of Amy requesting information and action from Dave, who provides both.

> AMY:   Ok, what, what's that word?
> JOE:   Don't ask me.
> AMY:   I'll ask him. What's that word (to Dave)?
> JOE:   Dave, do you know what we should write, like here?
> AMY:   Right here. (several seconds elapse)
> I want you to look at my paper. (several seconds elapse)
> Listen to this.
> I've got these words.
> I keep gettin mixed up, Dave.
> Dave, I keep gettin
> DAVE:   r, the the (the words requested by Amy are provided by Dave).
> (Wilkinson and Calculator, 1982, p. 97)

As the preceding example illustrates, descriptive tools can be used effectively to provide detailed records of what was said and done in a given situation at a given moment. The analyses of the transcriptions can provide insights that may not be gleaned merely by listening in to communication among students.

### Children's Production of Requests

In this section, several studies of children's production of requests will be discussed. The ability to make requests and receive adequate responses from others is essential to the teaching and learning processes in classrooms. The studies to be discussed concern several issues: the relationship between language forms and the request function, the ability to obtain appropriate responses to requests, and the relationship between the production of requests and reading achievement (in the school-age studies). Individual differences, including those that are age related, cultural, and individual, are addressed in these studies.

*Preschool children production of requests.*   The idea that one can use a variety of different language forms to convey the same communicative function is an aspect of competence that develops early. For example, consider the request for action. Any one of the following different forms can be used to convey the intention to a listener: "Give me a pencil." "I need a pencil." "Can I have a pencil?" In addition, some recent work on children's comprehension of requests for action provides evidence that, very early, children use available cues for context to understand intention and adjust their messages to meet the demands of specific situations (Shatz, 1978). Taken together, these studies suggest that young children possess an extensive repertoire of forms to convey the request function of language, and children are able to differentiate these forms according to a variety of contextual variables, such as the age or familiarity of the listener and the listener's probability of providing an appropriate response.

Read and Cherry (1978) conducted a study to examine the extent of the preschool child's communicative competence in producing requests for action. In a group of monolingual English-speaking preschool children, it was expected that there would be individual differences in production of requests for action: that children of different ages (2-, 3-, and 4-years-old) would not differ in the quantity of the requests produced but that they would differ in the quality of requests produced, that is, in the initial choice and subsequent revision of requests. The task was introduced to each child as a game that he or she was going to play with the Cookie Monster, a popular character from the television show "Sesame Street," and the experimenter, a game in which the child was to request the puppet to provide a desired object, juice, a cookie, or a crayon. A series of interactions resulted in the children's producing a sequence of requests when the puppet failed to provide the action requested. The requests were transcribed and coded according to the following categories: gestural (nonlexical nonverbal), imperative (command forms that are not embedded), embedded imperative (interrogative forms containing a modal verb), declarative statements (declarative statements with request, intention, and utterances that name the desired object), "please" standing alone, and expression of want/need.

The results showed that older and younger children did not differ in their overall production of the number of requests (a .13 correlation with age, not statistically significant). The absence of developmental trend suggests that 2-year-olds already possess many ways to manipulate their environment just as older children do. A correlation of −.49 was obtained between age and number of gestural requests, whereas the production of embedded imperatives correlated +.56 with age. Thus, the data show individual differences in the quality but not in quantity of production. The data provide evidence that children from 2 to 4 years of age possess extensive and flexible repertoires of directive forms. Older children were less likely than younger ones to produce gestural requests but were much more likely to use the polite embedded imperative form as well as the impolite imperative form. Children in the study did not have the full linguistic means to express the request function of language; nevertheless, they conveyed nuances by varying their strategies and employing both their limited linguistic and nonlinguistic means.

The results of this study provide evidence that even very young children act in a socially competent way. Even though linguistic knowledge was incompletely developed, young children used nonverbal behavior as an adaptation to an environment that was not optimally responsive. Individual differences were apparent. These children all showed to varying degrees that they understood the use of vocal, verbal, and nonverbal communication to operate in a social world, to influence the behavior of another social being vis-à-vis the child's goal. Using language in this way to influence others is an aspect of communicative competence that shows continuity in development from the preverbal through the verbal years. The task and measures developed for this study could serve as the basis for a an assessment instrument.

*School-age children's production of requests: The effective speaker.*    In a subsequent line of research, we developed the concept of the *effective speaker,* who uses knowledge of language forms, functions, and contexts to achieve communicative goals (Wilkinson & Calculator, 1982; Wilkinson & Spinelli, 1983). For example, in the case of requests for action, effective speakers are successful in obtaining appropriate responses to their requests from listeners. We proposed the model of the effective speaker that characterizes the use of requests and responses by young children. Our model (see Table 1) identifies the following characteristics of requests that predict obtaining appropriate responses from listeners. First, speakers may express acts clearly and directly in an attempt to minimize ambiguity and multiple interpretations of the same speech. For example, speakers may use *direct forms* and specifically *designate* them to one particular listener when making a request. Second, in the classroom, requests that are *on task,* that is, those that refer to the shared activities in the teaching-learning situation, are most likely to be understood by listeners, and thus these types of requests are the most likely to be successful in obtaining compliance from listeners. Third, requests that are understood by listeners as *sincere* are most likely to result in compliance. Finally, effective speakers are flexible in producing

**TABLE 1    Request Characteristics of the Effective Speaker**

A successful request is likely to be

1. **Direct:** Use of linguistic forms that directly signal the speaker's needs. For requests for action, the imperative or I want/I need statements; for requests for information, the Wh-, yes-no, or tag question.

    Direct requests: How do you do this one? I need a pencil.

    Indirect questions: I don't get this. Anybody have a pencil?

2. **Designated to a listener:** Unambiguously indicates the intended listener through verbal or nonverbal means.

    C: Sally, where do you put the dollar sign? or

    C: (looking at P) Did you get that one?

3. **Sincere:** A request is sincere if (a) the action, purpose, and need for the request are clear; for example, in a request for information, the listener believes that the speaker really wants the information and does not already know the information; (b) there is both an ability and an obligation of the listener to respond to the request; and (c) the speaker has a right to make the request.

    Sincere: "John, I can't find the price for the hamburger."

    Insincere: "Well, slow-poke, what one are you finally up to now?"

4. **Revised if unsuccessful:** A restatement of a request previously made by the same speaker to the same listener who had not responded appropriately:

    A: "Bob, I need a pencil:"

    B: "Uh:"

    A: "Bob, can I borrow a pencil?"

5. **On task:** Related to the academic content or procedures and materials of the assignment.

    On task: "Is this one add or subtract?"

    Off task: "Whaddya gonna do at recess?"

6. **Responded to appropriately:** The requested action or information was given or else a reason was given why the action and/or information could not be given.

    Appropriate response:    C: "Alice, what's five?"

                             A: "I got 22 for that one."

    Inappropriate response:  C: "Alice, what's five?"

                             A: "What did you get for it?"

---

their request; for example, as we have seen with the preschool children, speakers should *revise* their initial request when compliance from listeners is not obtained.

Our research on first and third grade monolingual English-speaking children provides support for a model of the effective speaker (Wilkinson & Calculator, 1982; Wilkinson & Spinelli, 1983). Data were collected on 65 children interacting in their all-student reading groups. These groups are common in elementary school classrooms and are used for teaching reading. Students in these groups work individually and together on "seatwork" assignments, with cooperation often encouraged. Using requests to exchange information and action are central to these groups. Reading, which occurred as a formal classroom activity every morning, lasting about 40 minutes, was audio and videotaped recorded in each classroom over a two-week period. The tapes were transcribed, requests produced by the children were identified and coded according to the Wilkinson model. An expressive language sample was obtained by informal interview with each student, and these samples were analyzed using the Loban (1976) method of structural language analysis. In addition, the Miller-Yoder Test of Grammatical Comprehension (Miller & Yoder, 1972) was administered, as was the Metropolitan Reading Achievement Test (McGauvran & Nurss, 1976).

The results show that school-age children are, on the whole, effective speakers, since they obtain appropriate responses to their requests from their listeners about two-thirds of the time. The typical school child produced requests that were direct, sincere, on task, and designated to a particular listener. When the listener did not comply with the speaker's request, the school-age children revised their requests two-fifths of the time. There were strong individual differences among the children. Not all children were effective in obtaining what they requested, and the requests of these children did not conform to our model. Further analysis of our two data sets provided strong evidence for the predictive nature of our model of the effective speaker's use of requests. A hierarchy of log-linear models was used to fit the data. The model that best fit all the data assumed that there were associations among the five characteristics identified (direct, sincere, on task, designated, and revised) and that these characteristics were associated with what was requested (action, information) and with whether the request obtained appropriate responses. The major conclusions from our analysis are that these characteristics of requests are correlated and whether a request obtains compliance depends on all the other characteristics identified by the model.

Reading achievement was positively related to obtaining appropriate responses to requests and to directness of requests. This positive relationship may reflect true causal associations between them, and they may be direct or indirect. In the direct case, students who obtain appropriate responses to their requests may learn reading content as a consequence. In the indirect case, some other intellectual ability promotes both effective production of requests and the development of reading skills. Further research is needed to examine these relationships, the sources of individual differences in language usage, and their consequences for reading achievement. It is interesting to note that measures of the subjects' structural knowledge of language was unrelated to the production of requests.

*Second language learners production of requests.* In a third study in this series, we investigated production of requests by second language learners (Spanish/English) to determine how well the Wilkinson model described the language production of students who were not from monolingual English-speaking homes. This issue is important when teachers instruct students about how to communicate in their all-student reading groups; it is also necessary to delineate cultural differences before assessing children with disordered language.

Two third grade classrooms in an elementary school in an Hispanic neighborhood in San Antonio, Texas, were selected for this study (Wilkinson, Milosky, & Genishi, 1986). Forty-eight of the 50 subjects were of Mexican-American descent and demonstrated the phonological and prosodic features that are characteristic of Chicano English. Two black children in the class were included in the analysis because their interactions in the groups could not be separated out without disrupting the integrity of the analysis. Of the 48 Hispanic students, 34 reported that both Spanish and English were spoken in the home, 5 said that Spanish only was spoken in the home, and 9 said that English only was spoken in the home. The children, upon entering school, had been given the Bilingual Syntax Measure (Burt, Dulay, & Hernandez, 1975), and 43 were found to be sufficiently proficient in English so as not to qualify for bilingual education in Texas. The students' English language ability was screened to rule out gross comprehension or production deficits. An expressive language sample was obtained by informal interview with each student, and these samples were analyzed using the Loban (1976) method of structural language analysis. In addition, the Peabody Picture Vocabulary Test-Revised (Dunn & Dunn, 1981) was adminis-tered, as was the Metropolitan Reading Achievement Test (Prescott, Balow, Hogan, & Farr, 1978). Reading, which occurred as a formal classroom activity every morning, lasting about 40 minutes, was audio and videotaped recorded in each classroom over a two-week period. Following the procedures in the previous two studies, the tapes were transcribed, with requests produced by the children identified and coded accord-ing to the Wilkinson model.

Analyses of these data showed that the children almost always spoke English during reading and that they were effective in obtaining responses to requests for action or information about 60 percent of the time. The typical third grader in this study produced requests that were direct, sincere, and on task. However, the students specifically designated the intended listener only one in five times and revised requests for a "second try" only one in three times. Thus, the data from second language learners essentially confirm the Wilkinson model of effective speakers' use of re-quests, with the exception that the designation of listeners and use of revisions were less frequent than for the monolingual English speakers. Again, we found that reading achievement was positively related to obtaining appropriate responses to requests. This positive relationship may reflect true causal associations between them, and they may direct or indirect, as discussed in the previous section.

Figure 1 displays the range of performance observed for requests and responses. Each characteristic of requests is listed on the x axis: *sincere, on task, designate, direct, response,* and *revise.* On the y axis is the proportion of requests that showed each characteristic. The performance levels of the individual children are distributed vertically for each characteristic. For each subject, the proportion of requests having the characteristic was calculated. For the purpose of illustrating the amount of variability among subjects and the range of scores for each characteristic, the figure symbols summarize these distributions as follows: the black circles indicate the lowest and highest proportions obtained among the subjects for a given characteristic, the dashed bar indicates the proportional values corresponding to the tenth and the ninetieth percentiles of the sample (e.g., 10 percent of the children used direct forms 46 percent of the time or less, 10 percent used them 92 percent of the time or more),

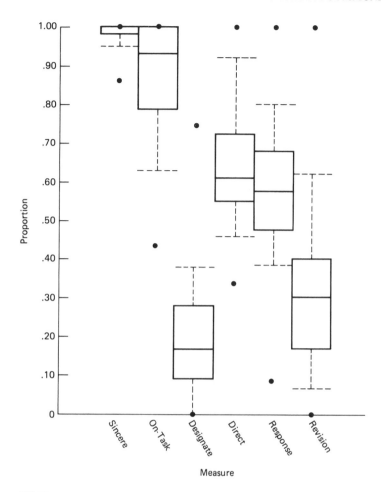

**FIGURE 1**

and the box indicates the interquartile range, with the medial the solid bar in the middle (e.g., half the sample used direct forms between 55 percent and 72 percent of the time, with a median value of 61 percent.)

Some interesting patterns in this figure can be noted. Scores for sincerity and on-task relevance were generally high and of limited variability. Thus, there seems to be a common competence among children in these aspects of producing requests. The remaining four characteristics show much greater variability in scores and a generally lower average performance. The variability suggests genuine individual differences in the degree to which requests are direct, designated, and revised and obtain appropriate responses.

Figure 2 displays the profiles of two children, Juanita and Enrique, on the characteristics of the production of requests and responses. Juanita is an effective

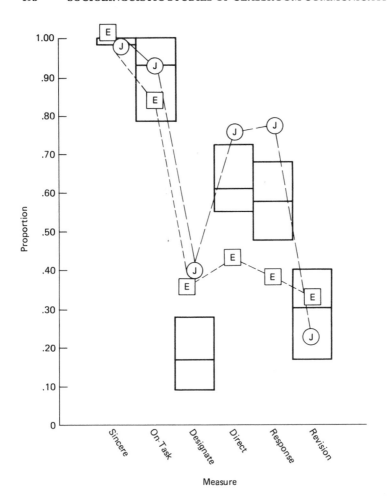

**FIGURE 2**

speaker, as defined by the Wilkinson model; that is, she usually obtains appropriate responses to her requests (78 percent of the time). She designates many more requests to specific listeners than do other students in this class, and she uses direct forms frequently; her requests are generally on task and sincere. Juanita assumes the role of the leader of the group and its taskmaster, pacing the other students and allotting tasks for each to do. She is in the top half of her class in reading achievement, and in the ninetieth percentile on vocabulary as measured by the Peabody Picture Vocabulary Test. In the following excerpt, taken from her reading group, Juanita's effectiveness as a speaker is apparent as she allocates turns to read aloud, confirms responses of other students, and restrains the others in the group until all are ready to proceed with the task:

CARMEN:  (reading aloud) On what page does Chapter Five begin and end?
JUANITA:  Wait, wait, wait.
PABLO:  Chapter Four (writes it down).
GLORIA:  Chapter Four.
JUANITA:  Wait (points to Pablo). He's still on Chapter Four.
PABLO:  How do you spell four?
CARMEN:  (erases her paper) OH.
JUANITA:  You put f-o-u-r (spells it aloud).
PABLO:  (reading aloud) Number four, on what page?
JUANITA:  Hey, no, no, no (points to Carmen). She does it.
CARMEN:  (reads the turn allocated to her by Juanita).

Enrique's profile suggests a markedly different quality in interaction with other students. He is an ineffective speaker, since he obtains appropriate responses to his requests only 40 percent of the time. Although the profile shows that he does designate his requests to particular listeners, a close examination of his conversations with other students reveals that almost all his designated requests are directed to one other student, Paula, who is not very helpful sometimes. Enrique is more often indirect than direct. As the following excerpt shows, his revisions are not more direct than his initial requests, and he does not specify why or where he is having a problem. In this exchange, Enrique receives only the answer to the problem, with no explanation or elaboration.

PAULA:  Let's do this, you start (points to E's paper).
ENRIQUE:  This is hard.
PAULA:  Write number 5 (turns to E). Number 5 is (turns back to her own work, and erases). Oh, I know which one it is. I'm finished, now I have to do the next page.
ENRIQUE:  I don't understand this one. This one's hard (taps Paula's arm). Paula, this one's tricky.
PAULA:  No, it's not.
ENRIQUE:  It says...yes it is.
PAULA:  I ready got it. It's this one (points to answer on E's paper).

Two findings in the present study differed in some important ways from the findings of the monolingual studies. In previous research, we saw that students who revised an initial unsuccessful request were likely to obtain an appropriate response with a "second try," as can be seen in the following example:

COLIN:  How do you do this one?
TRACY:  Uh, wait a minute.
COLIN:  Can you help me with this one, please?
TRACY:  Oh, on that one you gotta add the rabbits and pigs.

In the present study, however, when students followed an inappropriate or non-response with a revision, they were still unlikely to be successful in obtaining an appropriate response. Occasionally, some of the students indicated that a revised request was counterproductive to the group effort of "moving along," as can be seen in the following example:

DARIA:   Wait for me then.
SONIA:   (reads) Read the...
DARIA:   Wait.
SONIA:   No, I'm gonna read.
DARIA:   Don't read it. You just get me confused with my name.
SONIA:   Read.
DARIA:   Wait.

Another difference between the second language learners in the present study and the monolingual first langauge learners of English studied previously is that the directness of the request forms was not associated uniquely with reading achievement for these students. Production of indirect forms was just as likely to be associated with higher reading achievement. In addition, second langauge learners very rarely designated their requests to specific students (only 20 percent of the time), in sharp contrast to the performance of first language learners (83 percent of the time). These findings, taken together, suggest a cultural style on the part of the Hispanic children of using requests that are less verbally direct but focus on group interaction. During the group interactions, students spoke often while their heads were down, presumably directing their gaze to their work, with the communicative focus of the request often not specifically designated, but perhaps addressed to the group as a whole. This pattern of speech also may indicate that designation by either verbal or nonverbal means may be considered inappropriate because it is impolite to be too personal.

### Implications for Assessment

Implications that can be derived from sociolinguistic research can be applied to children who are having some kind of language problems in school, as well as to normally developing children. Those who use descriptive tools focus on and record exactly what is said as it unfolds in a particular situation. These original records, on audio and/or video tape, can be reviewed indefinitely. These records are transcribed into everyday language, which in turn can be used for illustrative and evaluative purposes. The descriptions are permanent records. The primary advantage is that there is a completely accurate record of what language was actually produced. Careful analysis can reveal the precise nature of any communicative difficulty and the aspects of the situation associated with it.

The advantages of the completeness of information and the infinite retrievability of information are offset, to some degree, by some disadvantages. First, new observers need training to use descriptive tools. The question of what to point the camera at and how to link audio and video recordings to obtain a clear record is difficult. Second, it is difficult to analyze the audio-visual record and turn them into transcriptions because of noise and other flaws within the technological record. Third, it is time consuming and expensive to make audio-video records and transcribe data, and code them. It is important that a clear focus be attended to; both the wide angle and narrow focus.

In applying a sociolinguistic analysis to assessment, it may be useful to observe the conditions under which the child is successful in obtaining appropriate responses to requests, the variety of patterns of requests that the child produces, and the nature of the child's behavior following the failure to obtain an appropriate response (e.g. after Wilkinson & Calculator, 1982). After obtaining such a *profile,* one could examine which differences may be cultural, situations, or individual. No one factor may necessarily be attributed to one source. However, identifying patterns may help to indicate when change is desirable. For example, if a child consistently produces indirect requests when other group members are using direct forms of requests, it may be desirable to assess the child's ability to differentiate these two types of requests. Furthermore, to ensure that the child can use the syntactic forms that are available in his or her repertoire, it may be necessary to require the production of both kinds of requests. It may also be necessary to teach the child how such usage may change according to the demands of the situation. For example, direct imperative requests for materials, which may be accepted in the situation of all-student instructional groups, may not be accepted by a teacher leading an instructional group. If a student receives no response to a request, repeats it without revising, and continues to receive no response, there may be a need to help the child evaluate why. Is it because the group perceives the request and its revisions and counterproductive to group goals? The findings of Bryan, Donahue, and Pearl (1981) and Donahue and Bryan (1983) suggest that language-impaired children may need to be taught explicitly how to control conversation. These ways include how to render their requests and statements more assertive and explicit, as well as how to soften them when appropriate.

Research suggests that an accurate assessment of students' knowledge of language usage in the classroom should be examined in relevant, multiple contexts. One problem with standard assessments is that assessment has been made of a particular language function or discourse unit in only on particular context. We cannot assume that performance of the appropriate behavior in that context necessarily predicts whether the student will perform the same behavior in another context. The generalizability of performance assessed in only one context is dubious. Ervin-Tripp (1982) observes that the forms of requests vary with context, and therefore, language should be evaluated in the context of concern, or else be evaluated in a context that attempts to duplicate the context of concern. Mehan, Hertweck, Combs, and Flynn (1982) point out that behavior varies with context, and they suggest observation of a given behavior in multiple contexts so that any conclusions about generalized deficit will be drawn cautiously. The background of the assessed individual must also be considered because, as Cook-Gumperz and Gumperz (1982) note, the judgment of behavior as appropriate varies with context.

Multiple methods of assessment are necessary. Observing that a student has produced a behavior conforming to the rules of language use in the classroom is often not sufficient for knowing whether the student has, in fact, achieved communicative competence in the broad sense. In addition to the multiple descriptions in a number of contexts, we need to develop tools that help us to assess what a student does and does not know about the use of language in the specific classroom situations. The importance of careful observation of students communicating and interacting in a variety of contexts that differ on a variety of dimensions is an important implication of sociolinguistic research. In addition, it may be possible to create contexts with high communicative demand or to manipulate contexts to see how a student responds to communicative error (e.g., Read & Cherry, 1978).

Descriptive tools can provide teachers and clinicians with both narrow- and wide-angle lenses to be aimed at a child with a communication problems. Dollaghan and Miller (1985) suggest that time could be well spent recording and transcribing the speech of the children exactly as it occurs and then conducting a fine-grained analysis of that speech sample to see the problem clearly and in detail. They provide the following example:

> one might construct a taxonomy that at least distinguished between answers to "wh" questions, yes-no questions, tag questions, and choice questions, or the clinician might conduct an exploratory observation of the subject's question answering skills by recording and examining the number of events preceding and following successful and unsuccessful responses to questions. This exploratory phase might lead the clinician to realize that the subject's question answering skill actually varies depending on the degree to which the question refers to some aspect of the "here-and-now" or the degree to which the answer can be produced through use of a comprehension strategy. The clinician could then proceed to construct a taxonomy distinguishing among these events and to write recognition rules for its categories; subsequent observations would yield a much better picture of the specific kinds of questions to which treatment should be addressed. (Dollaghan & Miller, 1986, p. 15)

After such information is gathered for individual students, the question arises of the norms to be used for comparison. Should they be those of a given culture? Should they reflect the environment of the student during the school day? Thus, the findings of a particular assessment cannot themselves be isolated from the values, expectations, and purposes for which the evaluation is to be used. The background against which the evaluation is being compared is as important as the data revealed in the evaluation itself.

# REFERENCES

BRYAN, T., DONAHUE, M., & PEARL, R. (1981). Learning disabled children's peer interactions during a small group problem solving task. *Learning Disability Quarterly, 4,* 13-22.

BURT, M., DULAY, H., & HERNANDEZ, E. (1975). *Bilingual syntax measure.* New York: Harcourt Brace Jovanovich

CAZDEN, C. (1988). *Classroom discourse.* Portsmith, NH: Heinemann.

CAZDEN, C., JOHN, V., & HYMES, D. (1972). *Functions of language in the classroom.* New York: Teachers College Press.

CHERRY, L. (1978). Teacher-student interaction and teachers' expectations of students' communicative competence. In P. Griffin & R. Shuy (Eds.), *The study of children's functional language and education in the early years.* Final report to the Carnegie Corporation. Arlington, VA: Center for Applied Linguistics.

CHERRY, L. (1979). A sociocognitive approach to language development and its implications for education. In O. Garnica & M. King (Eds.). *Language, children, and society,* pp. 115-134. New York: Pergamon.

COHEN, E. (1984). Talking and working together: Status, interaction and learning. In P. Peterson, L. Wilkinson, & M. Hallinan (Eds.). *The social context of instruction,* pp. 171-189. Orlando, FL: Academic Press.

COOK-GUMPERZ, J., & GUMPERZ, J. (1982). Communicative competence in educational perspective. In L. Cherry Wilkinson (Ed.), *Communicating in the classroom,* pp. 13-26. New York: Academic Press.

COOPER, C., MARQUIS, A., & AYERS-LOPEZ, S. (1982). Peer learning in the classroom: Tracing developmental patterns and consquences of children's spontaneous interactions. In L. Cherry Wilkinson (Ed.), *Communicating in the classroom,* pp. 69-84. New York: Academic Press.

DOLLAGHAN, C. & J. MILLER (1986). Observational methods in the study of communicative competence. In R. Shecklebush (Ed.), *Language competence and instruction,* pp. 99-124. San Diego, CA: College Hill Press.

DONAHUE, M. & BRYAN, T. (1983) Conversational skills and modeling in learning disabled boys. *Applied Psycholinguistics 4,* 251-278.

DUNKIN, B. & BIDDLE, B. (1974). *The study of teaching.* New York: Holt, Rinehart and Winston.

DUNN, L., & DUNN, L. (1981). *Peabody Picture Vocabulary Test-Revised.* Circle Pines, MN: American Guidance Service.

EDER, D. (1982). Differences in communicative styles across ability groups. In L. Cherry Wilkinson (Ed.), *Communicating in the classroom,* pp. 245-264. New York: Academic Press.

ERICKSON, F. (1982). Classroom discourse as improvisation: Relationships between academic task structure and social participation structure in lessons. In L. Cherry Wilkinson (Ed.)., *Communicating in the classroom,* pp. 153-182. New York: Academic Press.

ERICKSON, F., & SHULTZ, J. (1982). *The counselor as gatekeeper: Social interaction in interviews.* New York: Academic Press.

ERVIN-TRIPP, S. (1977). Wait for me roller-skate. In S. Ervin-Tripp & C. Mitchell-Kernan (Eds.), *Child discourse.* New York: Academic Press.

ERVIN-TRIPP, S. (1982). Structures of control. In L. Cherry Wilkinson (Ed.), *Communicating in the classroom,* pp. 27-48. New York: Academic Press.

FLANDERS, N. (1970). *Analyzing teaching behavior.* Reading, MA: Addison-Wesley.

FLORIO, S., & SHULTZ, J. (1979). Social competence at home and at school. *Theory into Practice, 18,* 234-243.

GREEN, J. & SMITH, D. (1983). Teaching and learning: A linguistic perspective. *The Elementary School Journal, 83,* 353-391.

GREEN, J., & WALLAT, C. (1981). Mapping instructional conversations: A sociolinguistic ethnography. In J. Green, & C. Wallat, (Eds.), *Ethnography and language in educational settings*, pp. 161-208. Norwood, NJ: Ablex.

GRIFFIN, P. & SHUY, R. (Eds.). (1978). *The study of children's functional language and education in the early years*. Final report to the Carnegie Corporation. Arlington, VA: Center for Applied Linguistics.

HEATH, S. (1982). Questioning at home and at school: A comparative stdy. In G. Spindler (Ed.), *Doing the ethnography of schooling*. New York: Holt, Rinehart and Winston.

LOBAN, W. (1976). *Language development*. Champaign, IL: National Council of Teachers of English.

MCGAUVRAN, M., & NURSS, J. (1976). *Metropolitan Reading Test*. New York: Harcourt Brace Jovanovich.

MEHAN, H. (1979). *Learning lessons*. Cambridge, MA: Harvard University Press.

MEHAN, H., HERTWECK, A., COMBS, S., & FLYNN, P. (1982). Teachers' interpretations of students behavior. In L. Cherry Wilkinson (Ed.), *Communicating in the classroom*, pp. 297-322. New York: Academic Press.

MERRITT, M. (1982). Distributing and directing attention in primary classrooms. In L. Cherry Wilkinson (Ed.), *Communicating in the classroom*, pp. 223-244. New York: Academic Press.

MICHAELS, S. (1986). Narrative presentations: An oral preparation for literacy with first grade. In J. Cook-Gumperz (Ed.), *The social construction of literacy*, pp. 94-116. New York: Cambridge University Press.

MILLER, J., & YODER, D. (1972). *The Miller-Yoder Test of Grammatical Comprehension (MY Test)*. Madison: University of Wisconsin Press.

PRESCOTT, G., BALOW, I., HOGAN, T., & FARR, R., (1978). *Metropolitan Reading Achievement Test*. New York: Harcourt Brace Jovanovich.

READ, B., & CHERRY, L. (1978). Preschool children production of directives. *Discourse Processes, 1*, 233-245.

SHATZ, M. (1978). Children's comprehension of question directives. *Journal of child language, 5*, 39-46.

SINCLAIR, J., & COULTHARD, R. (1975). *Towards an analysis of discourse: The English used by teachers and pupils*. London: Oxford University Press.

WILKINSON, L. CHERRY (1982a). *Communicating in the classroom*. New York: Academic Press.

WILKINSON, L. CHERRY (1982b). Introduction: A sociolinguistic approach to communicating in the classroom. In L. Cherry Wilkinson (Ed.), *Communicating in the classroom*, pp. 3-12. New York: Academic Press.

WILKINSON, L. CHERRY, & CALCULATOR, S. (1982). Requests and responses in peer-directed reading groups. *American Education Research Journal, 19*, 107-122.

WILKINSON, L. CHERRY, MILOSKY, L., & GENISHI, C. (1986). Second language learners' use of requests and responses in elementary classrooms. *Topics in Language Disorders, 6*, 57-70.

WILKINSON, L. CHERRY, & SPINELLI, F. (1983). Using requests effectively in peer-directed instructional groups. *American Education Research Journal, 20*, 479-501.

# 12

# TEACHERS COPING WITH CHANGE: ASSESSING THE EARLY LITERACY CURRICULUM

*Dorothy S. Stricklanu*
*Teachers College, Columbia Universii y*

*Donna M. Ogle*
*National College of Education*

### Abstract

Strickland and Ogle describe an investigation into the nature and characteristics of kindergarten programs and kindergarten teachers beliefs about
what is essential in an effective up-to-date curriculum. Special attention
was given to observing instructional contexts for language and literacy
development. An outcome of the investigation was a data source for early
childhood teachers to examine and reflect on their own instructional
settings.

## INTRODUCTION

The current interest in literacy instruction in early childhood settings is highly
significant and controversial. One group of educators contends that the years just prior
to first grade should be used to get children ready for the introduction to formal
reading. They advocate systematic instruction in a variety of discrete prereading and
prewriting skills, which include direct instruction on letter names, letter-sound relationships, and an assortment of visual-perceptual tasks. Those who hold this *aca-
demic/readiness perspective* of early literacy tend to view learning to read and write
as the acquisition of a set of hierarchically arranged skills, that the teacher imparts in

a predetermined manner. This approach to early literacy has become increasingly prevalent in kindergarten classrooms, and it is making its appearance at earlier and earlier levels as well (Fox, 1987; Larrick, 1987).

Another view of literacy in early childhood reflects a traditional concern for putting the young child's social, emotional, and physical development first. Although educators holding this view also envision the years prior to first grade as a period of readiness, they would protect the child from paper and pencil activities and concentrate on play, emphasizing oral language expansion and motor activities. Theirs might be called a *nonacademic/readiness perspective* in which activities specifically designed for "reading readiness" would be put on hold until first grade. The demands of parents and the expectations of the public have brought about a steady decline in the number of educators holding this view. An increasing number, particularly those responsible for kindergarten-age pupils, have reluctantly joined the ranks of the academic/readiness camp.

A third small, but steadily growing, group of early childhood educators have embraced a view of early literacy known as an *emergent literacy perspective.* Grounded in recent research on young children's reading and writing, these researchers take a developmental view of young children's learning. Rather than separate literacy from other aspects of learning, they would nurture it as a natural part of the child's total development. Proponents of this perspective point to the recent research that demonstrates how young children begin developing concepts of reading and writing even during their first year of life. They remind us that by the time some children begin formal schooling, they have been read hundreds of books, memorized whole stories, begun to match speech to print, and in some cases have even begun to read independently (Ferreiro & Teberosky, 1982; Hiebert, 1978; Wells 1986). Other research has documented how young children begin exploring with writing and invent their own graphic systems modeled from the standard system they observe around them (Chomsky, 1979; Clay, 1975; Read, 1975). Most important, the literacy learning of these children is accomplished in an environment in which a playful, meaningful context is maintained.

Regardless of the point of view teachers of young children hold, it is clear that they are being pressured to reconsider their literacy programs. Proposals for the introduction of reading and writing into the early childhood curriculum vary considerably. Reflecting on the theoretical positions described earlier, it is not surprising that some argue for formal step-by-step introduction of skills accompanied by workbooks and frequent testing (Bereiter, Engleman, Osborn & Reidford, 1966). Others take their lead from informal schooling in England and the United States and argue for rich literacy environments in which the teacher reads to children; models written language through the use of experience charts, notes, and labels; provides opportunities for children to do their own writing; and encourages children to attempt to read easy materials (Holdaway, 1979; Loughlin & Martin 1987; Schickendanz, 1986; Strickland, 1989).

It is clear from the numbers of states reconsidering their directives on kindergarten education that a dramatic reconceptualization of kindergarten is underway (Egertson, 1987; Hills, 1987; position statement of the National Association of Early Childhood Specialists in State Departments of Education, 1987). Generally, the trend is toward more formalized literacy instruction in kindergarten. This shift has created great concern among kindergarten and prekindergarten teachers who view it as contrary to their understandings of child growth and development.

This chapter describes a study initiated to examine the instruction occurring in the classrooms of kindergarten teachers in varied settings. The teachers had been identified as exemplary by their supervisors. We wanted to learn about their priorities and practices in a time of change. We focused on the instructional contexts for language and literacy development, hoping to learn how these teachers were actually providing instruction in literacy and what influenced their instructional decisions. One purpose was the generation of a corpus of classroom descriptions that might be used by teachers to assess their own literacy environments. It is our hope that this study will add to the growing body of data on this topic (Meyer, Linn, & Hastings, 1985; Durkin, 1987). The following questions guided its development.

1. What are the classroom priorities of good kindergarten teachers? How do these teachers apportion the content of their instructional time? Specifically, we were interested in knowing how much of their time was devoted to literacy activities and how those activities were conducted.
2. How do good kindergarten teachers organize their classrooms for instruction? We wanted to know the degree to which they worked with the whole class, small groups, and individuals.
3. What patterns of interaction exist in the classrooms of good kindergarten teachers? We were interested in the kind and quality of opportunities given children to talk with their teachers and to initiate their own verbal interactions.

Five teachers, two suburban, two urban, and one from a rural setting were selected to participate in the study. The schools were located in suburban Illinois, suburban New York, Chicago, New York City, and rural New Hampshire. Twelve children were in the rural class, others ranged from 23 to 25 students. The teachers were selected to participate on the basis of having been identified (to the researchers) by principals or supervisors as excellent kindergarten teachers. Each teacher volunteered to participate willingly upon being so identified. Their particular philosophies about reading and writing development were not determined, although they all were involved in some form of literacy instruction. Each teacher was experienced in kindergarten and primary grades (more than five years), and each had received specialized early childhood training.

Initial interviews were conducted with the teachers to determine what they considered their priorities and how they organized for instruction. Our purpose was explained along with the procedures that would be followed during classroom observations. Three observers were trained to record the events in the school day using a modification of the Stallings's kindergarten snapshot (Stallings & Kaskowitz, 1974) combined with a running record of all transactions. The observation sheet included information about when the activity was initiated, what the activity was, the participants, the verbal interactions that occurred, and any qualitative features recorders were able to note. The teacher served as the focal point of the observations. Snapshots were filled out five times during the session to provide information about the activities of all those in the classroom. The snapshot is a tally of what all the members of the class are doing and with whom they are interacting precisely within one particular minute of time. Three separate mornings (approximately 8:30 A.M. to 11:30 A.M.) data was collected through the observation of each teacher. All the teachers agreed that this was the time period in which their literacy programs were most evident. With the exception of New Hampshire, the programs were all full-day kindergartens. The observers recorded all interactions in the classroom in which the teacher was a part. After each observation the notes were coded so that the information could be tallied. The observation scheme allowed us to determine the number of verbal interactions between the teacher and the whole class, small groups, and individuals; the content of the teacher-student interactions; and the numbers of teacher versus student verbal initiatives. Records of the instruction provided and the time frame of each activity helped make the picture of the classroom more complete.

Interactions centered on literacy events, socialization, management, and discipline. Teacher feedback to a child's response (acknowledgment, correction, praise) was recorded separately. All literacy events were recorded. Included in our definition of literacy events were teachers reading to students, teachers developing new vocabulary and helping children elaborate on oral language, teachers acting as scribe for students' dictation, teachers helping students write and label their own work, students working on independently written pieces, students' independent "reading" (includes any extended interaction with a book) or listening to taped storybooks on headsets, and instruction in reading readiness workbooks or other formal skill work.

Social interactions were defined as occasions when teacher and children talked about events outside the classroom, such as family activities, how the children felt, what they were wearing, and so on. Management interactions involved the teacher structuring the events of the classroom and helping students "get the show on the road" to use Stallings' phrase. Kindergarten teachers typically place a high priority on helping children learn how to function in school settings. For example, how to move from center to center and appropriate ways to walk in the classroom, stand in line, and fill out worksheets often receive a great deal of attention. Discipline interactions consisted of those instances in which students stepped outside the boundaries of appropriate behavior and were reprimanded or when students reported such behavior to teachers.

### Brief Overviews of Each of the Five Classrooms

*Suburban Illinois.* This school is located in a primarily white middle-class neighborhood in a university town just outside of Chicago. A typical literacy interaction in this classroom involves the children dictating and "reading" group-generated stories. The teacher reads aloud frequently and pauses to discuss stories, illustrations, and allow children to make predictions. Students are also given daily opportunities to engage in independent writing. Management consists of assisting students in manipulating the school environment and in providing structure for transitions.

*Suburban New York.*    Located in a Long Island suburb, this school district is primarily composed of working-class and middle-class white families. The large percentage of literacy interactions in this room reflect the teacher's method for handling phonics instruction. Children would bring in pictures of objects whose names began with the specific initial consonant being studied. The teacher would call on each child who would then produce a quick one-word response. Literature was often used as the basis of a writing activity in which children completed a sentence pattern corresponding with one in a story and drew a picture to create their own books. Management interactions focused on helping children learn to cope with the demands of school behaviors.

*Urban Chicago.*    This is an inner-city school in which the children come from black, low-socioeconomic-status families. Workbooks and worksheets provide the major instructional format for literacy in this classroom. Thus, teacher questions with one-word responses and teacher directions followed by little or no verbal response were typical. Very little reading aloud occurred in this classroom, and no chart work or children's writing was in evidence. Management interaction focused on directions for the use of tools and materials.

*Urban New York City.*    The population in this school is largely black and Hispanic. It is located on the edge of the Harlem area of New York City. Most of the literacy interactions in this classroom revolve around workbook instruction. Other literacy events do occur on a daily basis, however. Books are often brought from home by individual students and are shared in a large group setting. Except for the signing of names to their work, children's writing was not in evidence. A large proportion of the management interactions center around passing out materials, scissors, and books.

*Rural New Hampshire.*    These children come from a mixture of poor, working-class, and lower-middle-class families. Like the suburban Illinois classroom, these children are given many opportunities to write as well as to enjoy books. However, in contrast to that school, the writing is more teacher oriented and dependent. Therefore, children are less likely to invent their own spellings but to depend on the teacher for help. Books are shared much as a family might share stories. The teacher pauses for discussion, questions, and predictions. The classroom environment is full of examples of print in use, such as student mailboxes, news charts, and recipes. A large number of the management interactions occurred during the many cooking activities provided and revolve around the assembling of utensils.

Interviews revealed that these five teachers were very similar in the way they described their program goals. Literacy and management considerations were high priorities, facts our observations corroborated. Districtwide curriculum guides were in place in each setting, and these provided a general framework for decision making. Opinions of other teachers also influenced their ideas about the kindergarten curriculum. Teachers said that although they did some long-range planning for the year, most units of work lasted for a two week period. All the teachers said they saw some differences in the children they teach now as opposed to children five or ten years ago. Most of today's children know some letters of the alphabet, and most have had some prior school experience. Two teachers complained that many children appeared more hyperactive and less knowledgeable about traditional things such as nursery rhymes, even with previous schooling. All the teachers stressed that a change in parents' and administrators' attitudes about the nature of kindergarten had done more to alter their behavior than their feelings about any change in the abilities of the children.

### What Are the Classroom Priorities of Good Kindergarten Teachers?

To determine teachers' priorities for how they spent their time, all interactions were coded according to content. The categories used were literacy instruction, other instruction, feedback, social interaction, play, management, and discipline. When interactions were totaled across teachers and schools, 2,244 or nearly 25 percent of the 9,147 interactions involved literacy instruction. The largest amount of time, 33 percent, was spent on management. Teacher-student interactions during play only accounted for slightly over 1 percent of the total. Table 1 shows the summaries of classroom interactions according to content.

When schools were analyzed individually, substantial variation in several categories existed. The percentage of time spent in literacy instruction varied from a low of 13.8 percent to a high of 44.5 percent. Not surprisingly, the city schools had lower than average amounts of time devoted to literacy: 13.8 percent and 21.6 percent. Management consumed from 20.3 percent to 42 percent of the interactions. Discipline was involved in less than 3 percent of the interactions of the suburban and rural schools; it did account for 7.8 percent and 14.8 percent of the city interactions. In none of the schools did much more than 2 percent of the teacher-student interactions occur during play.

These data do not reflect the traditional concept of kindergarten life in which play is viewed as the medium through which most learning occurs. Teachers did not focus on the playtime as central in their involvement with students. When children were at play, they were doing so with little or no direct involvement with the teacher. The teachers arranged play areas and scheduled play times before students arrived, and students engaged in these activities independently. Teachers were not using these as resources for observation or language and social development. Rather, they chose to use the time they spent with children focused on instruction and training for school life. In the verbal reports from teacher interviews as well as in their behavior, teachers

**TABLE 1  Percentage Total Interactions by Content**

| School | Management | Literacy Instruction | Other Instruction | Feedback | Social Interaction | Playtime | Discipline |
|---|---|---|---|---|---|---|---|
| Suburban | | | | | | | |
| Illinois | 32.5 | 25.6 | 21.2 | 8.0 | 8.0 | 2.4 | 2.3 |
| New York | 20.3 | 44.5 | 4.8 | 18.8 | 8.5 | 2.1 | 1.0 |
| Urban | | | | | | | |
| Chicago | 42.0 | 13.8 | 13.1 | 9.6 | 5.9 | 0.9 | 14.8 |
| New York City | 26.8 | 21.6 | 12.5 | 9.1 | 20.8 | 1.4 | 7.8 |
| Rural | | | | | | | |
| New Hampshire | 38.3 | 19.5 | 10.0 | 9.5 | 21.8 | 0.5 | 0.5 |
| Totals across teachers and schools (approx.) | 33.0 | 25.0 | 12.0 | 11.0 | 13.0 | 1.0 | 5.0 |

stressed one of their major roles as preparing children to move easily through the routines of school life. A great deal of time was devoted to instructing them in how to find materials, clean up, move from one area to another, and turn in completed work. By handling these problems before they occurred, teachers sought to minimize the need for corrective discipline.

An analysis of the content of the individual teacher's instruction revealed that the type of literacy instruction provided varied considerably. In three of the schools (two urban and New York suburban), phonics instruction was central to literacy. The urban schools used workbooks for letter-sound instruction during which the interactions were characterized by short question-answer cycles. In all schools carpet time was used for the teacher to read to students, although in the two urban schools, this was not done on a daily basis. Children in the New York suburban school also engaged in writing their own stories based on models of stories read to them such as Bill Martin's *Brown Bear, Brown Bear.* A large proportion of the literacy interaction in this classroom reflected the way phonics instruction was handled. Children would bring in pictures of objects whose names began with a specific initial consonant under study. The teacher would call on each child, who would then produce a one-word response.

In the other two schools (Illinois suburban and rural) little workbook instruction was used. In the Illinois suburban school the teacher had two centers for writing. One center was devoted to children's independent writing/drawing and invented spelling was encouraged. The other center provided the *Breakthrough to Literacy* (Mackay, Thompson, & Schaub, 1984) materials for children to use in constructing sentences using words from the large corpus provided by word banks based on vocabulary collected from group charts. Independently written pieces were shared with the teacher or with the group. During carpet time, when she read to the children, this teacher often paused to share illustrations and encourage student predictions and other types of discussion. In the rural school, many opportunities were provided for students to write. Here, the writing was more teacher directed, however. Children frequently worked at the writing center on a one-to-one basis with her and relied on her for the spelling of unfamiliar words. Carpet time was rich in language experiences. The teacher shared books much as a family might share stories with stops for discussion, questioning, and prediction. A large number of the management interactions occurred during cooking activities and revolved around assembling supplies.

### How Do Good Kindergarten Teachers Organize Their Classrooms for Instruction?

Not only is the content of the teachers' interactions important in describing classroom interaction, the way in which teachers interact with children is also important. Therefore, we examined each interaction to determine with whom the teacher was speaking: individual child, pairs of children, small group, or whole group. Table 2 provides the summaries for each teacher. It was clear that these teachers geared most of their interactions to either the whole class or to individual students.

TABLE 2    Percentage Interactions by Instructional Organization

| School | Whole Group | Small Group | Pairs | Individuals |
|---|---|---|---|---|
| Suburban | | | | |
|   Illinois | 21.9 | 6.47 | 3.0 | 65.7 |
|   New York | 31.4 | 3.1 | 1.1 | 64.3 |
| Urban | | | | |
|   Chicago | 43.9 | 4.9 | 2.1 | 49.1 |
|   New York City | 41.0 | 5.4 | 1.2 | 52.4 |
| Rural | | | | |
|   New Hampshire | 16.0 | 0 | 0.9 | 83.1 |

Individual interactions have to be interpreted further, however, since in some cases teachers would initiate individual questions while children were in a large group setting. For example, a teacher might call on one particular child to answer a question during the reading of a story to the whole class. This would be coded as a teacher to individual child interaction. Individual question-response interaction during whole group instruction was most common in the two urban schools. It is also important to note that the one school where the teacher did almost no small group interacting (the rural school) also had the fewest children in the class, only 12. Therefore, interacting with the whole group was much easier than in the larger setting.

When literacy instruction was examined specifically, three of the teachers focused most of their interactions on individual children: only in the two urban schools was the whole group a major unit for teacher interactions around literacy. Even then, in one of the urban schools, the teacher's interactions were evenly divided between individual and whole group interactions.

While the interaction data provides a clear pattern of how teachers talk with children individually and as a whole class, a further examination of the data was necessary to gain a fuller picture of how the classrooms worked. For example, at the Illinois suburban school the teacher used two basic structures for classroom organization: the carpet time, often used twice a session, where she interacted with the whole group, reading to them, discussing the calendar, singing, and talking about a variety of instructional topics. She would often introduce pertinent sentences on a sentence maker and encourage students to read them to her. Twice in each session the children worked at designated centers around the room. There were math, block, listening, art, writing, Sentence Maker, games, and water centers from which to choose. While the children were at centers, the teacher would circulate and spend somewhat extended times with individuals. Another point of interest in the Illinois suburban school is that a large portion of mathematical instruction was done in pairs. This is not evident in our data because we focused on interactions between teacher and student rather than between students.

In contrast, in the Chicago urban school, teachers were required to use a workbook program for part of their literacy and math instruction. Using these materials, the teacher would provide introductory instruction to the whole class and then have children work independently at their desks while she circulated. At tables children engaged in activities with shapes and math manipulatives. Most of these were whole group activities, but there was time for individual interactions. This teacher also used two carpet times daily with the whole class to introduce the calendar, take roll, sing, read aloud, and introduce content themes.

### What Patterns of Interaction Exist in the Classrooms of Good Kindergarten Teachers?

For children to expand their oral language facility they need opportunities to engage in meaningful verbal exchange in the classroom. Therefore, as a part of the larger analysis we coded both student and teacher initiatives in the interactions. We wanted to know with what frequency children could initiate their own communications with the teacher. Unfortunately, we could not maintain a record of the child-child interactions.

Both teacher and student initiatives and responses were coded by the content of the interactions: literacy, other instruction, social, management, play, and discipline. Summaries of interaction patterns are presented in Table 3. It is clear that most of the initiatives come from the teachers. However, there are interesting variations in the patterns of student initiatives. In the two classrooms most characterized by informal organization and work in centers student initiatives are substantially higher than in the other three classrooms. The summary chart indicates that in these schools 32.1 percent and 37.5 percent of the interactions are student initiated. In the other three schools only 10-12 percent of the initiatives are by students.

TABLE 3    Patterns of Interaction: Classroom Initiatives*

| Schools | Teacher initiatives | | Student initiatives | | Total |
|---|---|---|---|---|---|
| | No. | % | No. | % | No. |
| Suburban | | | | | |
| Illinois | 412 | 67.9 | 195 | 32.1 | 607 |
| New York | 734 | 87.6 | 104 | 12.4 | 838 |
| Urban | | | | | |
| Chicago | 513 | 90.0 | 57 | 10.0 | 570 |
| New York City | 812 | 89.2 | 98 | 10.8 | 910 |
| Rural | | | | | |
| New Hampshire | 1,381 | 62.5 | 827 | 37.5 | 2,208 |

One major outcome of this study was the rich data source it provided for the examination and reflection of classroom environments. Early childhood teachers can use what was learned about these five classrooms as content for discussion and analysis of their own instructional settings. By focusing their attention first on classrooms of teachers unknown to them, they are able to approach the information in a dispassionate and objective manner. The transition from that kind of discussion to a close look at their own classrooms becomes a very natural one. Following are some questions designed to give teachers a start toward self-assessing their early literacy curricula.

### LITERACY PRIORITIES

1. How much of my instructional time is spent on housekeeping and management as opposed to student involvement with materials and ideas?
2. Approximately how much of my time is spent on literacy instruction?
3. What forms does the literacy instruction in my classroom take?
4. Are opportunities for both reading and writing offered?
5. What part does oral language play in the literacy activities?
6. What, if any, proportion of the time devoted to literacy do workbooks and worksheets play?
7. Is play used as a resource for interacting with students and for observing students language and literacy behaviors?

### INSTRUCTIONAL ORGANIZATION

1. How much of my time is spent with individuals and small groups as opposed to whole group instruction?
2. Is there variation in the organizational pattern throughout the day?
3. Do the literacy activities in my classroom reflect varied instructional organization.

### PATTERNS OF INTERACTION

1. Are there numerous opportunities for students to talk during the day?
2. Are opportunities provided for teacher-guided discussion and meaningful verbal exchange?
3. Do students initiate a significant proportion of the talk during the day?
4. Do I take time to listen to student-initiated talk and encourage them to express their ideas through speech?

## SUMMARY AND CONCLUSIONS

The teachers involved in this study clearly accept children's literacy development as one of their priorities. A substantial part of their interactions with children is focused on reading and writing activities. All the teachers read aloud to children and discussed books with them. Children were encouraged to compose through drawing and writing. Written language was displayed around the rooms. Beyond these similarities, these exemplary teachers reflect a variety of approaches to the best way to introduce children to literacy. Workbooks and formal phonics instruction were used in three of the classrooms. Yet, when the teachers were interviewed, we discovered that the decision to use these materials was not theirs. Teachers reported that workbooks were used because they had been adopted or prescribed by higher levels of administration. It is interesting to note that teachers who used workbooks actually spent less time on literacy than did those who did not, suggesting that the use of these materials may be viewed as synonymous with the total literacy program. It should be also be noted that one of the teachers who was not using a phonics workbook confided that she was under pressure to begin using one the following year. All the teachers reported that they wanted to expand children's understandings of literacy, but they preferred to do it in an informal way. Since the completion of the study, one urban district has changed its curriculum so that workbooks are no longer required. These changes in curriculum and materials reflect the uncertainty within the profession over these issues.

These teachers consider helping children function appropriately in school a high priority. Each spent a good portion of time on the positive aspects of management, preparing children to handle themselves in school. Their low levels of problems with discipline may be reflective of the care with which they prepared their students.

All the teachers spent considerable time talking with children individually. When literacy interactions were considered specifically, whole group interactions ranged from 19.8 percent to 62.4 percent. The two extremes were provided by the rural school and the city schools with highly formalized workbook instruction.

Children also had many opportunities to initiate interactions with their teachers. The frequency of their doing so varied by settings with a low of 10 percent of all interactions to a high of 37.5 percent. Class size was obviously a factor here. In all schools, management concerns were one of the two highest categories of student initiatives. The other high categories were centered around literacy instruction (two suburban schools), social (rural and one urban), and discipline (one urban). These findings have important implications for those interested in helping young children gain control over oral language and use it effectively.

What we have described, based on the data, is a mosaic of classrooms alive with language learning. We suspect that these teachers are not atypical. Today's kindergarten teachers are finding a variety of ways to cope with the changing perspectives on literacy instruction for young children. The children are active participants in the process, too. They are making use of what they have learned in and out of school. They initiate language exchanges and respond to teacher queries.

These teachers, like so many teachers around the country reflect a diversity of approaches to instruction—a diversity that we have observed within school districts and even within school buildings. Phonics, language experience activities with groups and individuals, children's independent writing with invented spellings, experiences with literature, and handwriting practice were all observed during our visits. Our purpose was not to critique the relative merits of one approach over another. Rather, our interest was in beginning to build a database that describes what is occurring in kindergarten and to help teachers become more aware of the need to examine their own behavior. We believe that classroom teachers and curriculum specialists can use this information, along with the growing body of research on young children's literacy development, as they reflect on their own situations and plan curriculum change.

As researchers holding an emergent literacy view of young children's reading and writing development, we have our own opinions about which classroom practices are most consistent with current research and theory. Certainly more detailed studies of the impact of these activities on children's literacy development are needed. What is very clear is that we are in a period of change. Literacy development is a important part of kindergarten, and this trend will undoubtedly have an impact on the curriculum for 4-year-olds as well. How this is accomplished may have far-reaching effects beyond literacy to influence children's social, emotional, and physical well-being — something that kindergarten has always been about.

## REFERENCES

BEREITER, C., ENGLEMAN, S., OSBORN, J., & REIDFORD, P. (1966). An academically oriented pre-school for culturally deprived children. In Fred Hechinger (Ed.), *Pre-school education today*, pp. 105–135. Garden City, NY: Doubleday.

CHOMSKY, C. (1979). Approaching reading through invented spelling. In L. Resnick & P. Weaver (Eds.), *Theory and Practice of Early Reading,* pp. 43–67. Hillsdale, NJ: Erlbaum.

CLAY, M. (1975). *What did I write?* Auckland, NZ: Heinemann.

DURKIN, D. (1987). A classroom-observation study of reading instruction in kindergarten, *Early Childhood Research Quarterly, 2.*

EGERTSON, H. A. (1987). Recapturing kindergarten for five-year-olds. *Education Week, 6,* 28, 19.

FERREIRO, E., & TEBEROSKY, A. (1982). *Literacy before schooling.* Portsmouth, NH: Heinemann.

FOX, B. (1987). Literacy and state funded prekindergarten programs: Speaking out on the issues. *The Reading Teacher, 41,* 58–65.

HIEBERT, E. H. (1978). Preschool children's understandings of written language. *Child Development, 49,* 1231–1234.

HILLS, T. (1987). Children in the fast lane: Implications for early childhood policy and practice. *Early Childhood Research Quarterly, 2,* 265–273.

HOLDAWAY, D. (1979). *The foundations of literacy.* Portsmouth, NH: Heinemann.

LARRICK, N. (1987). Illiteracy starts too soon. *Phi Delta Kappa, 69,* 184–189.

LOUGHLIN, C., & MARTIN, M. (1987). *Supporting literacy.* New York: Teachers College Press.

MACKAY, D., THOMPSON, B., & SCHAUB P. (1984). *Breakthrough to literacy: The theory and practice of teaching initial reading and writing.* Essex, England: Longman for the Schools Council.

MARTIN, W. (19  ). *Brown bear, brown bear, what do you see?* New York: Holt.

MEYER, L. A., LINN, R. L., & HASTINGS, C. N. (1985). *A look at instruction in kindergarten: Observations of interaction in three school districts* (Tech. Rep. No. L-3). Urbana: University of Illinois, Center for the Study of Reading.

MITCHELL, A. (1988). *The public school early childhood study: The case studies.* New York: Bank Street College of Education.

National Association of Early Childhood Specialists in State Departments of Education. (1987). Unacceptable trends in kindergarten entry and placement.

READ, C. (1975). *Children's categorization of speech sounds in English* (Research Report No. 17). Urbana, IL: National Council of Teachers of English.

SCHICKENDANZ, J. A. (1986). *More than the ABC's: The early stages of reading and writing.* Washington, DC: National Association for the Education of Young Children.

STALLINGS, J. A., & KASKOWITZ, D. (1974). *Follow-through observation, 1972-73.* Menlo Park, CA: Stanford Research Institute.

STRICKLAND, D. (1989). A model for change: Framework for an emergent literacy curriculum. In D. Strickland & L. Morrow (Eds.), *Emerging literacy: Young children learn to read and write.* Newark, DE: International Reading Association.

WELLS, G. (1986). *The meaning makers.* Portsmouth, NH: Heinemann.

## AUTHOR NOTE

The authors wish to thank Joyce Jennings, Denny Taylor, and Beatrice Teitel for their assistance in collecting and analyzing the data for this study.

# 13

# CONTEXTS

*Janet Emig*

*Rutgers, The State University of New Jersey*

### Abstract

In the concluding chapter, Janet Emig considers the issues discussed in this text and places emergent literacy in the broader context of the national political and philosophical debates concerning literacy.

In the service of presenting how literacy in young children can best be assessed, what the papers in this volume may have accomplished as well is presenting with eloquence and compelling substantiation a model of emergent literary, a model that has the potentiality for transforming attitudes and practices in the learning and teaching of writing for students of all ages.

Perhaps ironically, however, in a volume where again and again is stressed the significance of context—for what a child makes of a text, for how an assessor can appraise what that child has made of that text—two enclosing contexts have not yet been sketched, much less drawn. These contexts that may determine all else, including how literacy itself can be defined, are the current intellectual milieu and the prevailing political environment. (Since this is the United States, they may be too intertwined to tease apart.)

Emergent literacy as a model for presenting writing and reading to learners must compete for attention and respect with two other models of immense influence and power. These models are cultural literacy as espoused by E. D. Hirsch, Jr. as chief spokesperson, and the philosophical/literary theory of deconstruction as espoused, say, by J. Hillis Miller. Cultural literacy holds the vast attention of the public, the politicians, and the school managers—principals, superintendents, school boards. Deconstruction is a major mode of analysis among faculty and graduate students in key English departments at major research universities. Both set forth markedly different views of what literacy is and how it can be attained.

Before turning to an explication of these, let me make and briefly support the claim, however, that emergent literacy as a model is not confined to how very young children may or may not develop their abilities to write and to read. Rather, emergent literacy is a mode of humanistic education that already finds analogs, even direct transformations, in the learning and teaching of literacy at all levels. Assuredly, the whole language movement, under the guidance of such leading reading researchers as Kenneth and Yetta Goodman, that is growing more and more influential within elementary school English/language arts education shares central assumptions with this work concerning the young child. These assumptions include that (1) the processes of writing, reading, listening, and speaking should be organically presented in the classroom as they are in all other settings of our lives; (2) consideration of wholes such as complete texts must supplant the focus on small, discrete, and often unrelated parts—practices misguidedly called the learning of basic skills; and (3) learning must direct evaluation, rather than assessment driving learning and the shaping of the curriculum.

*Democracy Through Language,* the recommendations coming out of the major Coalition on the Future of English, held in July 1987, and sponsored by nine of the chief English/language arts associations such as the Modern Language Association and the National Council of Teachers of English, support very similar tenets for the learning and teaching of literacy. Some of the documents are particularly strong in recommending that secondary schools emulate elementary schools espousing whole language learning if the high school curriculum in English is to serve effectively its current and future constituencies who are very different in profile from the students it has served in the past.

Comparable humanistic theories and practices are being set forth for the teaching of writing and reading in colleges and universities by such groups as the College Conference on Composition and Communication. Steadily in its journal and other publications, students are encouraged to find their own voice as writers, to make significant meaning of texts as independent and autonomous readers, and to take both sets of abilities into their learning of all subject matters and disciplines.

Against all these variants of humanistic presentations of literacy, E. D. Hirsch, Jr., has set out with great canniness and skill, his concept of cultural literacy. Hirsch claims that Americans, particularly American children, currently lack the knowledge of our shared Western cultural tradition and that schools and universities must return to the transmission of this culture to the young if our democracy is to survive. One difficulty many of Hirsch's critics have with his notions, even beyond the vast epistemological one of how he defines knowing, is how these concepts of cultural literacy are to be presented.  In total contrast to emergent literacy which posits contextualizing learning and presenting literacy organically in the lives of learners, Hirsch proposes a decontextualized, at times even rote, learning of a catalog he specifies of central cultural items (a list significantly short on names of women and minority contributors).  To that end, with two colleagues, he has published *The Dictionary of Cultural Literacy*, an annotated catalog of facts and allusions "Americans need to know," a volume that stayed number one on *The New York Times'* "Advice and How To" list for many weeks after its publication.  He is also preparing a curriculum for elementary and secondary schools that specifies items, grade by grade, to be learned by the students and upon which they are to be tested at regular intervals.  How extremely Hirsch at times believes that concepts can be divorced from context came clear in a remark he made before the English Coalition when he claimed that students could as readily gain a sense of *Hamlet* from reading *Cliff Notes* as from reading the tragedy itself.

Presenting a stance toward literacy vastly different from both emergent and cultural literacy is the theory of deconstruction being propounded in many major college departments of English.  As the rhetorician W. Ross Winterrowed notes in his introduction to Sharon Crowley's invaluable new *A Teacher's Introduction to Deconstruction;*

> In bare essence, the project of deconstruction is to obliterate the doctrine of presence in Western metaphysics—that is, to deconstruct the all-pervasive notion that behind the words is a truth that the words express…Deconstruction, then, razes determinate meaning and from the rubble constructs the indeterminate text, behind which or within which there is no simple, unvarying meaning.

The implications of this theory, bare, for reading and the assessment of that reading are immediately apparent and overwhelming.  Finding the meaning in and of the text has served as the occupation and preoccupation of initial and continuing reading instruction throughout the centuries:  "What color are Spot's spots?"  "How does Joyce's concept of epiphany reveal itself in 'The Dead?'"

Almost all standardized tests have been predicated upon determining the invariant meaning of a decontextualized passage—*a, b, c, none of the above*—as well as the intention of the author:  "What does Sylvia Plath mean when she compares her father to a Nazi in her poem 'Daddy?'"  But what if there is no invariant meaning of a text?  What if a text is just what and no more than what each individual reader makes of it, at least in part because of her individuality?  And what if much of what she makes of it can be attributed to her age, gender, religion, politics, her situatedness in a culture that is as relative as the text's to that culture?

Critics have been fierce in their response to deconstruction, both as to its essential concepts and to its implications for the presentation of literacy, particularly to naive readers and writers.  Richard A. Schweder of the University of Chicago satirizes these concepts in an essay in the January 8, 1989, issue of *The New York Times Book Review:*

> That truth is castrating and humanism oppressive. That the ego is infinitely dissolvable. That a person is made up of syllables and that life is really a run-on sentence that only death can bring to an end. That nihilism is the only defensible philosophy for modern times...

The linguist C. Jan Swearingen, who calls this position relativism versus Hirsch's reactionaryism, asks:

> How can students who have not yet learned to read as "naive" or "sentimental" readers jump in at the level of problematizing such reading? How can anyone learn to problematize something that has not yet been known or imparted? Do we impart traditional modes of reading and writing only to hastily—and cruelly—grab them away? Our writing classrooms are full of students whose "self" is mute because they have never come into contact with the cultural conventions of post-Cartesian, post-enlightenment, or post-romantic conceptions and practices of self and voice. To tell such students that there is no such thing as accurate reference because there is no reality is—many feel—a pathologically arrogant pedagogical act.

Those concerned with the initial imparting of literacy may ask, "What does this debate have to do with us or with children who are just in the process of learning to write and to read?" If inculcation into deconstruction is the program and the practice within many major departments of English, and of other literatures, as it is, their graduate students will teach the high school teachers who will, in turn, develop expectations, or nonexpectations, that will influence the course of literacy education for children.

With deconstruction one can hope that it will not be introduced as mode of reading and of analysis until late undergraduate or graduate school. Its influence may more likely be felt upon efforts at standardized testing for any admission, placement, or even diagnostic purposes. There is the strong likelihood that any evaluation that is posited upon invariant meanings of texts and monolithic intentions and purposes of writers will undergo severe criticism. Assessment of early literacy, if it proceeds from these assumptions, will not be immune.

There are striking differences in those espousing emergent literacy from those espousing cultural literacy or deconstruction. The differences are biographical: Who is proposing emergent literacy? To a person, they share the world with children and have daily dealings with them. They teach learners of many ages and backgrounds, not only graduate students in research universities but also students in preschools, public elementary and secondary schools, community colleges, and even senior centers. The relativists and the reactionaries scarcely mention young children. If they teach at all, they confine themselves to gifted students at elite universities. Many espousing emergent literacy are women. There are no major women players in the relativist/reactionary debate. Perhaps for some of the reasons just cited, those in emergent literacy reject the ungrounded, the artificial, the abstruse that mark the other two stances.

Those in emergent literacy have a vivid sense of actual rather than of gauzy and glorified and curiously revisionist American and Western educational history. Unlike Allan Bloom, they know that the great educational theorist of antiquity like Plato did not envision education as a few nubile aristocratic youths lounging under a plane tree toying with their syllogisms, but, as Nussbaum points out in her essay, "Undemocratic Vistas," Socrates, Aristotle, the Stoics, and Cicero care deeply about "politics, ethics, and pedagogy in their own pluralistic cultures," including at times education for women. As for the United States, those young marvels of the past who knew their Sisyphus and all nine (?) labors of Hercules probably represented, say, in 1890, when only one in six eighth graders finished high school, fewer than 10 percent of their age group. Those in emergent literacy know, as the Resnicks (1980) point out in their overview, *The Nature of Literacy: A Historical Exploration*, the current American ambition to help all achieve a higher literacy is almost unique in human history.

The implication of many of the essays in this collection is the necessity for a marked reform in teacher education. If teachers and other caretakers come to hold the chief responsibility for the inculcation and assessment of early literacy, clearly they will need to possess and to demonstrate attributes not previously required of them.

Underlying all others will be their own profound literacy as writers and as readers. If they themselves do not engage deeply in these two complex, epigenetic processes, they will be unable to sponsor and to evaluate the literacy of others. They will need as well to possess formal knowledge of the growing body of theories and research findings about early literacy found in diverse disciplines, from literary theory to neural science.

How they learn what they will need to know will prove as significant (more?) than the "what." The curriculum in early childhood and elementary education—indeed, the teacher education curriculum across all age levels, including graduate school—must consequently undergo marked revisions and expansions. The classes and seminars must provide, must exemplify, literacy events themselves of significance and power, with the instructors embodying the strongest possible models of sponsoring adult behavior. If a model such as emergent literacy is espoused, teachers must not only understand the arguments of others; they must also build their own powerful arguments for its validity if it is to withstand the force of such powerful and literally supported concepts as cultural literacy and deconstruction. And all inquiries need to be set against the contexts, explicitly considered, of a given culture's sets of values and political aspirations.

For the immediate future, literacy will avowedly be a significant focus of the White House agenda for education, but it is too early to know how substantive that attention will prove to be. If literacy comes to be regarded merely as yet another form of cost-effective volunteerism, the attention will not be helpful. If the interest represents serious, funded concentration upon a major national problem, among adults as well as among children, theories, models, practices, and even the concepts and assumptions of assessment could undergo transformation. With assessment we might as educators and as citizens even come to address the questions: "Why are we doing it?" "To what educational purposes?" "For what political ends?"

If learning to write and read require (1) safe and steady home structures; (2) time that can regularly be devoted to reading and writing; and (3) adults present to assure concentration, introspection, and reflection, what do our demographic actualities and projections tell us about the likelihood of most American children now and in the future finding these in their contexts? Today only 7 percent of American children live in a nuclear family with a working father, a housewife mother, and one brother or sister. Of 100 children born in 1985

- Twelve were born out of wedlock.
- Five were born to parents who separate.
- Two were born to parents one of whom would die before the child reached age 18.
- Only 41 would reach 18 as members of an intact classical nuclear family.

And if these figures are supplemented by the fact that over 20 percent of American children are being raised by single, working mothers and that children form the majority of the desperately poor of this country, the scope and grimness of the problem become inescapable.

Can we as educators and as citizens provide for our children of any age environments that can substitute in a compelling way for the homes and schools that once provided for some American children, probably never the majority, at least the chance to become literate? And, if so, how? A theme for our own deliberations, far more crucial, an immediate national political and educational agenda has already been determined for us.

# REFERENCES

CROWLEY, S. (1989). *A teacher's introduction to deconstruction.* Urbana, IL: National Council of Teachers of English.

FLOWER, L. (1988, November). *Cognition, context and theory-building.* Berkeley and Pittsburgh: Center for the Study of Writing at Berkeley and Carnegie-Mellon.

HIRSCH, E. D., Jr. (1982). *Cultural literacy: What every American needs to know.* Buffalo, NY: Prometheus Books.

HIRSCH, E. D., Jr., KETT, J. F., TREFIL, J. (1988). *The dictionary of cultural literacy.* Boston: Houghton Mifflin Co.

LUNSFORD, A., & LLOYD-JONES, R. (1989). *Democracy through language: Papers from the English coalition.* Urbana, IL.: National Council of Teachers of English.

MILLER, J. H. (1987, October 9-15). But are things as we think they are? *Times Literary Supplement,* pp. 1104-1105.

NUSSBAUM, M. (1987, November 5). *Undemocratic vistas.* New York Review of Books.

RESNICK, D. P., RESNICK, L. B. (1980). The nature of literacy: An historical exploration. In M. Wolf, M. K. McQuillan and E. Radwin (Eds.) *Thought and Language/Language and*

*Reading*. Cambridge, MA.: Harvard Educational Review (Reprint series #14) pp. 396-411.

SCHWEDER, R. A. (1989, January 8). In Paris: Miniskirts of the Mind. *The New York Times Book Review*, p. 1.

SWEARINGEN, C. J. (1988, Fall). Bloomsday for literacy: How reactionaries and relativists alike undermine literacy while seeming to promote it. *Freshman English News, 17*, 1-5.

# ABOUT THE CONTRIBUTORS

**Irene Athey** received her Ph.D. in educational psychology from the University of California at Berkeley. At the present time she is a Professor at the Graduate School of Education at Rutgers University. Dr. Athey's area of specialization concerns the relationship of young children's growth in language and cognition to their ability to comprehend and appreciate reading. Her writings have appeared in numerous book chapters and journals such as *Journal of Educational Research* and the *Harvard Educational Review*. Dr. Athey has taught at every level from preschool to graduate school. She served as an administrator at the University of Rochester and as dean of the Graduate School of Education at Rutgers. She is past president of the National Reading Conference.

**Janet Emig** received her Ed.D. from Harvard University. She is a professor of English Education at Rutgers University and a member of the graduate faculty in English there. Her research interests deal with cross-age, cross-cultural studies of the composing process. She has published several books and numerous journal articles. Dr. Emig is the co-founder of the New Jersey Writing Project and is president of the National Council of Teachers of English.

**Connie Juel** received her Ph.D. from Stanford University. She is a professor at the University of Texas at Austin and was a former elementary reading teacher. Her area of specialization is curriculum and instruction.  Recently she completed a four-year longitudinal study investigating how children learn to read and write from first to fourth grade.  She is an associate editor of *Reading Research Quarterly* and has been published widely in book chapters and journals.

**Martin Kling** received his Ph.D. in educational psychology from the University of California at Berkeley.  He has been with Rutgers University since 1965.  He is professor and chair of the Department of Learning and Teaching; and is also director of the Reading Center.  His main interests are theories of reading and diagnosis and correction of reading/learning problems.  Dr. Kling is known for his publication of *The Targeted Reading Collection,* a critical review of research on theory in language development as it relates to the reading process.  He has numerous contributions in books and professional journals.

**Jana M. Mason** received her Ph.D. from Stanford University and is a professor at the University of Illinois (Urbana-Champaign) with appointments in the College of Education and the Center for the Study of Reading.  She has published many articles on children's reading and reading instruction.  These include a reading methods textbook published by Scott, Foresman; a book on reading and writing connections published by Allyn & Bacon; and a book on children who are at risk for academic failure published by Heinemann.  Mason's current work is directed toward evaluation of intervention techniques for at-risk preschool and kindergarten children.  This work involves reading Little Books to children, extending book concepts with dramatic play and writing activities, and developing new classroom instructional procedures.

**Lesley Mandel Morrow** received her Ph.D. from Fordham University in New York City.  She is coordinator of the Early Childhood/Elementary Graduate Programs at the Graduate School of Education at Rutgers University.  Dr. Morrow's area of research deals with early childhood literacy development and specifically focuses on promoting voluntary reading and comprehension of story through the use of children's literature. She has received several awards for her research from the International Reading Association and Rutgers University.  Dr. Morrow has numerous publications in journals, book chapters, and books.  Some of her work has appeared in *Reading Research Quarterly, Research in the Teaching of English, Journal of Reading Behavior,* and *Reading Teacher.*  She is the author of *Literacy Development in the Early Years: Helping Children Read and Write,* a book published by Prentice Hall.

**Donna Ogle** is on the faculty at the National College of Education at Evanston, Illinois, where she chairs the Reading/Language Department.  Her research interests focus on comprehension and staff development.  She has recently published *Teaching and Reading as Thinking Skills* and *Strategic Thinking and Learning Cognitive Instruction in the Content Areas* (with Palinscar, Jones, and Carr).  She currently serves on the board of directors of the National Reading Conference and the Publications Committee for the International Reading Association.

**Robert P. Parker** is a professor of education at the Graduate School of Education at Rutgers University. He received his Ph.D. from Northwestern University in English education. His area of specialization and research focuses on children's literacy development; teachers' personal theories; and language, thinking, and learning. He has several publications in journals and book chapters. His most recent book is entitled *The Consequences of Writing: Enhancing Learning in the Disciplines,* published by Boynton/Cook with Vera Boodkin.

**P. David Pearson** received his Ph.D. in education from the University of Minnesota. He is director of the Center for the Study of Reading at the University of Illinois, Urbana-Champaign. His research interests focus on reading instruction and assessment. Dr. Pearson has numerous publications. One of his most important is the *Handbook of Reading Research.* Dr. Pearson was editor of *Reading Research Quarterly* and is past president of The National Reading Conference.

**Jeffrey K. Smith** is associate professor of educational psychology and director of research and development for the Graduate School of Education at Rutgers University. He received his Ph.D. from the University of Chicago in measurement, evaluation, and statistical analysis. He has published research on test wiseness, test bias, and test interpretation in the *Journal of Educational Measurement, Applied Psychological Measurement,* and *Educational and Psychological Measurement,* among other journals.

**Anne C. Stallman** received her B.S. and M.A. in education from the Ohio State University. She is currently a research assistant completing her Ph.D. at the University of Illinois at Urbana-Champaign. Her research interests deal with vocabulary knowledge, reading comprehension, and assessment.

**Janice P. Stewart** is a graduate of the University of Illinois, Urbana-Champaign. She received her Ph.D. in elementary education and early childhood education. Presently Dr. Stewart is an assistant professor at Rutgers University Graduate School of Education and a research associate at the Center for the Study of Reading, University of Illinois. Her area of specialization is early literacy development in young children. She has publications on this topic in book chapters.

**Dorothy S. Strickland** is the Arthur I. Gates Professor of Education at Teachers College, Columbia University. She received an M.A. in educational psychology and a Ph.D. in early childhood and elementary education from New York University. A former classroom teacher, reading consultant, and learning disabilities specialist, Strickland has authored and edited numerous books, chapters, and articles concerning language development and reading. Recent titles include *The Administration and Supervision of Reading Programs* and *Emergent Literacy: Young Children Learn to Read and Write* (with Lesley Morrow). She is past president of the International Reading Association.

**Elizabeth Sulzby** received her Ph.D. from the University of Virginia. She is associate professor of education and a faculty associate in linguistics at the University of Michigan at Ann Arbor. She teaches courses in the following programs: reading and literacy, early childhood and elementary education, and educational psychology. Dr. Sulzby's research is in the area of emergent literacy, and she has had numerous publications, some of which have appeared in *Reading Research Quarterly, Research in the Teaching of English, Journal of Reading Behavior*, and *First Language*. Her most recent project is a study of emergent writing with and without the computer with low-income minority students, which is being funded by the Spencer Foundation.

**William H. Teale** is associate professor at the University of Texas at San Antonio. He received his doctorate from the University of Virginia in reading and English education. Dr. Teale specializes in studying the literacy development of young children in home and school settings. He has published widely on this topic in professional publications such as *Language Arts, The Reading Teacher*, and *Elementary School Journal*. He is the editor of the book *Emergent Literacy: Writing and Reading* with Elizabeth Sulzby.

**Louise Cherry Wilkinson** received her Ed.D. from Harvard University in human development and is an expert in classroom communication. Her preparation in educational psychology and child development and her research and publications have focused on the development of normal children's language and communicative skills in school. She takes a sociolinguistic approach to peer communication, classroom instructional grouping, and cultural differences in children's communicative styles and the consequences for learning. She is the author of more than 60 articles and chapters, the editor/co-editor of three volumes on classrooms published by Academic Press, and author of a new volume on classroom communications with Dr. Elaine Silliman. Dr. Wilkinson is a fellow of the American Psychological Association and is presently dean of the Rutgers Graduate School of Education.

# INDEX